ARE 4.0

Structural Systems

QUESTIONS & ANSWERS John Hardt

KAPLAN AEC EDUCATION

This publication is designed to provide accurate and authoritative information in regard to the subject matter covered. It is sold with the understanding that the publisher is not engaged in rendering legal, accounting, or other professional service. If legal advice or other expert assistance is required, the services of a competent professional person should be sought.

President: Mehul Patel
Vice President & General Manager: David Dufresne
Vice President of Product Development and Publishing: Evan M. Butterfield
Editorial Project Manager: Jason Mitchell
Director of Production: Daniel Frey
Production Editor: Caitlin Ostrow
Production Artist: Cepheus Edmondson
Creative Director: Lucy Jenkins
Senior Product Manager: Brian O'Connor

Published by Kaplan AEC Education
30 South Wacker Drive, Suite 2500
Chicago, IL 60606-7481
(312) 836-4400
www.kaplanaecarchitecture.com

Printed in the United States of America.

08   09   10   10 9 8 7 6 5 4 3 2

ISBN-13: 978-1-4277-7034-9

ISBN: 1-4277-7034-4

CONTENTS

WELCOME

Thank you for choosing Kaplan AEC Education for your ARE study needs. We offer updates annually to keep abreast of code and exam changes and to address any errors discovered since the previous update was published. We wish you the best of luck in your pursuit of licensure.

ARE OVERVIEW

Since the State of Illinois first pioneered the practice of licensing architects in 1897, architectural licensing has been increasingly adopted as a means to protect the public health, safety, and welfare. Today, all U.S. states and Canadian provinces require licensing for individuals practicing architecture. Licensing requirements vary by jurisdiction; however, the minimum requirements are uniform and in all cases include passing the Architect Registration Exam (ARE). This makes the ARE a required rite of passage for all those entering the profession, and you should be congratulated on undertaking this challenging endeavor.

Developed by the National Council of Architectural Registration Boards (NCARB), the ARE is the only exam by which architecture candidates can become registered in the United States or Canada. The ARE assesses candidates' knowledge, skills, and abilities in seven different areas of professional practice, including a candidate's competency in decision making and knowledge of various areas of the profession. The exam also tests competence in fulfilling an architect's responsibilities and in coordinating the activities of others while working with a team of design and construction specialists. In all jurisdictions, candidates must pass the seven divisions of the exam to become registered.

The ARE is designed and prepared by architects, making it a practice-based exam. It is generally not a test of academic knowledge, but rather a means to test decision-making ability as it relates to the responsibilities of the architectural profession. For example, the exam does not expect candidates to memorize specific details of the building code, but requires them to understand a model code's general requirements, scope, and purpose, and to know the architect's responsibilities related to that code. As such, there is no substitute for a well-rounded internship to help prepare for the ARE.

4.0 Exam Format

The seven ARE 4.0 divisions are outlined in the table below.

DIVISION	QUESTIONS	VIGNETTES
Building Design & Construction Systems	85	Accessibility/ Ramp Roof Plan Stair Design
Building Systems	95	Mechanical & Electrical Plan
Construction Documents & Services	100	Building Section
Programming, Planning & Practice	85	Site Zoning
Schematic Design	-	Building Layout Interior Layout
Site Planning & Design	65	Site Design Site Grading
Structural Systems	125	Structural Layout

The exam presents multiple-choice questions individually. Candidates may answer questions, skip questions, or mark questions for further review. Candidates may also move backward or forward within the exam using simple on-

ARCHITECTURAL HISTORY

Questions pertaining to the history of architecture appear throughout the ARE divisions. The prominence of historical questions will vary not only by division but also within different versions of the exam for each division. In general, however, history tends to be lightly tested, with approximately three to seven history questions per division, depending upon the total number of questions within the division. One aspect common to all the divisions is that whatever history questions are presented will be related to that division's subject matter. For example, a question regarding Chicago's John Hancock Center and the purpose of its unique exterior cross bracing may appear on the Structural Systems exam.

Though it is difficult to predict how essential your knowledge of architectural history will be to passing any of the multiple-choice divisions, it is recommended that you refer to a primer in this field—such as Kaplan's *Architectural History*—before taking each exam, and that you keep an eye out for topics relevant to the division for which you are studying. It is always better to be overprepared than taken by surprise at the testing center.

screen icons. The vignettes require candidates to create a graphic solution according to program and code requirements.

Actual appointment times for taking the exam are slightly longer than the actual exam time, allowing candidates to check in and out of the testing center. All ARE candidates are encouraged to review NCARB's *ARE Guidelines* for further detail about the exam format. These guidelines are available via free download at NCARB's Web site (*www.ncarb.org*).

Exam Format

It is important for exam candidates to familiarize themselves not only with exam content, but also with question format. Familiarity with the basic question types found in the ARE will reduce confusion, save time, and help you pass the exam. The ARE contains three basic question types.

The first and most common type is a straightforward multiple-choice question followed by four choices (A, B, C, and D). Candidates are expected to select the correct answer. This type of question is shown in the following example.

Which of the following cities is the capital of the United States?

A. New York

B. Washington, DC

C. Chicago

D. Los Angeles

The second type of question is a negatively worded question. In questions such as this, the negative wording is usually highlighted using all caps, as shown below.

Which of the following cities is NOT located on the west coast of the United States?

A. Los Angeles

B. San Diego

C. San Francisco

D. New York

The third type of question is a combination question. In a combination question, more than one choice may be correct; candidates must select from combinations of potentially correct choices. An example of a combination question is shown below.

Which of the following cities are located within the United States?

I. New York
II. Toronto
III. Montreal
IV. Los Angeles

A. I only
B. I and II
C. II and III
D. I and IV

The single most important thing candidates can do to prepare themselves for the vignettes is to learn to proficiently navigate NCARB's graphic software. Practice software can be downloaded free of charge from their Web site. Candidates should download it and become thoroughly familiar with its use.

Recommendations on Exam Division Order

NCARB allows candidates to choose the order in which they take the exams, and the choice is an important one. While only you know what works best for you, the following are some general considerations that many have found to be beneficial:

1. The Building Design & Construction Systems and Programming, Planning & Practice divisions are perhaps the broadest of all the divisions. Although this can make them among the most intimidating, taking these divisions early in the process will give a candidate a broad base of knowledge and may prove helpful in preparing for subsequent divisions. An alternative to this approach is to take these two divisions last, since you will already be familiar with much of their content. This latter approach likely is most beneficial when you take the exam divisions in fairly rapid succession so that details learned while studying for earlier divisions will still be fresh in your mind.

2. The Construction Documents & Services exam covers a broad range of subjects, dealing primarily with the architect's role and responsibilities within the building design and construction team. Because these subjects serve as one of the core foundations of the ARE, it may be advisable to take this division early in the process, as knowledge gained preparing for this exam can help in subsequent divisions.

3. Take exams that particularly concern you early in the process. NCARB rules prohibit retaking an exam for six months. Therefore, failing an exam early in the process will allow the candidate to use the waiting period to prepare for and take other exams.

EXAM PREPARATION

Overview

There is little argument that preparation is key to passing the ARE. With this in mind, Kaplan has developed a complete learning system for each exam division, including study guides, question-and-answer handbooks, mock exams, and flash cards. The study guides offer a condensed course of study and will best prepare you for the exam when utilized along with the other tools in the learning system. The system is designed to provide you with the general background necessary to pass the exam and to

THE EXAM TRANSITION

ARE 3.1

In November 2005 NCARB released *ARE Guidelines* Version 3.1, which outlines changes to the exam effective February 2006. These guidelines primarily detailed changes for the Site Planning division, combining the site design and site parking vignettes as well as the site zoning and site analysis vignettes. For more details about these changes, please refer to Kaplan's study guides for the graphic divisions.

The guidelines mean less to those preparing for multiple-choice divisions. Noteworthy points are outlined below.

- All division statements and content area descriptions were unchanged for the multiple-choice divisions.

- The number of questions and time limits for all exams were unchanged.

- The list of codes and standards candidates should familiarize themselves with was reduced to those of the International Code Council (ICC), the National Fire Protection Association (NFPA), and the National Research Council of Canada.

- A statics title has been removed from the reference list for General Structures.

ARE 4.0

In the spring of 2007, NCARB unveiled ARE 4.0, available as of July 2008. According to NCARB, the 4.0 version of the exam will be more subject-oriented than 3.1, and is intended to better assess a candidate's ability to approach projects independently. The format combines the multiple-choice and graphic portions of different divisions, reducing the number of divisions from nine to seven.

The transition will be gradual, with a one-year overlap during which both ARE 3.1 and ARE 4.0 will be administered. Provided you pass at least one ARE 3.1 division prior to May 2008, you can continue to take ARE 3.1 divisions until July 2009.

If you have not passed all ARE 3.1 divisions by June 2009, you will be transitioned to the ARE 4.0 format. You will be given credit for ARE 4.0 divisions according to which 3.1 divisions you have passed. Visit *www.kaplanaecarchitecture.com* for more details.

In order to avoid being retested on subjects you have already passed, you should develop a strategy for which divisions you take in which order. Here are some key points to keep in mind:

- Building Technology is a key division in the transition; its vignettes will be dispersed across four ARE 4.0 divisions. Be sure to pass Building Technology if you have passed and want credit for any of the following ARE 3.1 divisions: Building Design/Materials & Methods; Construction Documents & Services; General Structures; Lateral Forces; or Mechanical & Electrical Systems.

- Pre-Design and Site Planning content will be shuffled in ARE 4.0: If you pass one, pass the other.

- General Structures, Lateral Forces, and the Structural Layout vignette from Building Technology are being merged into the Structural Systems division. If you pass any of these and want to avoid being retested on material you have already seen, pass all three.

provide an indication of specific content areas that demand additional attention.

In addition to the Kaplan learning system, materials from industry-standard documents may prove useful for the various divisions. Several of these sources are noted in the "Supplementary Study Materials" section below.

Understanding the Field

The subject of structures may fall under the direct responsibility of the architect or under the responsibility of a structural consultant, depending on the scale and complexity of the project. In either case, however, properly designed building structures are critical in protecting the safety of building occupants. This significant role means that the subject of structural systems must be thoroughly understood in order for architects to properly integrate structural elements into their designs and permit constructive interaction with other members of the building design team.

Understanding the Exam

The Structural Systems exam is among the most daunting of the ARE exams due to the technical nature of the subject and the wide array of problems that may be presented. Candidates will find questions covering statics, wood construction, concrete, steel, foundations, long-span structural systems, and connections frequently on the exam. Many candidates, however, allow the breadth of the exam to intimidate unnecessarily.

Candidates must be familiar with the *Manual of Steel Construction* published by the American Institute of Steel Construction, but it is not necessary to memorize any part of this volume. Rather, candidates should be aware of how to utilize the charts and tables found in the book. Tables and charts needed to solve problems within the ARE will be provided during the

exam. Additionally, candidates should be aware that a series of equations, tables, and formulas are available within the ARE software by clicking on the References button. Therefore, candidates should not waste time memorizing formulas, but rather should focus their studies on practicing their use.

Many have also found that the question-and-answer books and mock exams published by Kaplan are especially useful for this exam as they provide additional opportunities to practice working through structural problems.

Preparation Basics

The first step in preparation should be a review of the exam specifications and reference materials published by NCARB. These statements are available for each of the seven ARE divisions to serve as a guide for preparing for the exam. Download these statements and familiarize yourself with their content. This will help you focus your attention on the subjects on which the exam focuses.

Prior CAD knowledge is not necessary to successfully complete vignettes. In fact, it's important for candidates familiar with CAD to realize they will experience significant differences between CAD and the drawing tools used on the exam.

Though no two people will have exactly the same ARE experience, the following are recommended best practices to adopt in your studies and should serve as a guide.

Set aside scheduled study time.
Establish a routine and adopt study strategies that reflect your strengths and mirror your approach in other successful academic pursuits. Most importantly, set aside a definite amount of study time each week, just as if you were

taking a lecture course, and carefully read all of the material.

Take—and retake—quizzes.

After studying each lesson in the study guide, take the quiz found at its conclusion. The quiz questions are intended to be straightforward and objective. Answers and explanations can be found at the back of the book. If you answer a question incorrectly, see if you can determine why the correct answer is correct before reading the explanation. Retake the quiz until you answer every question correctly and understand why the correct answers are correct.

Identify areas for improvement.

The quizzes allow you the opportunity to pinpoint areas where you need improvement. Reread and take note of the sections that cover these areas and seek additional information from other sources. Use the question-and-answer handbook and online test bank as a final tune-up for the exam.

Take the final exam.

A final exam designed to simulate the ARE follows the last lesson of each study guide. Answers and explanations can be found on the pages following the exam. As with the lesson quizzes, retake the final exam until you answer every question correctly and understand why the correct answers are correct.

Use the flash cards.

If you've purchased the flash cards, go through them once and set aside any terms you know at first glance. Take the rest to work, reviewing them on the train, over lunch, or before bed. Remove cards as you become familiar with their terms until you know all the terms. Review all the cards a final time before taking the exam.

Practice using the NCARB software.

Work through the practice vignettes contained within the NCARB software. You should work through each vignette repeatedly until you can solve it easily. As your skills develop, track how long it takes to work through a solution for each vignette.

Supplementary Study Materials

In addition to the Kaplan learning system, materials from industry-standard sources may prove useful in your studies. Candidates should consult the list of exam references in the NCARB guidelines for the council's recommendations and pay particular attention to the following publications, which are essential to successfully completing this exam:

- International Code Council (ICC) *International Building Code*
- American Institute of Steel Construction *Manual of Steel Construction: Allowable Stress Design,* Ninth Edition

Test-Taking Advice

Preparation for the exam should include a review of successful test-taking procedures—especially for those who have been out of the classroom for some time. Following is advice to aid in your success.

Pace yourself.

Each division allows candidates at least one minute per question. You should be able to comfortably read and reread each question and fully understand what is being asked before answering. Each vignette allows candidates ample time to complete a solution within the time allotted.

Read carefully.

Begin each question by reading it carefully and fully reviewing the choices, eliminating those that are obviously incorrect. Interpret language

literally, and keep an eye out for negatively worded questions. With vignettes, carefully review instructions and requirements. Quickly make a list of program and code requirements to check your work against as you proceed through the vignette.

Guess.

All unanswered questions are considered incorrect, so answer every question. If you are unsure of the correct answer, select your best guess and/or mark the question for later review. If you continue to be unsure of the answer after returning the question a second time, it is usually best to stick with your first guess.

Review difficult questions.

The exam allows candidates to review and change answers within the time limit. Utilize this feature to mark troubling questions for review upon completing the rest of the exam.

Reference material.

Some divisions include reference materials accessible through an on-screen icon. These materials include formulas and other reference content that may prove helpful when answering questions in these divisions. Note that candidates may *not* bring reference material with them to the testing center.

Best answer questions.

Many candidates fall victim to questions seeking the "best" answer. In these cases, it may appear at first glance as though several choices are correct. Remember the importance of reviewing the question carefully and interpreting the language literally. Consider the following example.

Which of these cities is located on the east coast of the United States?

A. Boston

B. Philadelphia

C. Washington, DC

D. Atlanta

At first glance, it may appear that all of the cities could be correct answers. However, if you interpret the question literally, you'll identify the critical phrase as "on the east coast." Although each of the cities listed is arguably an "eastern" city, only Boston sits on the Atlantic coast. All the other choices are located in the eastern part of the country, but are not coastal cities.

Style doesn't count.

Vignettes are graded on their conformance with program requirements and instructions. Don't waste time creating aesthetically pleasing solutions and adding unnecessary design elements.

ACKNOWLEDGMENTS

This introduction was written by John F. Hardt, AIA. Mr. Hardt is vice president and senior project architect with Karlsberger, an architecture, planning, and design firm based in Columbus, Ohio. He is a graduate of Ohio State University (MArch).

ABOUT KAPLAN

Thank you for choosing Kaplan AEC Education as your source for ARE preparation materials. Whether helping future professors prepare for the GRE or providing tomorrow's doctors the tools they need to pass the MCAT, Kaplan possesses more than 50 years of experience as

a global leader in exam prep and educational publishing. It is that experience and history that Kaplan brings to the world of architectural education, pairing unparalleled resources with acknowledged experts in ARE content areas to bring you the very best in licensure study materials.

Only Kaplan AEC offers a complete catalog of individual products and integrated learning systems to help you pass all seven divisions of the ARE. Kaplan's ARE materials include study guides, mock exams, question-and-answer handbooks, video workshops, and flash cards. Products may be purchased individually or in division-specific learning systems to suit your needs. These systems are designed to help you better focus on essential information for each division, provide flexibility in how you study, and save you money.

To order, please visit *www.KaplanAEC.com* or call (800) 420-1429.

1. Which of the diagrams below best represents the distribution of flexural stress in a homogeneous rectangular beam?

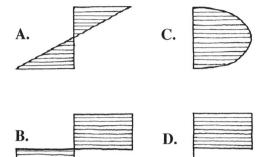

2. Truss members are generally subject to internal stresses that are axial. Which of the following will also cause bending stresses in truss members? Check all that apply.

   A. Using trusses without diagonals

   B. Closely spaced joists that span between trusses

   C. Truss joints that provide restraint against rotation

   D. Application of a load to a joint

3. During the design of a building, the deflection of a beam is calculated to be 0.90″. In order to limit the maximum deflection of the beam to ¾ inch, how should the design be changed?

   A. Substitute a beam having a section modulus 20 percent greater.

   B. Substitute a beam having a moment of inertia 20 percent greater.

   C. Substitute a beam having a moment of inertia 83 percent greater.

   D. Substitute a beam having a yield point 20 percent greater.

4. In designing a cantilever retaining wall, which of the following factors are considered?

   I. Overturning moment

   II. Sliding force

   III. Soil pressure under the footing

   IV. Bending moment in the stem

   A. I, II, and III

   B. II and IV

   C. I, III, and IV

   D. I, II, III, and IV

5. Overturning effects are most critical for which of the following? Check all that apply.

   A. Buildings with a high height-to-width ratio

   B. Buildings with a low height-to-width ratio

   C. Tall, slender buildings

   D. Short, squat buildings

   E. Top-heavy buildings

   F. Pyramid-shaped buildings

6. All of the following statements about shear walls are correct, *EXCEPT*

   A. a shear wall resists lateral forces from wind or earthquake by developing shear in its own plane.

   B. a shear wall must be made of reinforced concrete or structural steel.

   C. shear walls may be used with moment-resisting frames to form a dual system.

   D. a shear wall is analogous to a vertical cantilever beam.

7. A cantilever beam supports a uniformly distributed load as shown below. Which of the following is the appropriate moment diagram?

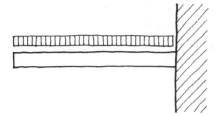

A.

B.

C.

D.

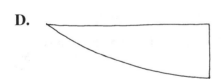

8. The stress at which a ductile material continues to deform without an increase in load is called the _____.

9. Which of the four beams below are statically indeterminate?

I.

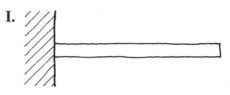

II.

III.

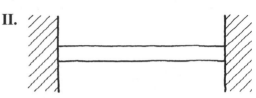

IV.

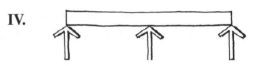

A. I, II, and IV

B. II and IV

C. III and IV

D. I, II, and III

10. What does redundancy in a structure refer to?

A. Providing more structural members than are necessary to support the anticipated loads

B. Having the ability to redistribute loads to other structural elements in case of overload or failure

C. Having a structural system that is statically indeterminate

D. Having main girders that consist of two members each

11. A commercial building assigned to SDC D has a fundamental period of 0.4 seconds, $S_{DS} = 1.0g$, $S_{DI} = 0.55g$, $R = 6$, and $W = 1,000,000$ pounds. What is the base shear?

   A. 114 kips

   B. 121 kips

   C. 167 kips

   D. 209 kips

12. A building with steel moment-resisting frames assigned to SDC D is 120 feet high and has a fundamental period of vibration of 1.29 seconds. If the building height were 240 feet and all other factors remained the same, the period would

   A. double.

   B. decrease by half.

   C. remain the same.

   D. increase about 75 percent.

13. The bracing of nonstructural elements must be designed to resist seismic forces that are

   A. the same as those used for the design of the building.

   B. usually smaller than those used for the design of the building.

   C. usually greater than those used for the design of the building.

   D. zero, since nonstructural elements are not required to be braced.

14. A hole or notch for a pipe must be provided in a reinforced concrete beam. Which of the diagrams below shows the hole or notch that will *LEAST* affect the beam's load-carrying capacity?

A.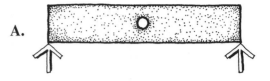

B.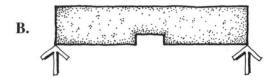

C.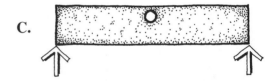

D.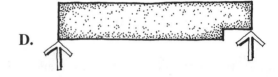

15. Which of the following statements about prestressed concrete construction is *NOT* true?

   A. Precast, prestressed members usually require end anchorages.

   B. Pretensioned members require no end anchorages.

   C. Prestressing a beam results in a smaller section.

   D. Posttensioned members usually require end anchorages.

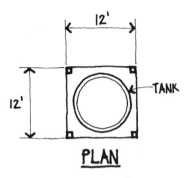

PLAN

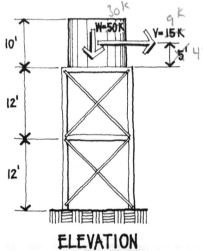

ELEVATION

DIAGRAM IS WRONG

16. A water tank, plus its contents, weighs 30 kips and is supported on the four-legged braced frame shown. The seismic load is equal to 0.30W and is assumed to act parallel to either axis of the frame. What is the total overturning moment on the frame?

A. Overturning moment = 126 ft.-kips

B. Overturning moment = 216 ft.-kips

C. Overturning moment = 252 ft.-kips

D. Overturning moment = 288 ft.-kips

17. The allowable shear in a plywood diaphragm depends on all of the following, *EXCEPT*

A. plywood grade and thickness.

B. direction of framing.

C. nail size and spacing.

D. width of framing members.

18. Compared to a steel frame building, a reinforced concrete building has

I. greater seismic load.

II. greater wind load.

III. greater weight.

A. I and II

B. I and III

C. II and III

D. I, II, and III

19. Select the correct statement about the steel frame shown below.

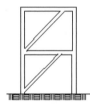

A. It is more ductile than a concentric braced frame.

B. It is not permitted to be used to resist seismic loads.

C. It may be used to resist seismic loads except in SDC D and higher.

D. It is called a special moment-resisting frame.

20. A special moment-resisting frame has an R value of 8. A concrete shear wall has an R value of 5. If all other factors are the same, the special moment-resisting frame should be designed to resist a seismic force that

  A. is 50 percent greater than that for the shear wall.

  B. is 37.5 percent smaller than that for the shear wall.

  C. is the same as that for the shear wall.

  D. may be greater or smaller than that for the shear wall, depending on the SDC.

21. Which of the following types of stress are important in building design? Check all that apply.

  A. Shear

  B. Tension

  C. Compression

  D. Strain

22. The load capacity of a structural steel column depends on the slenderness ratio Kl/r. In this ratio, K depends on

  A. the length of the column.

  B. the grade of steel.

  C. the moment of inertia and area of the column.

  D. the end conditions of the column.

23. A wide flange floor beam in a building is required to support a new piece of equipment, which will overstress the beam in bending. It is therefore necessary to strengthen the beam. Access is only from below. Which of the methods shown would be most effective, assuming there is sufficient headroom?

  A. 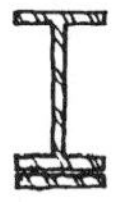 Weld a horizontal plate to the bottom flange.

  B.  Weld two angles to the bottom flange.

  C.  Weld a vertical plate to the bottom flange.

  D.  Weld a T plate to the bottom flange.

24. A steel column supports a dead load of 120 kips and a live load of 150 kips. The allowable soil bearing value is 4,000 pounds per square foot. What is the smallest pad footing that may be used?

  A. 5′-6″ × 5′-6″

  B. 6′-2″ × 6′-2″

  C. 6′-9″ × 6′-9″

  D. 8′-3″ × 8′-3″

25. What is the total lateral force exerted by the earth against the retaining wall shown, per lineal foot of wall? Assume the pressure of the retained earth to be equivalent to a fluid weighing 30 pounds per cubic foot.

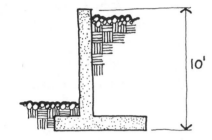

A.   150#

B.   300#

C.   1,500#

D.   3,000#

26. All of the following may increase the sliding resistance of a retaining wall, *EXCEPT*

A.   adding an integral key to the footing.

B.   making the footing wider.

C.   making the footing deeper.

D.   increasing the amount of reinforcing steel in the footing.

27. What is the purpose of the footing shown?

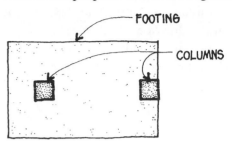

PLAN

A.   To resist differential settlement

B.   To fix the column bases against rotation

C.   To distribute the column loads over a large area when soil conditions are poor

D.   To support two columns where one of the columns is too close to the property line to have a symmetrical footing

28. The soil boring log for a building site shows that the upper 15 feet of subsurface material is a loose fill, below which is a thick layer of dense sand. Which of the following foundation systems might be appropriate on this site?

I.   Footings placed after the fill is removed and recompacted

II.   Footings extending through the fill into the dense sand

III. Belled caissons bearing on the dense sand

IV.   Piles extending through the fill into the dense sand

A.   I and II

B.   III and IV

C.   II, III, and IV

D.   I, II, III, and IV

29. In the seismic evaluation of existing wood frame buildings, which of the following statements are correct? Check all that apply.

   A. Wood frame buildings do not generally pose a significant life safety hazard during an earthquake.

   B. Diaphragms consisting of straight sheathing, such as 1 × 6 boards, are generally as satisfactory as plywood diaphragms.

   C. Cripple walls below the first floor level must be braced to resist shear forces.

   D. Friction between the sill and foundation of a bearing wall is often sufficient to preclude the need for anchor bolts.

30. The wind speed at site 1 is 85 mph, and the wind speed at site 2 is 90 mph. If the wind pressure at site 1 is 12.6 psf, what is the wind pressure at site 2?

   A. 26.8 psf

   B. 14.1 psf

   C. 12.6 psf

   D. 10.0 psf

31. Select the correct statement regarding earthquake design.

   A. In seismic design, the vertical seismic forces are assumed to be equal in magnitude to the horizontal seismic forces.

   B. The seismic forces are always considered to act simultaneously in the two horizontal directions parallel to the axes of the building.

   C. The seismic forces are always considered to act in the two horizontal directions parallel to the axes of the building, and may act simultaneously.

   D. Since earthquakes cause only horizontal ground motions, design for vertical seismic forces is not required.

32. Which of the following buildings resists wind loads by acting as a huge trussed tube?

   A. Lake Point Tower in Chicago

   B. Kresge Auditorium at M.I.T.

   C. John Hancock Building in Chicago

   D. Federal Reserve Bank Building in Minneapolis

33. A steel bar two inches in diameter and 20 feet long resists a tensile load of 50,000 pounds. What is the unit tensile stress in the bar?

   A. 7,958 psi

   B. 12,500 psi

   C. 15,915 psi

   D. 25,000 psi

34. Which of the beams below are statically indeterminate?

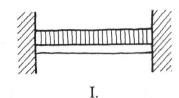

I.

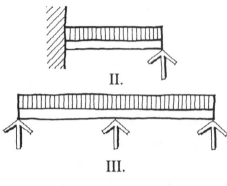

II.

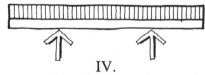

III.

IV.

- **A.** I, II, and III
- **B.** I and III
- **C.** II and IV
- **D.** I and II

35. What is the purpose of seismic isolation?

- **A.** To separate adjacent buildings in order to prevent pounding during an earthquake
- **B.** To reduce the total displacement of a building caused by earthquake forces
- **C.** To reduce seismic forces by allowing displacement to occur at the isolators
- **D.** To allow a building to respond elastically to earthquake ground motions

36. Which of the following statements about earthquake design is correct?

- **A.** Firm ground tends to amplify earthquake motion.
- **B.** Because of the great strength of steel, structures built of steel tend to sway less than those built of concrete.
- **C.** If the period of ground motion waves coincides with the natural period of the building, the acceleration of the building will be much less than the ground acceleration.
- **D.** Placing infill walls between columns stiffens the columns, thereby attracting greater seismic forces.

37. Two framing plans are shown below. Compared to the girders in plan A, how much greater is the required section modulus of the girders in plan B?

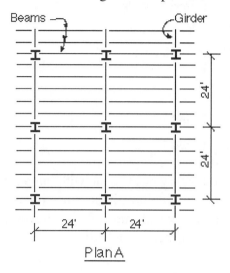

Plan A

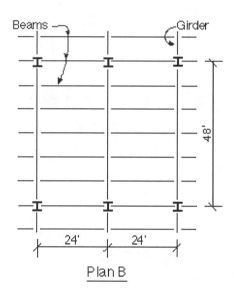

Plan B

A. 50 percent greater

B. Twice as great

C. Four times as great

D. Eight times as great

38. The moment diagram for a beam is shown below. Which of the following is the corresponding shear diagram?

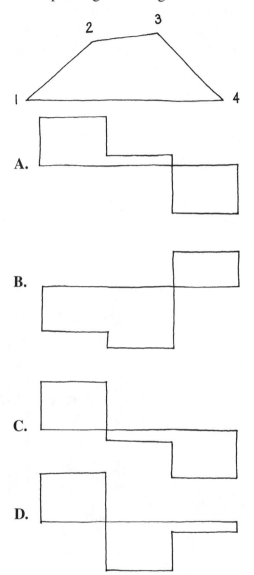

39. A structural steel beam spans 28 feet and supports a uniformly distributed load of 1,500 pounds per lineal foot. The maximum permissible deflection of the beam is 1 inch. What is the required I for the beam, if the value of E is 29,000,000 psi? Use the formula $\Delta = 5wL^4/384EI$.

- **A.** 255 in.^{4}
- **B.** 715 in.^{4}
- **C.** 858 in.^{4}
- **D.** 2,747 in.^{4}

40. This sketch illustrates which of the following?

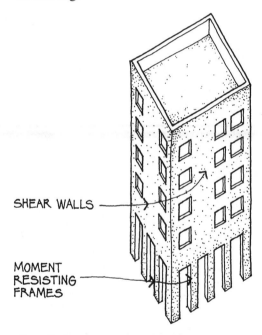

SHEAR WALLS

MOMENT RESISTING FRAMES

- **I.** Soft story
- **II.** Re-entrant corner
- **III.** Torsional irregularity
- **IV.** Stiffness irregularity
- **A.** II and III
- **B.** I and IV
- **C.** I and III
- **D.** I, II, III, and IV

41. Which of the following are most vulnerable to earthquake damage?

- **I.** Masonry chimneys
- **II.** Exterior walls
- **III.** Diaphragms
- **IV.** Masonry parapets
- **A.** I and II
- **B.** I and IV
- **C.** II and III
- **D.** II and IV

42. A one-story rigid frame with hinged bases supports a uniformly distributed load as shown below. Which of the following is the correct moment diagram for the frame?

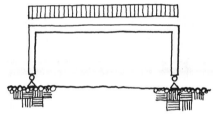

A.

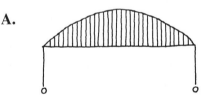

B.

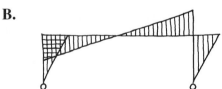

C.

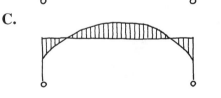

D.

43. The ability of a structural material or system to sustain inelastic deformations without collapse is called _____.

44. In the detail shown, the purpose of the anchors is to

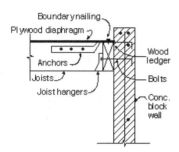

A. provide vertical support for the joists.

B. transfer diaphragm shear into the wall.

C. provide lateral support for the wall.

D. provide vertical support for the ledger.

45. Given the following reinforcing bar data:

Bar Size	Area
#4	0.20 in.^{2}
#5	0.31 in.^{2}
#6	0.44 in.^{2}
#7	0.60 in.^{2}
#8	0.79 in.^{2}
#9	1.00 in.^{2}

If the ultimate tensile capacity of 2-#6 grade 40 reinforcing bars is compared with that of 1-#8 grade 60 reinforcing bar,

A. the #6 bars have the greater capacity.

B. the #8 bar has the greater capacity.

C. the capacities of both sets of bars are identical.

D. the capacity cannot be determined without knowing the 28-day compressive strength (f'_c) of the concrete in which the reinforcing bars are used.

46. Which of the following statements concerning the flat plate floor system are generally correct?

I.   The construction depth is shallow.

II. Shear stresses near the columns are high.

III. The system is inherently very stiff.

IV. Beams between the columns are required in both directions.

V.   The system is economical for live loads of 100 psf or more and for spans of about 30 feet.

A. I and II only

B. II, III, and V

C. I, IV, and V

D. I, II, and V

47. Considering the two beams shown below, the three-span continuous beam and the simple beam, which of the following is *NOT* a correct statement?

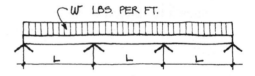

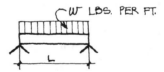

A. The maximum positive bending moment in the simple beam is greater than in the continuous beam.

B. The maximum negative bending moment in the continuous beam is greater than in the simple beam.

C. The maximum positive bending moment is greater in the end spans of the continuous beam than in the center span.

D. The maximum deflection of the continuous beam is the same as that of the simple beam.

48. In a simple beam supporting a concentrated load, as shown below, where do the beam fibers lengthen and where do they shorten?

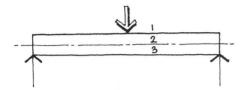

- **A.** Lengthen at 1, shorten at 3
- **B.** Lengthen at 3, shorten at 1
- **C.** Lengthen at 1 and 2, shorten at 3
- **D.** Lengthen at 2 and 3, shorten at 1

49. Which of the following statements concerning the seismic design of buildings is correct?

- **A.** In an earthquake, the ground moves horizontally and vertically, but the effects of the vertical motion are usually neglected in the design.
- **B.** The acceleration of the ground beneath the building and the acceleration of the building usually have the same value.
- **C.** Special moment-resisting frames have less ability to resist earthquakes without failure than shear walls.
- **D.** The overturning moment due to seismic forces need not be considered in design, since earthquakes reverse direction and thus buildings cannot overturn.

50. Building I has a fundamental period of vibration of one second. Building II has a fundamental period of vibration of two seconds. If all other factors are equal

- **A.** building I will have greater seismic acceleration and therefore greater seismic force.
- **B.** building II will have greater seismic acceleration and therefore greater seismic force.
- **C.** both buildings will have the same seismic acceleration and therefore the same seismic force.
- **D.** building I will have less seismic acceleration and therefore greater seismic force.

51. The seismic loads on the building shown in the plan are resisted by shear walls 1, 2, 3, and 4. The diaphragm is rigid, and the center of rigidity does not coincide with the center of mass. Which walls will have increased shears caused by horizontal torsional moment for seismic loads in the north-south direction?

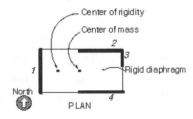

- **A.** Wall 1 only
- **B.** Wall 3 only
- **C.** Walls 1 and 3
- **D.** Neither wall 1 nor wall 3

52. The natural or fundamental period of vibration of a building is primarily a function of the building's

- **A.** width.
- **B.** height.
- **C.** acceleration.
- **D.** location.

53. In the seismic formula $V = C_s W$, the value of C_s generally depends on

   A. the location of the building and its occupancy.

   B. the type of structural system used.

   C. the height of the building.

   D. all of the attributes in A, B, and C.

54. Which of the following is the correct moment diagram for the beam shown?

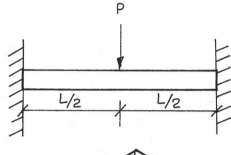

   A.

   B.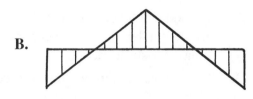

   C.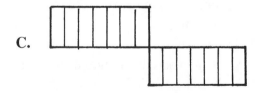

   D.

55. A square column pad is overstressed in shear. A solution is to

   A. increase the pad size.

   B. increase the area of reinforcing steel.

   C. use more bars of smaller diameter.

   D. increase the pad thickness.

56. Select the correct statement(s) about the bracing of nonstructural (architectural) elements in areas of high seismic risk.

   I. Nonstructural elements are not required to be braced.

   II. The seismic factor used in designing the bracing for nonstructural elements is the same as that used for the building structure.

   III. The seismic factor used in designing the bracing for nonstructural elements is greater than that used for the building structure.

   IV. Bracing for nonstructural elements must be designed for seismic forces coming from any horizontal direction.

   A. I only

   B. II and IV

   C. III only

   D. III and IV

57. The International Building Code allows two different methods for determining seismic forces: dynamic lateral force procedures and a static lateral force procedure. In this regard, which of the following is a correct statement?

   A. All buildings are permitted to be designed using either method.

   B. Some buildings must be designed using the static method, while the design of other buildings must use the dynamic method.

   C. The static method is always permitted, while the dynamic method is only allowed under certain conditions.

   D. The dynamic method is always permitted, while the static method is only allowed under certain conditions.

58. The two-span continuous beam shown supports a uniform load on span AB only and is connected to supports A, B, and C. Neglecting the weight of the beam, the reaction at C

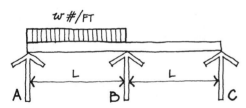

   A. acts upward.

   B. acts downward.

   C. may act upward or downward, depending on the magnitude of the uniform load.

   D. is zero.

59. Which of the following diagrams best shows the deflected shape of the rigid frame shown below?

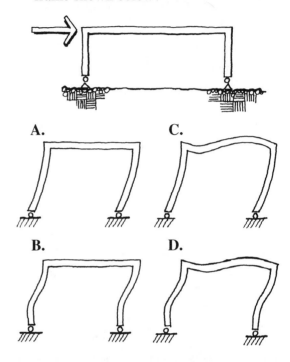

60. Select the correct statements about plywood diaphragms.

   I.   Plywood diaphragms are not permitted in buildings with concrete or masonry shear walls.

   II. Plywood diaphragms are not subject to horizontal torsional moments.

   III. A plywood diaphragm acts as a simple beam between the vertical resisting elements.

   IV. A plywood diaphragm distributes horizontal wind or seismic forces to the vertical resisting elements in proportion to their relative rigidities.

   A. I, II, and III

   B. II and IV

   C. I and IV

   D. II and III

61. A two-story moment-resisting frame with hinged bases resists the lateral earthquake loads as shown. Neglecting dead loads, what resists the overturning caused by the lateral loads?

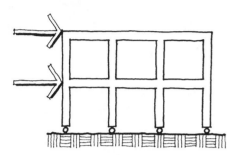

A. Moment at the column bases

B. Shear in the columns

C. Torsion in the columns

D. Uplift in two columns and compression in two columns

62. Select the correct statements about the three-hinged arch shown.

I. It is statically determinate.

II. It is capable of supporting both vertical and horizontal loads.

III. The connection at the center must be able to resist moment.

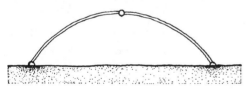

A. I only

B. II only

C. I and II

D. I, II, and III

63. When a member undergoes stress, its length changes. If the member does not return to its original length when the stress is removed, the action is called _____.

64. A 15-foot-long pin-ended column of A36 steel supports a load of 200 kips. The column's dimensions and properties are as follows: area = 14.1 in.^{2}, depth = 8.50″, web thickness = 0.400″, flange width = 8.110″, flange thickness = 0.685″, $r_{x\text{-}x}$ = 3.6″, $r_{y\text{-}y}$ = 2.08″. What is the compressive stress in the column?

A. 2.9 ksi

B. 14.2 ksi

C. 22.3 ksi

D. 24.0 ksi

65. A frame with tension-only diagonal braces resists a horizontal wind load of 15 kips acting to the right, as shown. What is the internal tension in each brace?

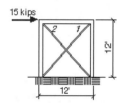

A. Brace 1 = 0, brace 2 = 21.2 kips

B. Brace 1 = 10.6 kips, brace 2 = 10.6 kips

C. Brace 1 = 21.2 kips, brace 2 = 0

D. Brace 1 = 15.0 kips, brace 2 = 0

66. A shear wall is subject to the wind loads and dead loads shown. What is the overturning moment and the dead load resisting moment?

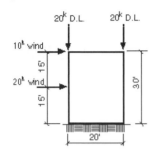

A. Overturning moment = 600 ft.-kips, dead load resisting moment = 800 ft.-kips

B. Overturning moment = 600 ft.-kips, dead load resisting moment = 400 ft.-kips

C. Overturning moment = 900 ft.-kips, dead load resisting moment = 400 ft.-kips

D. Overturning moment = 450 ft.-kips, dead load resisting moment = 800 ft.-kips

67. A cantilever beam is loaded as shown. What is the magnitude of the reaction V and the moment M at the fixed end, neglecting the weight of the beam?

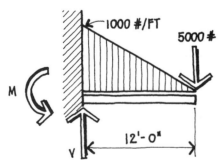

A. V = 11,000#; M = 84,000 ft.-lbs.

B. V = 11,000#; M = 96,000 ft.-lbs.

C. V = 17,000#; M = 108,000 ft.-lbs.

D. V = 17,000#; M = 132,000 ft.-lbs.

68. The load-carrying capacity of a wood column is determined by which of the following? Check all that apply.

A. The species and grade of lumber

B. The dimensions of the column section

C. The unbraced height of the column

D. The applied load

69. The strength of a complete penetration groove weld in tension or compression is

A. based on the shear strength through the throat of the weld.

B. equal to that of a fillet weld.

C. the same as that of the connected material.

D. less than that of the connected material.

70. Which of the following statements concerning the maximum size of coarse aggregate in a concrete mixture is *INCORRECT*?

A. The maximum size of coarse aggregate is limited by the narrowest dimension between forms.

B. The maximum size of coarse aggregate is less than the minimum clear spacing between reinforcing bars.

C. The smaller the maximum size of coarse aggregate, the greater the amount of water required.

D. For economy, the maximum size of coarse aggregate should be as small as possible.

71. A stub girder system is analogous to

    A. a triangulated truss.

    B. a rigid frame.

    C. a Vierendeel truss.

    D. an open web joist.

72. A column of ASTM A992 steel is 16 feet long and supports a load of 200 kips. What is the most economical W10 column section that can support the load? Use the chart on page 108.

    A. W10 × 33

    B. W10 × 39

    C. W10 × 45

    D. W10 × 49

73. What is the total force in member a of the cantilever truss shown below?

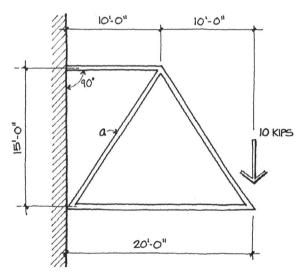

    A. 12.02 kips tension

    B. 12.02 kips compression

    C. 6.67 kips compression

    D. 13.33 kips compression

74. The weld symbol shown indicates

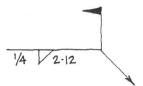

    A. a 1/4 inch intermittent bevel weld to be made in the field.

    B. a 1/4 inch intermittent fillet weld to be made in the field.

    C. a 1/4 inch fillet weld that has been flagged to indicate required ultrasonic testing of 2 out of every 12 welds.

    D. a 1/4 inch fillet weld to be made in the field with class 2-12 electrodes.

75. In general, the most economical reinforced concrete framing system is one in which

    A. the amount of reinforcing steel is kept to a minimum by increasing the sizes of the members.

    B. the vertical loads are resisted by bearing walls and the lateral wind or earthquake loads by rigid frames.

    C. the areas in which the concrete is in tension are replaced with voids, as in a waffle slab, thus reducing the weight of the system.

    D. the forming is uniform and repetitive and the reinforcing layout is simple and repetitive.

76. What is the left reaction for the beam shown below?

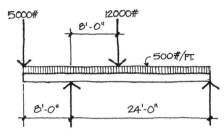

A. 25,333#

B. 7,667#

C. 21,333#

D. 23,000#

77. Each of the following items is associated with Roman architecture, *EXCEPT*

A. thermae.

B. basilica.

C. amphitheater.

D. stoa.

78. Which of the following best describes the P-delta effect in seismic design?

A. The increase in bending moments induced by the vertical loads acting on the laterally displaced building frame

B. Small differences between the lateral seismic design forces computed by the dynamic lateral force procedure and those based on the static lateral force procedure

C. The pattern of cracking found in concrete shear walls resisting high seismic forces

D. The amplification of building motion caused by certain site soil conditions

79. Which of the following are common causes of failure for old buildings as a result of earthquake? Check all that apply.

A. Complex building configurations

B. Lack of reinforcing in masonry walls

C. Inadequate connections

D. Low mortar strength

E. Indirect, irregular paths of load resistance

80. In seismic design, it is desirable to have a system such that if a particular element fails, the lateral load will be redistributed to other elements. What is this property called?

A. Rigidity

B. Redundancy

C. Elasticity

D. Ductility

81. Four different plans are shown for a 15-story building assigned to Seismic Design Category D. Assuming all other factors are equal, which plan arrangement is best for seismic resistance?

A.

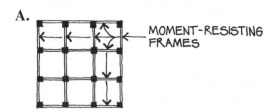

B.

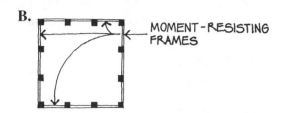

C.

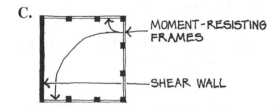

D.

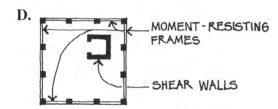

82. A reinforced concrete parapet wall weighing 100 pounds per square foot extends 4′6″ above the roof of a commercial building assigned to SDC D. What is the seismic moment on the parapet wall, per foot of length? $S_{DS} = 1.37g$

    A. 738 ft.-lbs.

    B. 1,661 ft.-lbs.

    C. 2,215 ft.-lbs.

    D. 3,322 ft.-lbs.

83. Several structural systems are being considered for a 20-story office building with columns 30 feet apart in each direction. Which of the following floor framing systems is *LEAST* likely to be economical?

    A. Concrete fill over steel deck over steel composite floor beams spaced at 10 feet on center that span 30 feet between steel girders

    B. Concrete on metal forms over open web joists spaced at 2 feet on center that span 30 feet between steel girders

    C. Concrete topping over precast prestressed concrete planks that span 30 feet between steel girder

    D. Flat plate spanning 30 feet in each direction directly to the columns

84. The vertical cylindrical tank shown is used to store water. The resulting stress in the tank wall is _____.

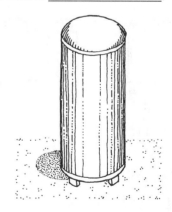

85. If the wind speed increases from 85 to 120 mph, the wind pressure in pounds per square foot increases by what percentage?

    A. 30 percent

    B. 43 percent

    C. 99 percent

    D. 204 percent

86. The design of a building to resist wind forces includes all of the following, *EXCEPT*

    A. inward pressure on windward walls.

    B. inward pressure on leeward roofs.

    C. upward pressure on flat roofs.

    D. inward or outward pressure on windward roofs, depending on the slope.

87. Which of the following diagrams correctly represents the wind pressures used to design a building?

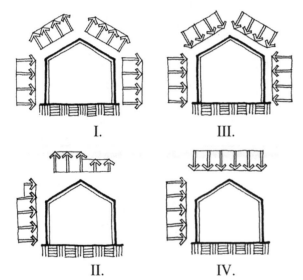

    A. I and II

    B. III and IV

    C. I and IV

    D. II and III

88. Select the correct statements about the horizontal thrust at the base of a three-hinged arch.

    I. The thrust is directly proportional to the vertical load supported by the arch.

    II. The thrust is directly proportional to the arch span.

    III. The thrust is directly proportional to the rise of the arch.

    IV. The thrust increases if the temperature rises and decreases if the temperature drops.

    A. I, II, and IV

    B. I and III

    C. II and IV

    D. I and II

89. Select the *INCORRECT* statement about long-span construction.

    A. Secondary stresses in long-span structures may justify an increase in factors of safety.

    B. Consideration should be given to using different factors of safety for site-assembled and factory-assembled building components.

    C. The factors of safety for long-span building components should not exceed those specified in the building code.

    D. The effects of temperature are more critical in long-span structures than in conventional structures.

90. The structural action of a membrane is based on its _____ strength.

91. How does the dead load of a building affect the lateral forces from wind and earthquake?

   I. The lateral earthquake force is directly proportional to the dead load.

   II. The lateral wind force is directly proportional to the dead load.

   III. The dead load has no effect on the lateral earthquake force.

   IV. The dead load has no effect on the lateral wind force.

   A. I and II

   B. I and IV

   C. II and III

   D. III and IV

92. A building is constructed on a sloping site, and the lateral wind or earthquake forces are resisted by moment-resisting frames, as shown. Which column resists the greatest amount of lateral force, assuming all the columns have the same cross section?

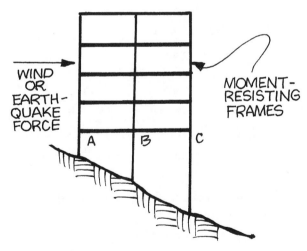

   A. Column A

   B. Column B

   C. Column C

   D. Columns A, B, and C equally

93. A beam is loaded as shown. Which of the following is the corresponding shear diagram?

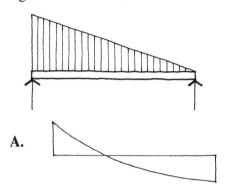

A.

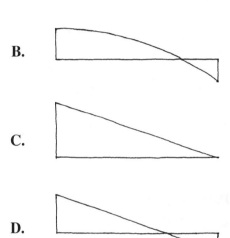

B.

C.

D.

94. Which of the following statements concerning the dome of the Florence Cathedral is *NOT* correct?

   A. It was designed by the great Renaissance architect Brunelleschi.

   B. It consists of a thick inner dome connected to a thinner outer dome.

   C. The construction of the dome required the largest temporary structure ever used up to that time for shoring.

   D. A series of built-in iron chains act to resist tensile forces and prevent the dome from cracking or collapsing.

95. Select the correct statement about the Pantheon.

    A. Built-in iron chains were used to resist hoop tensile stresses in the dome.

    B. Its dome was constructed of individual stones carefully fitted together.

    C. It was destroyed in the great earthquake of 1847.

    D. Its concrete dome, the largest of antiquity, still stands today.

96. Which of the following men were important figures in the evolution of the skyscraper?

    I.   Elisha Graves Otis

    II. Fazlur Khan

    III. William LeBaron Jenney

    IV. Robert Maillart

    A. I and III

    B. II and IV

    C. I, II, III, and IV

    D. I, II, and III

97. The roof of the Dulles Airport terminal is supported by a series of monumental concrete piers. Why do these piers lean outward?

    A. To express the concept of flight

    B. To counteract the pull of the roof cables

    C. To counteract the thrust of the roof arches

    D. To provide greater resistance to lateral forces from wind or earthquake

98. When the outside temperature increases, the top of a dome will

    A. move up.

    B. move down.

    C. remain in the same location.

    D. move sideways.

99. A sign above a roof is 10 feet by 20 feet and is supported by a diagonally-braced steel column at each end, as shown. If the wind load is 13 psf and the braces can only resist tension, what is the force in one of the braces?

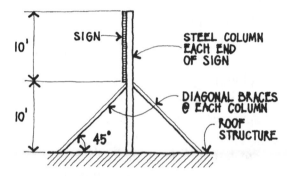

    A. 1,950# tension

    B. 2,758# tension

    C. 3,900# tension

    D. 5,515# tension

100. In lateral force resisting systems, diaphragms perform in which ways? Check all that apply.

    A. Transfer lateral loads from the roof and floors to the foundation

    B. Resist shear in their own plane, and tension

    C. Transfer lateral forces by torsion if they are rigid

    D. Transfer lateral loads to the vertical shear walls or frames below

101. A shear wall is subject to lateral wind load as shown. Which of the following diagrams correctly shows the soil pressure under the wall footing resulting from combined vertical load and overturning?

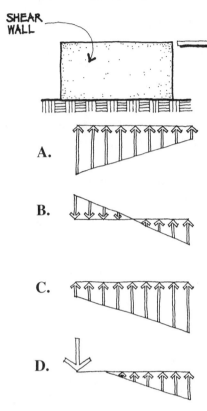

102. The John Hancock Building in Chicago and the Sears Tower have what in common?

I. They were designed by Skidmore, Owings, and Merrill.

II. They employ tubular systems to resist lateral loads.

III. They utilize reinforced concrete framing.

A. I only

B. II only

C. I and II

D. II and III

103. Which of the following statements about live load is correct?

A. In order to provide an adequate factor of safety, the live load may not be less than the dead load.

B. Live load is the load superimposed by the use and occupancy of the building, not including the wind load, earthquake load, or dead load.

C. If approved by the building official, the live load may be neglected in the design of a building, if it is less than the dead load.

D. Because of their greater vulnerability to failure, long-span structures must be designed for a greater live load than conventional structures.

104. Thin shells and membranes are able to resist load because of their

A. compressive strength.

B. shear strength.

C. form.

D. tensile strength.

105. A water tank weighing 50 kips is supported on a four-legged braced frame as shown. The seismic load is 15 kips and is assumed to act parallel to either axis of the frame. What is the overturning moment on the frame?

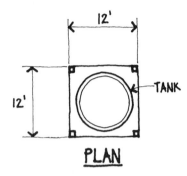

PLAN

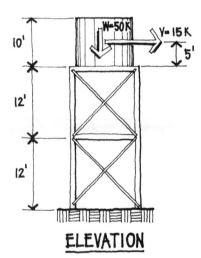

ELEVATION

A. Overturning moment = 217 ft.-kips

B. Overturning moment = 360 ft.-kips

C. Overturning moment = 435 ft.-kips

D. Overturning moment = 510 ft.-kips

106. Which of the following factors are more critical for long span buildings than for conventional buildings? Check all that apply.

A. Field inspection and testing

B. Snow drift loads and partial snow loads

C. The effects of temperature, creep, and shrinkage

D. Secondary stresses caused by deflection and the interaction of building elements

107. Which of the following statements about the continuous beam shown is *INCORRECT*? Neglect the weight of the beam.

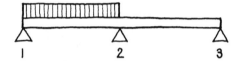

A. The moment in span 1-2 is always negative.

B. The moment over support 2 is negative.

C. The reaction at 3 is downward.

D. The moment in span 2-3 is always negative.

108. Which of the following statements concerning an object in equilibrium is *INCORRECT*?

A. There is no unbalanced force acting on the object.

B. The resultant force on the object passes through the centroid.

C. There is no unbalanced moment acting on the object.

D. The resultant force on the object is equal to zero.

109. For which of the following building types is long-span construction likely to be used? Check all that apply.

    A. Exhibition hall

    B. Basketball pavilion

    C. Library

    D. Auditorium

    E. University science building

110. Which surface in reinforced concrete can be formed using straight planks?

    A. Hyperbolic paraboloid

    B. Folded plate

    C. Geodesic dome

    D. Lamella

111. In what system used in Gothic cathedrals is load supported by piers at its four corners?

    A. Lamella

    B. Groined vault

    C. Dome

    D. Folded plate

112. What is the essential structural element of all suspension structures?

    A. Arch

    B. Dome

    C. Cable

    D. Plate girder

113. Select the correct statements concerning lateral forces, according to the allowable stress design requirements of the International Building Code.

    I. Because of the dynamic nature of seismic forces, the calculated seismic overturning moment is modified by a factor which effectively decreases the moment.

    II. The dead load resisting moment must be at least 1.67 times the overturning moment caused by wind forces.

    III. The dead load resisting moment must be at least 1.5 times the overturning moment caused by seismic forces.

    IV. The lateral seismic force applied at each floor line is proportional to the dead load located at that floor.

    V. Because of the excellent performance of symmetrical buildings in earthquakes, no provision for horizontal torsional moments is required for such buildings.

    A. I, II, III, IV, and V

    B. I, II, and III

    C. III and IV

    D. II only

114. In designing a building for earthquakes in accordance with the International Building Code, the lateral seismic force depends on which of the following? Check all that apply.

    A. Soil conditions at the site

    B. Live load

    C. Building's location

    D. Type of lateral load resisting system

115. A component that has the principal purpose to spread the column load so that the bearing pressure on the foundation is not excessive is called a

_____.

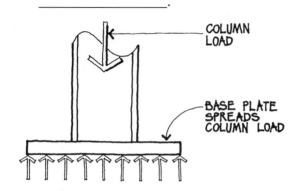

116. Which of the following are advantages of a conventional truss over a Vierendeel truss?

I. Less deflection

II. Less material

III. Less conflict between truss members and doors or windows

IV. Ability to have loads applied between panel points

A. I and II

B. I and IV

C. II and III

D. I, II, and IV

117. In a structural steel rigid frame, moment resistance at the beam-column joints may be provided by which of the following?

I. Two clip angles bolted to the beam web and the column flange

II. Groove welds between the top and bottom beam flanges and the column flange

III. Plates welded to the column flange and bolted to the top and bottom beam flanges

IV. A seat angle welded to the column flange and bolted to the bottom flange of the beam

A. I and II

B. I and III

C. I, II, III, and IV

D. II and III

118. A wood column is used to support an axial load of 40 kips. The column is 16 feet long, and its ends are restrained against lateral movement. The design stress in compression parallel to the grain has been determined to be 732 psi. What is the smallest column that may be used?

A. 6×6

B. 6×8

C. 8×8

D. 8×10

119. In the detail shown, the item labeled "A" provides lateral support for the wall in case of earthquake. This item is a _____.

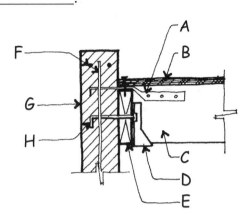

120. A two-hinged moment-resisting frame resists a lateral seismic load of 60 kips, as shown. Both columns have the same cross section. What is the moment at the beam-column intersection?

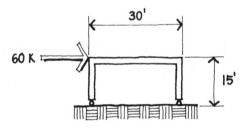

A. Zero
B. 225 ft.-kips
C. 450 ft.-kips
D. 900 ft.-kips

121. The U.S. Pavilion at Expo 70 in Osaka had an air-supported roof spanning 262 feet by 460 feet. Its occupied space was pressurized, and its roof was subject to upward suction from wind. Its concrete foundation ring was primarily subject to what type of stress?

A. Compression
B. Tension
C. Shear
D. Flexure

122. A series of parallel arches, skewed with respect to the axes of a building, which intersect another series of skewed arches, is known as a

A. groined vault.
B. lamella.
C. Schwedler dome.
D. hyperbolic paraboloid.

123. Which of the following statements are true? A long-span shell structure

I. is suitable for resisting concentrated loads.
II. can resist both compression and tension in its own plane.
III. cannot resist any substantial bending stress.
IV. cannot resist any shear stress.

A. II, III, and IV
B. I and II
C. III and IV
D. II and III

124. The four basic structural systems shown below are being considered for a long-span roof. Which of them supports uniform vertical loads primarily by compression?

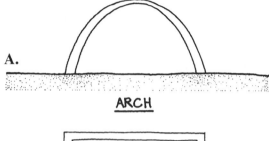

A.

ARCH

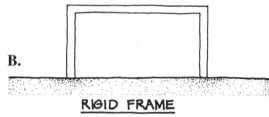

B.

RIGID FRAME

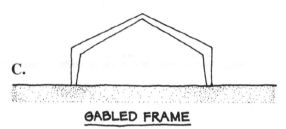

C.

GABLED FRAME

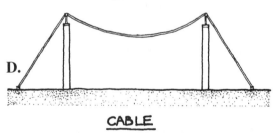

D.

CABLE

125. Which of the following is the best definition of "space frame"?

A. A two-way system of rigid frames

B. A moment-resisting frame

C. A two-way system of trusses

D. Any three-dimensional structural system

126. Long-span steel joists spanning 60 feet between girders are used to support a roof. The joists are spaced 6 feet on center, the dead load is 20 pounds per square foot (including the joist weight), the live load is 20 pounds per square foot, and the live load deflection is limited to 1/360 of the span. What is the lightest joist that can support the load? Use the table on page 104, which is reproduced from the Standard Specifications for Steel Joists.

A. 32LH06

B. 36LH07

C. 36LH08

D. 36LH09

127. A roof truss spans 80 feet and supports panel point loads of 15 kips each, as shown below. What is the maximum internal force in the top chord?

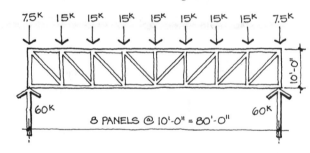

A. 15 kips

B. 60 kips

C. 112.5 kips

D. 120 kips

128. Reinforced concrete circular domes

A. generally resist flexural stresses.

B. are economical in the use of concrete.

C. are effective in resisting concentrated loads.

D. are inexpensive to form.

129. The roof of a building is supported by steel joists that span between joist girders. The typical bay is 60 feet by 60 feet, the joists are spaced at 6 feet on center, and the total dead and live load, including the joist girder weight, is 40 psf. What is the load at each panel point of a typical joist girder?

   A. 7.2 kips

   B. 12.0 kips

   C. 14.4 kips

   D. 24.0 kips

130. Which of the four space frame plan layouts shown below is most economical?

A.
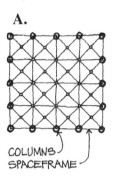
COLUMNS
SPACEFRAME

C.
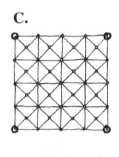

B.
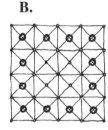

D.
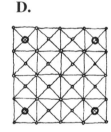

131. In the design of steel columns, the factor K is a function of the

   A. length of the column.

   B. radius of gyration of the column.

   C. yield strength of the steel.

   D. end conditions of the column.

132. The wind pressures used in the design of buildings depend on

   I. wind speed.

   II. terrain.

   III. occupancy category.

   IV. the part of the building under consideration.

   A. I and III

   B. II and IV

   C. I, II, and IV

   D. I, II, III, and IV

133. Which of the following most closely represents the distribution of wind forces used to design a building?

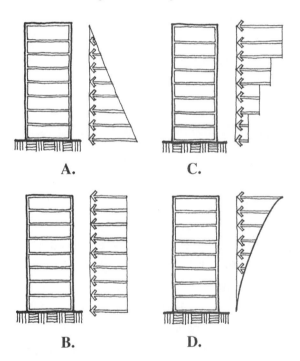

      A.   **C.**

      B.   **D.**

134. The beam shown has a reaction of 80 kips. It is attached to the column by an end plate welded to the beam web and bolted to the column flange. How many inches of 1/4-inch fillet weld are required on each side of the beam web? Use E70XX electrodes with an allowable shear stress of 21.0 ksi.

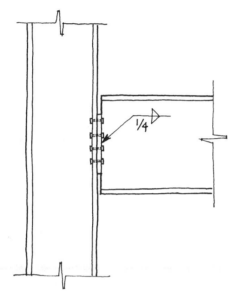

A. 8″

B. 11″

C. 16″

D. 22″

135. Select the correct statement about reinforced concrete columns.

A. Reinforced concrete columns are normally designed for axial compression only.

B. Spiral columns have greater axial load capacity than tied columns.

C. Spiral and tied columns are both designed with the same strength reduction factor ϕ.

D. Tied columns are more expensive than spiral columns.

136. Wind and seismic forces are fundamentally different. In this regard, which of the following statements are correct?

I. Wind is an actual surface-applied force, while seismic forces are simulated.

II. Wind forces are unrelated to dead load, while seismic forces are directly proportional to dead load.

III. Wind forces are independent of the type of lateral load resisting system, while seismic forces vary according to the type of lateral load resisting system.

A. I and II

B. II and III

C. I and III

D. I, II, and III

137. Which of the following loads is *NOT* required to be combined with seismic loads in the design of building components when using strength design load combinations?

A. Roof live load

B. Floor live load

C. Dead load

D. Snow load

138. Select the correct statements about the Eiffel Tower.

    I. It was the first great structure built of steel.

    II. Its shape is ideally suited to resist wind forces.

    III. It is the tallest freestanding tower in the world.

    IV. It was originally designed to be dismantled after the International Exposition of 1889 in Paris.

    A. II and IV

    B. I, II, and III

    C. I and III

    D. I, II, III, and IV

139. Select the correct statements about diaphragms.

    I. They are analogous to horizontal girders.

    II. They resist shear in their own plane.

    III. They transfer lateral loads to the vertical resisting elements.

    A. I and II

    B. I and III

    C. II and III

    D. I, II, and III

140. Select the correct statements about Load and Resistance Factor Design (LRFD) for steel structures.

    A. The actual dead, live, and other loads are multiplied by their respective load factors.

    B. The nominal strength is multiplied by a resistance factor ϕ, which is generally less than 1.

    C. The actual unfactored loads are used in design.

    D. The factor of safety is obtained by using allowable stresses that are less than the yield stress.

141. Wide flange steel beams are efficient bending members because

    A. they have thick webs.

    B. most of their material is in the flanges.

    C. they are symmetrical about both axes.

    D. their strength is the same about both axes.

142. The footing shown in the plan is called a

    A. mat foundation.

    B. combined footing.

    C. cantilever footing.

    D. pile cap.

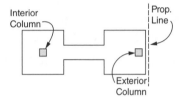

143. In comparing wind and earthquake forces, which of the following statements are correct?

    I. Both depend on the geographic location of the site.

    II. Both involve design for horizontal forces.

    III. For both, a 33⅓ percent increase in allowable stresses is permitted.

    IV. The magnitude of earthquake forces depends on the type of lateral force resisting system used.

    A. I, II, and IV

    B. I, II, III, and IV

    C. I only

    D. II only

144. Providing resistance to lateral wind or earthquake forces always requires some additional cost. In this regard, which of the following statements are true?

A. The additional cost will usually be minimized if the structural members used to resist vertical loads are also used to resist the lateral loads.

B. The additional cost will usually be minimized if a separate structural system, independent of the vertical load carrying system, is used to resist the lateral loads.

C. The additional cost will usually be minimized if the lateral force resisting system is expressed visually, as in the John Hancock Building.

D. The additional cost will always be minimized if a base isolation system is used.

145. Given the building and forces shown below, what is the maximum diaphragm shear in the north-south direction?

A. 540#/ft.

B. 1,080#/ft.

C. 120#/ft.

D. 240#/ft.

146. Radial cables support the roof of a circular building, as shown below. Which of the following statements is correct concerning the stress in the inner and outer rings?

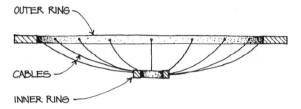

A. Both inner and outer rings are in tension.

B. Both inner and outer rings are in compression.

C. The inner ring is in tension and the outer ring is in compression.

D. The inner ring is in compression and the outer ring is in tension.

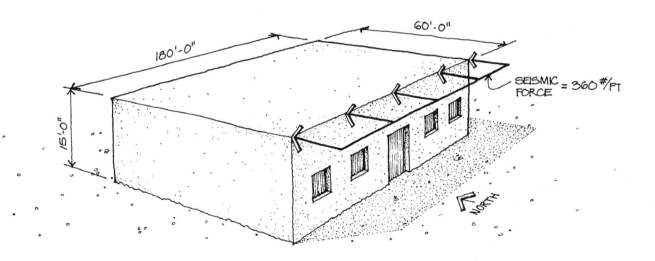

147. Select the correct statement concerning the structural member shown.

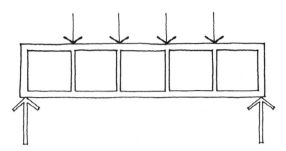

A. It tends to deflect less than a comparable triangulated truss.

B. It is unstable, as it is not composed of triangles.

C. In addition to axial stresses, the chord members must also resist bending moments, which are greater close to the supports than at midspan.

D. The joints must be pinned to avoid excessive stresses caused by deformation.

148. The braced frame shown below resists a wind load of 10 kips acting to the left. If the braces can resist tension only, what is the force in the left column caused by the wind?

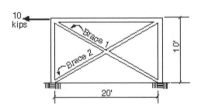

A. 5 kips compression

B. 5 kips tension

C. 10 kips compression

D. 10 kips tension

149. Which of the following are likely to be critical for overturning caused by wind forces? Check all that apply.

A. A large height-to-width ratio of the vertical resisting elements

B. The orientation of the building

C. Heavy equipment located on upper floors

150. When designing buildings for wind forces, which of the following effects are *NOT* considered?

I. Drift

II. Liquefaction

III. Tsunamis

IV. Overturning moment

A. I only

B. II and III

C. I, II, and III

D. I, II, III, and IV

151. Which of the following statements about long-span open web steel joists is correct?

A. Long-span joists generally have sufficient stiffness so that cambering the joists to prevent ponding of water is not necessary.

B. The most economical way to prevent ponding of water is to build pitch into the top chords of the joists.

C. Because of the possibility of ponding, long-span joists must be designed to support the weight of two inches of water uniformly over the entire roof surface.

D. Long-span joists should be provided with sufficient camber or pitch to prevent the accumulation of rainwater.

152. A parking structure is to have a clear span of 62 feet. Which of the following systems are likely to be practical and economical?

   I. Conventional cast-in-place reinforced concrete

   II. Glued laminated beams with heavy planking over

   III. Posttensioned concrete girders with pretensioned concrete planking over

   IV. Prestressed concrete tees

   V. Exposed steel girders with conventional cast-in-place concrete slab over

   A. All of the above

   B. IV and V

   C. III and IV

   D. III and V

153. You have selected a typical bay size 20 feet by 50 feet for a building for which you are the architect. The floor system consists of a concrete slab connected by studs to composite structural steel beams and girders. The beam spacing is 10 feet. You are investigating two different framing schemes: (1) 50-foot beams and 20-foot girders, and (2) 20-foot beams and 50-foot girders. Select the correct statement.

   A. Scheme 1 usually requires less weight of structural steel and less depth of construction.

   B. Scheme 2 usually requires less weight of structural steel and less depth of construction.

   C. Scheme 1 usually requires more weight of structural steel and less depth of construction.

   D. Scheme 2 usually requires more weight of structural steel and less depth of construction.

154. In the design of long-span buildings, the process that provides an additional safeguard against design deficiencies is called _____.

155. The detail shown below is to be used in an area of seismic risk to (1) transfer vertical load from the framing to the wall and (2) anchor the wall to the diaphragm for seismic load. Which of the following statements is correct?

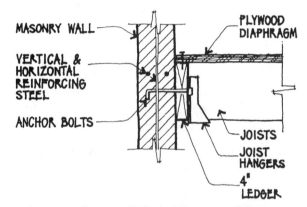

   A. The detail is acceptable for both transferring vertical load and anchoring the wall.

   B. The detail is unacceptable for both transferring vertical load and anchoring the wall.

   C. The detail is acceptable for anchoring the wall but unacceptable for transferring vertical load.

   D. The detail is acceptable for transferring vertical load but unacceptable for anchoring the wall.

156. A parapet must be designed to resist a seismic force equal to what percentage of its weight? $S_{DS} = 1.0g$.

   A. 20 percent

   B. 30 percent

   C. 120 percent

   D. 200 percent

157. A membrane inflated by air pressure encloses an occupied space and is anchored to a reinforced concrete ring at its perimeter. Which of the following statements is correct?

   I.   The ring is in compression.

   II. The ring is in tension.

   III. The membrane tends to lift off the ring.

   IV. The membrane tends to push down on the ring.

   A. I and IV

   B. I and III

   C. II and IV

   D. II and III

158. A tank is filled with water to a depth of ten feet. Which of the following diagrams correctly shows the pressure exerted on the tank walls? The unit weight of water is 62.4 pounds per cubic foot.

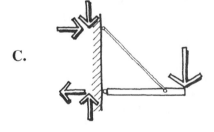

159. Which of the following diagrams correctly shows the reactions acting on the structure shown?

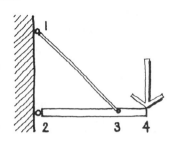

A.

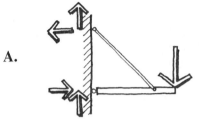

B.

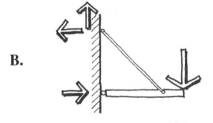

C.

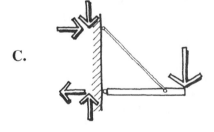

D.

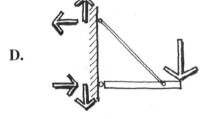

160. An eight-story office building is to be designed for a site in Los Angeles and is assigned to SDC D. The lateral force resisting system consists of special moment-resisting frames (R = 8). The design accelerations SDS and SDI are equal to 1.50g and 0.59g, respectively, and the fundamental period of the structure (T) equals one second. What is the seismic base shear as a percentage of the building weight?

- **A.** 5.66 percent
- **B.** 7.04 percent
- **C.** 14.2 percent
- **D.** 56.6 percent

161. The earthquake regulations in the International Building Code are intended to make buildings resistant to which of the following?

- **I.** Earth slides
- **II.** Soil liquefaction
- **III.** Ground shaking
- **IV.** Faulting near the structure
- **A.** I and II
- **B.** III and IV
- **C.** III only
- **D.** I, II, III, and IV

162. An existing storage facility, designed and constructed in accordance with the latest edition of the International Building Code, is to be converted to a restaurant seating 200 people. The building's lateral force resisting system must be adequate to resist how much more seismic force than in the original design.

- **A.** No additional seismic force
- **B.** 15 percent more seismic force
- **C.** 25 percent more seismic force
- **D.** 50 percent more seismic force

163. The roof of a convention hall has a column-free space that is 150 feet square. Two systems being considered are a space frame and a system of one-way parallel trusses. What are the advantages of the space frame over the parallel trusses?

- **I.** The space frame tends to deflect less.
- **II.** The space frame can be made shallower.
- **III.** Loads are resisted by all the members of the space frame.
- **IV.** The space frame spans in two directions.
- **A.** III and IV
- **B.** II and IV
- **C.** I and II
- **D.** I, II, III, and IV

164. The deflection of a reinforced concrete beam is affected by which of the following?

- **I.** The load supported by the beam
- **II.** The duration of the load
- **III.** The span of the beam
- **IV.** The yield point of the reinforcing steel
- **V.** The moment of inertia of the beam section
- **VI.** The strength of the concrete
- **A.** All of the above
- **B.** I, III, and V
- **C.** II, IV, and VI
- **D.** I, II, III, V, and VI

165. What is the purpose of stirrups in reinforced concrete beams?

    A. To resist shear stresses

    B. To resist compressive stresses

    C. To resist negative moment

    D. To restrain the main reinforcement against buckling

166. What is the correct shear diagram for the beam shown?

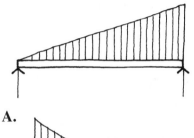

    A.

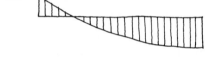

    B.

    C.

    D.

167. Complete the following statement. A rigid frame is a

    A. system of beams and columns with diagonal bracing.

    B. structural steel frame in which all the joints are welded.

    C. frame restrained against rotation at its bases.

    D. frame with rigid joints that is able to resist vertical and lateral loads.

168. A one-story rigid frame with fixed bases resists a horizontal load as shown. Neglecting the weight of the frame, which of the following correctly shows the directions of the reactions and moments at the bases?

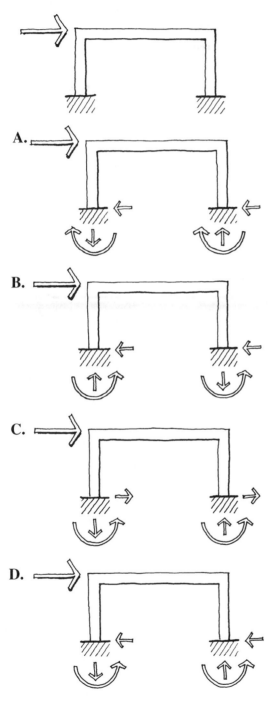

169. What is a soft story?

  A. A story whose strength is much less than that of the story above

  B. A story whose stiffness is much less than that of the story above

  C. A story that has no moment resistance

  D. A story that has no torsional resistance

170. Infilling a moment-resisting frame with a nonstructural wall tends to

  A. strengthen the frame.

  B. weaken the frame.

  C. have no effect on the frame.

  D. stiffen the frame.

171. The displacement caused by lateral loads of one level of a building relative to the level above or below is called _____ .

172. The rigidity of a building under wind loading can be substantially increased (the displacement decreased) by sloping the exterior columns to form a pyramid. A good example of this is the

  A. Marina City Towers in Chicago.

  B. ABC Building in Los Angeles.

  C. Transamerica Building in San Francisco.

  D. Seagram Building in New York.

173. Select the correct statement about the three-hinged arch shown below.

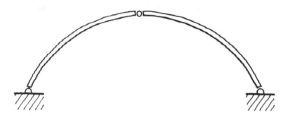

    A. There is no horizontal reaction at the bases if the arch supports only one concentrated load at midspan.

    B. When supporting vertical loads, the arch has horizontal reactions at its bases, which are equal in magnitude and opposite in direction.

    C. For stability, the arch must be able to resist bending moment at the crown.

    D. The arch can support upward or downward vertical loads, but is unable to resist horizontal loads.

174. Which of the following connectors are generally *NOT* used in moment-resisting structural steel connections?

    A. ASTM A325-SC high-strength bolts

    B. ASTM A307 machine bolts

    C. Full penetration groove welds

    D. Fillet welds

175. A 24-foot-long steel beam is installed when the temperature is 60°F. How much will it expand if the temperature rises to 90°F? The coefficient of expansion of steel is 0.0000065.

    A. 0.047″

    B. 0.056″

    C. 0.112″

    D. 0.168″

176. Which of the following diagrams most closely approximates the vertical distribution of earthquake forces in a short, stiff building?

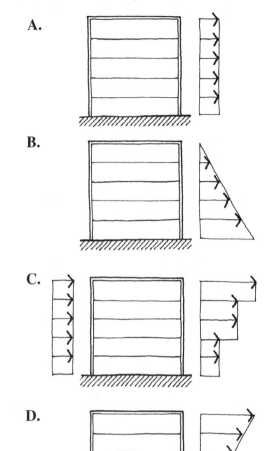

177. A re-entrant corner is considered to be a(n)

    A. vertical structural irregularity.

    B. plan structural irregularity.

    C. diaphragm discontinuity.

    D. out-of-plane offset.

178. The roof of a circular building is supported by a series of radial cables, which connect to a ring at the center of the roof and to another ring at the perimeter. Which of the following statements is correct?

    A. The center ring is higher than the perimeter ring.

    B. Both rings are in tension.

    C. The center ring is in tension and the perimeter ring is in compression.

    D. Both rings are in compression.

179. A beam supports the loads shown below. What is the reaction at R_1, neglecting the weight of the beam?

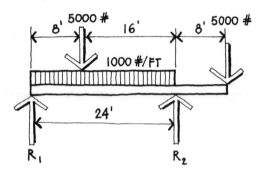

    A. 20,333#

    B. 17,000#

    C. 15,333#

    D. 13,667#

180. A bar two inches in diameter and 10 feet long stretches 0.159″ when subject to a tensile load of 50 kips. What is the modulus of elasticity of the bar?

    A. 1,001,000 psi

    B. 10,010,000 psi

    C. 12,012,000 psi

    D. 29,000,000 psi

181. Floor plans of four reinforced concrete buildings are shown. Which will have the greatest amount of torsion when resisting lateral forces?

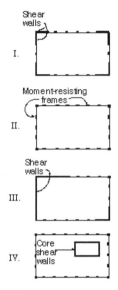

    A. I and III

    B. II and IV

    C. I and II

    D. III and IV

182. A wall that functions as a vertically oriented cantilever beam is a _____.

183. Buildings must be designed to resist

    A. wind forces only, not earthquake.

    B. earthquake forces only, not wind.

    C. wind or earthquake forces, but not both acting at the same time.

    D. wind and earthquake forces acting at the same time.

184. Which of the systems shown are stable under the action of horizontal wind or earthquake forces?

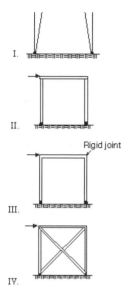

I.

II.

Rigid joint

III.

IV.

A. I and III
B. I, III, and IV
C. IV only
D. I, II, III, and IV

185. All of the following statements about wind and seismic design are correct, *EXCEPT*

A. structures are expected to yield inelastically during a major earthquake.
B. wind forces are exterior surface-applied forces.
C. seismic forces are simulated forces caused by a building's inertia.
D. except for buildings in areas of high seismic risk, wind forces generally exceed seismic forces.

186. The main cables in a suspension-type roof structure are stressed in

A. compression and bending.
B. compression only.
C. tension and bending.
D. tension only.

187. The load carrying capacity of a square or rectangular wood column is determined by all of the following *EXCEPT* the

A. radius of gyration of the column section.
B. unbraced height of the column.
C. species of lumber.
D. dimensions of the column section.

188. Which of the following statements about composite design is *NOT* true?

A. Composite design should only be used when conventional steel framing cannot support the design loads.
B. Composite design is generally more economical than conventional steel framing.
C. Deflection is more critical in composite design than in conventional steel framing.
D. The shear connectors used in composite design can develop the ultimate capacity of the steel or the concrete, whichever is less.

189. A W24 × 68 steel beam supports a uniformly distributed load of 2,000 pounds per lineal foot on a simple span of 28 feet. How much does it deflect, if I for the beam is 1,830 in.4 and E is 29,000,000 psi? See the beam formulas provided in the table on page 105.

    A. 0.11″

    B. 0.19″

    C. 0.38″

    D. 0.52″

190. A braced frame resists a horizontal wind load of 10 kips acting to the right, as shown. The diagonal brace can resist either tension or compression. What are the internal forces in the left and right columns caused by the 10 kip wind load acting to the right?

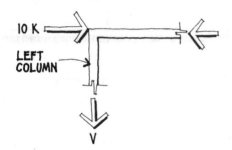

    A. Left column = zero, right column = 13.3 kips compression

    B. Left column = 13.3 kips tension, right column = zero

    C. Left column = 13.3 kips compression, right column = 13.3 kips tension

    D. Left column = zero, right column = 13.3 kips tension

191. Which of the following statements is correct?

    A. Seismic forces are exterior surface applied forces.

    B. Wind forces are inertially applied forces.

    C. During a major earthquake, structures are likely to behave inelastically.

    D. During a major windstorm, structures are likely to behave inelastically.

192. In the glued laminated roof system shown, what is the main purpose of connections A and B?

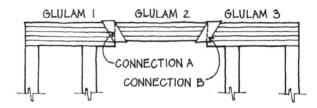

    A. To transfer the vertical reactions of glulam 2 to glulams 1 and 3

    B. To transfer the vertical reactions of glulams 1 and 3 to glulam 2

    C. To provide a moment splice between the glulams

    D. To transfer the horizontal reactions of glulam 2 to glulams 1 and 3

193. A steel beam supports a load of 1,000 pounds per foot on a simple span of 24 feet. The deflection is not to exceed L/360. What is the minimum required moment of inertia? $E = 29 \times 10^6$ psi and $\Delta = 5wL^4/384EI$.

    A. 321.8 in.[4]

    B. 1,609 in.[4]

    C. 2,234 in.[4]

    D. 3,218 in.[4]

194. A steel truss supporting equally spaced concentrated loads from a floor or roof system is called a _____.

195. For the building shown below in the plan, the lateral earthquake force in the east-west direction is equal to 100 kips. What is the magnitude of the torsional moment?

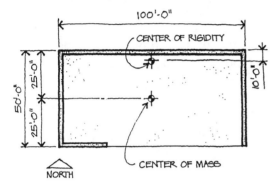

A. 1,000 ft.-kips

B. 1,500 ft.-kips

C. 2,500 ft.-kips

D. 5,000 ft.-kips

196. Select the correct statement. Base isolation is

A. permitted only in SDC C and SDC D.

B. an alternative structural design technique for buildings in seismic areas.

C. not permitted.

D. another term for seismic separation.

197. An eight-story office building with a special steel moment-resisting frame is to be designed for a site in Phoenix, Arizona. What is the seismic base shear as a percentage of the building weight? Assume $T = 1.20$ seconds, $S_{DS} = 0.41g$, and $S_{DI} = 0.15g$.

A. 1.6 percent of the building weight

B. 16.0 percent of the building weight

C. 3.2 percent of the building weight

D. 8.6 percent of the building weight

198. The load capacity of a structural steel column depends on the ratio Kl/r. In this regard, which of the following statements is correct?

I. K is a constant determined by the end conditions of the columns.

II. l is the effective length of the column.

III. r is the radius of gyration, which depends on the yield strength of the steel.

A. I only

B. I and II

C. I and III

D. II and III

199. What is the force in bolt A resulting from the handrail detail shown below?

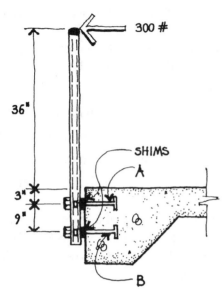

A.   1,300 lbs. tension

B.   1,600 lbs. tension

C.   300 lbs. tension

D.   1,300 lbs. compression

200. Select the correct statement concerning strength design of reinforced concrete.

I.   The minimum amount of reinforcing steel permitted is that which would produce balanced design.

II. The maximum amount of reinforcing steel permitted is less than that which would produce balanced design.

III. The design must ensure that yielding of the steel will occur before crushing of the concrete.

A.   I and II

B.   II and III

C.   I and III

D.   I, II, and III

201. A steel column supports an axial load of 200 kips and bears on a 16″ × 16″ base plate. What is the bearing pressure under the base plate?

A.   1,563 psi

B.   781 psi

C.   391 psi

D.   125 psi

202. Which of the following methods of splicing reinforcing bars is allowed?

I.   Lapped splices

II. Welded splices

III. Mechanical connection splices

A.   I only

B.   I and III

C.   II and III

D.   I, II, and III

203. Which of the following statements about shell structures is correct?

I.   A shell structure can only resist compression in its own plane.

II. Shell structures are suitable for resisting concentrated loads.

III. Shell structures are too thin to resist any appreciable bending stresses.

A.   I and II

B.   II and III

C.   III only

D.   I, II, and III

204. The reaction at support C of the continuous beam shown below is 1.5 kips downward. Neglecting the weight of the beam, what is the reaction at support A?

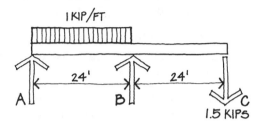

A.   10.5 kips

B.   12.0 kips

C.   13.5 kips

D.   15.0 kips

205. The floor framing of a building uses I-shaped wood joists spaced at 16 inches on center. The joists consist of solid wood flanges and a board web, which is inserted and glued into grooves in the flanges. What type of stress is resisted by the glue?

A.   Compression

B.   Tension

C.   Shear

D.   Bending

206. Four causes of earthquake damage to buildings are listed below. The earthquake regulations of the International Building Code are intended to provide resistance to which of them?

I.   Ground rupture in fault zones

II.   Ground failure

III. Tsunamis

IV.   Ground shaking

A.   I, II, III, and IV

B.   II and IV

C.   IV only

D.   I and II

207. The earthquake regulations in the International Building Code consider all of the following factors, *EXCEPT*

A.   building configuration.

B.   occupancy category.

C.   soil characteristics.

D.   Richter magnitude.

208. The purpose of the earthquake regulations in the International Building Code, as well as other codes, is

A.   to safeguard against major failures and loss of life.

B.   to maintain building functions during and after an earthquake.

C.   to limit damage in the event of a major earthquake.

D.   to provide for easy repair of earthquake damage.

209. Select the correct statements about cable roof structures.

I.   A cable is always under tension.

II.   High strength cable is about four times as strong as structural steel.

III. In a suspension roof, the cable material represents the largest part of the structural framing cost.

IV.   The dynamic behavior of cable-supported roofs is more critical than that of conventionally framed roofs.

V.   When supporting a load that is uniformly distributed horizontally across its entire span, a draped cable will assume the shape of a hyperbol

A.   III and V

B.   I, III, and IV

C.   I, II, IV, and V

D.   I, II, and IV

210. What is the horizontal thrust at each end of the three-hinged arch shown below?

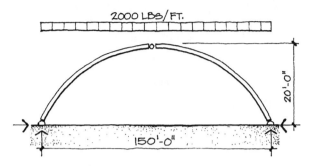

2000 LBS/FT.

20'-0"

150'-0"

A. 75 kips

B. 150 kips

C. 281.25 kips

D. 562.5 kips

211. Select the correct statements about composite steel beam and concrete slab construction.

I. Welded studs transfer moment between the steel beam and the concrete slab.

II. For the same load and span, a composite beam is generally shallower than a noncomposite beam.

III. A composite beam has greater stiffness than a noncomposite beam of equal depth, size, load, and span.

IV. Deflection, particularly of the steel beam alone under construction loads, may be critical and should be calculated.

A. I and II

B. II and IV

C. I and III

D. II, III, and IV

212. Select the correct statements about reinforced concrete columns.

I. A spiral column has more axial load-carrying capacity than an otherwise identical tied column.

II. A spiral column has greater fire resistance than an otherwise identical tied column.

III. Spiral columns are generally round, while tied columns are generally square.

IV. Spiral columns have simpler forming than tied columns.

A. I only

B. I and III

C. II and III

D. I, II, III, and IV

213. Which of the structures shown below is able to resist a lateral load from wind or earthquake?

I.

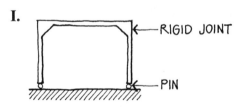

RIGID JOINT

PIN

II.

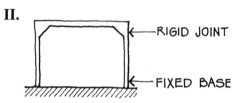

RIGID JOINT

FIXED BASE

III.

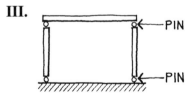

PIN

PIN

A. I and II

B. II only

C. I only

D. I, II, and III

214. A member that collects and transfers lateral forces to a shear wall, braced frame, or moment-resisting frame is called a _____.

215. Which of the following is the best definition of live load?

   A. The load superimposed by the use and occupancy of a building, not including the wind, earthquake, or dead load.

   B. Any continuously applied load, except the dead load.

   C. The load superimposed by the use and occupancy of a building, including the wind or earthquake load, but not including the dead load.

   D. The weight of a building's occupants and movable furniture.

216. For which of the following building types does the structural cost represent the lowest percentage of the total cost of construction?

   A. Hospital
   B. Warehouse
   C. Parking garage
   D. Shopping mall

217. You are designing a parking garage with a span of 62 feet. Which of the following systems would probably be practical and economical?

   I. One-way concrete joist and beam
   II. Prestressed concrete tees
   III. Flat slab
   IV. Posttensioned concrete girders with pretensioned concrete planking

   A. I and III
   B. I and IV
   C. II and IV
   D. I, II, III, and IV

218. Which of the following correctly shows the reactions at A and B for the structure shown?

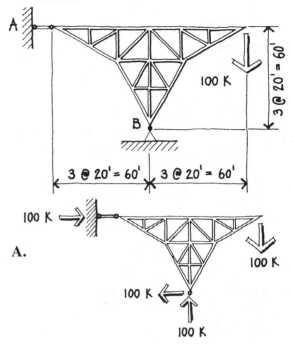

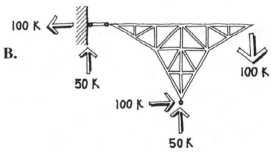

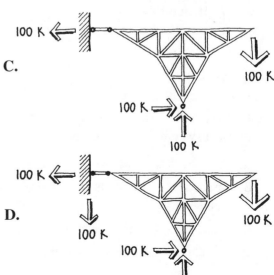

219. For rigid diaphragm structures, shear walls resist lateral seismic loads in proportion to their

   A. length.

   B. rigidity.

   C. thickness.

   D. height.

220. Which of the systems shown are stable under the action of horizontal wind or earthquake forces?

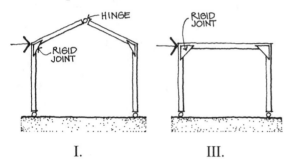

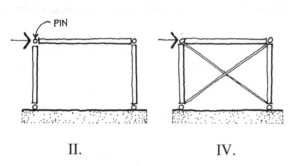

   A. I, III, and IV

   B. I, II, III, and IV

   C. III only

   D. IV only

221. In earthquake design, it is most desirable to use a system that comprises

   A. bearing walls that also resist shear.

   B. braced frames that also resist vertical loads.

   C. concrete eccentric braced frames.

   D. special moment-resisting frames.

222. A steel column in a moment-resisting steel frame is to be constructed as shown below. To determine the value of K for the column, the top of the column is assumed to be

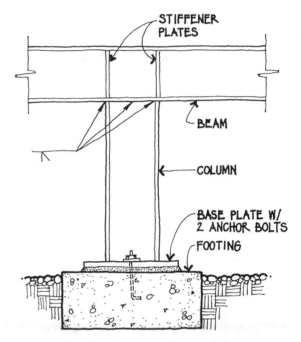

   A. fixed against rotation and free to translate.

   B. free to rotate and fixed against translation.

   C. free to rotate and free to translate.

   D. fixed against rotation and fixed against translation.

223. Which of the following types of soil is most susceptible to volumetric change caused by change of moisture content?

   A. Sand

   B. Gravel

   C. Rock

   D. Clay

224. The strength of a fillet weld is

  A. equal to that of a complete penetration groove weld.

  B. the same as that of the connected material.

  C. based on the shear strength through the throat of the weld.

  D. based on the tensile strength through the throat of the weld.

225. Reinforcing steel in the side opposite the tension side of a reinforced concrete beam does which of the following?

  I. Resists compression

  II. Resists shear stress

  III. Resists tension

  IV. Reduces the beam deflection resulting from creep

  A. I only

  B. I and III

  C. I and IV

  D. II, III, and IV

226. The purpose of the effective length factor K used in the design of structural steel columns is to

  A. evaluate the earthquake force that a column must resist.

  B. provide a method for designing columns with varying end restraints.

  C. modify the allowable column loads for different grades of steel.

  D. provide a method for designing columns that resist both moment and direct stress.

227. A building with a long period is associated with which of the following?

  A. Flexibility, low acceleration, low seismic force

  B. High overturning moments

  C. Rigidity, high acceleration, high seismic force

  D. Flexibility, high acceleration, high seismic force

228. A one-story building resists a seismic load of 200 pounds per foot, as shown. What is the maximum shear in the roof diaphragm?

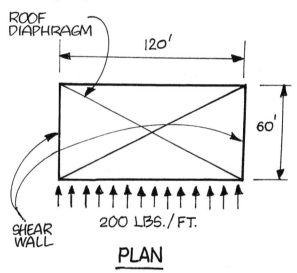

  A. 100 pounds per foot

  B. 150 pounds per foot

  C. 200 pounds per foot

  D. 400 pounds per foot

229. The Modified Mercalli scale is used to measure the

    A. ground acceleration of an earthquake.

    B. period of an earthquake.

    C. intensity of an earthquake as determined by subjective reactions.

    D. total energy released in an earthquake.

230. The resistance to sliding of a retaining wall should equal at least

    A. 75 percent of the total lateral pressure of the retained earth.

    B. 90 percent of the total lateral pressure of the retained earth.

    C. the total lateral pressure of the retained earth.

    D. 1.5 times the total lateral pressure of the retained earth.

231. The basic stress in an arch is

    A. compression.

    B. tension.

    C. flexure.

    D. shear.

232. How are the design values for wood adjusted for the duration of the load?

    A. The shorter the duration, the greater the design values.

    B. The shorter the duration, the lower the design values.

    C. The shorter the duration, the greater the design values for members, but not for mechanical fasteners.

    D. The duration does not affect the design values.

233. Your design calculations for a retaining wall show that the dead load resisting moment is equal to 1.5 times the overturning moment from earth pressure. Which of the following statements is correct?

    A. The design is satisfactory.

    B. The footing should be made wider.

    C. The footing should be made deeper.

    D. The amount of reinforcing steel in the wall and footing should be increased.

234. Buildings must be designed to resist which of the following allowable stress load combinations?

    I. Dead + 0.75 (floor live) + 0.75 (wind)

    II. Dead + 0.75 (floor live) + 0.75 [0.7 (seismic)]

    III. Dead + floor live + wind + seismic

    IV. Dead + one-half wind + 0.5 (seismic)

    A. I and II

    B. III only

    C. I, II, and III

    D. I, II, and IV

235. For a building with a rigid diaphragm, the lateral wind or earthquake load is distributed to the vertical resisting elements in accordance with their

    A. rigidities.

    B. strengths.

    C. locations.

    D. lengths.

236. For a plywood sheathed shear wall, which of the following statements is most correct?

   A. The minimum width of a plywood shear wall is determined by the height of the shear wall.

   B. The minimum width of a plywood shear wall is two feet.

   C. The minimum width of a plywood shear wall is equal to the total shear force divided by the allowable shear for the plywood used in the wall.

   D. The minimum width of a plywood shear wall is not limited.

237. The shear wall shown resists a lateral load of 10,000 pounds, and supports a dead load of 10,000 pounds at each end. What is the net uplift at point 1?

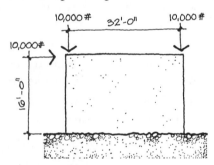

   A. Zero

   B. 5,000 pounds

   C. 10,000 pounds

   D. 20,000 pounds

238. The stresses in the one-story rigid frame shown are correctly identified in which of the following diagrams? (T = tension, C = compression.

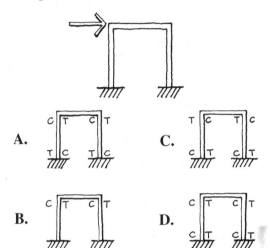

239. A column has a tributary area of 500 square feet and supports a roof and one floor. The loads are as follows: Roof dead load—20 lbs. per square foot; Roof live load—20 lbs. per square foot; Floor dead load—75 lbs. per square foot; Floor live load—100 lbs. per square foot. Neglecting the weight of the column, what is the smallest pad footing that may be used, if the allowable soil bearing value is 3,000 pounds per square foot?

   A. 4'-6" × 4'-6"

   B. 5'-6" × 5'-6"

   C. 6'-0" × 6'-0"

   D. 7'-0" × 7'-0"

240. Select the correct statement about long-span structures.

    A. Long-span structures generally have more redundancy than conventional structures.

    B. Connections in conventional structures are more critical than those in long-span structures.

    C. Long-span structures are more vulnerable to overall collapse than conventional structures.

    D. Because of their inherent instability, long-span structures generally require a dynamic load analysis.

241. Doubly reinforced concrete beams refer to

    A. beams with twice the required reinforcing steel, in order to provide a greater factor of safety.

    B. beams with compression as well as tension reinforcement.

    C. beams with shear as well as tension reinforcement.

    D. beams with tension reinforcement placed in two layers.

242. A reinforced concrete wall resists lateral seismic load as shown. Select the correct statement.

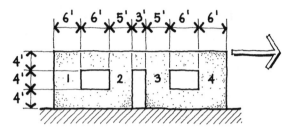

    A. Piers 1 and 4 resist more lateral load than piers 2 and 3.

    B. Piers 2 and 3 resist more lateral load than piers 1 and 4.

    C. Piers 1 and 2 resist more lateral load than piers 3 and 4.

    D. Each pier resists an equal amount of lateral load.

243. The seismic loads on the building shown are resisted by shear walls 1, 2, 3, and 4. The center of rigidity does not coincide with the center of mass. Which walls will have increased shears caused by horizontal torsional moment for seismic loads in the east-west direction?

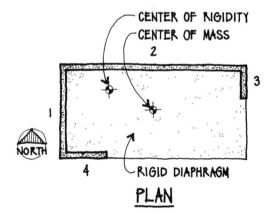

PLAN

    A. Walls 2 and 4

    B. Wall 4 only

    C. Wall 2 only

    D. Neither wall 2 nor wall 4

244. Which of the beam to column connections shown below might be used for a moment-resisting steel frame?

    A. I and II

    B. I and III

    C. III only

    D. I, II, III, and IV

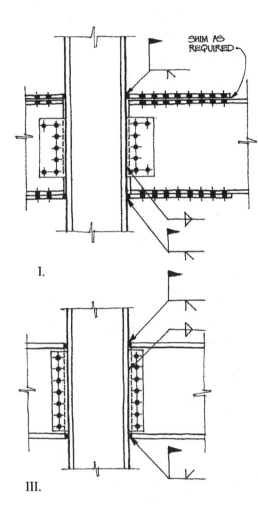

I.

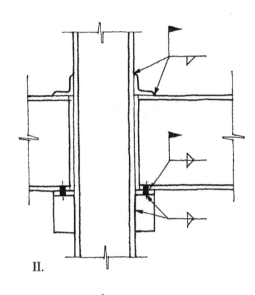

II.

III.

IV.

245. What is the midspan deflection of the beam shown to the right? Neglect the weight of the beam. Assume $E = 29 \times 10^6$ psi and $I = 2,100$ inches^4. See the beam formulas on page 109.

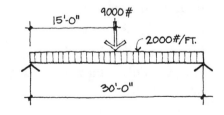

    A. 0.346″

    B. 0.498″

    C. 0.599″

    D. 0.743″

246. A moment-resisting frame with fixed bases resists a seismic load, as shown. Which of the following choices correctly shows the shape of the distorted frame?

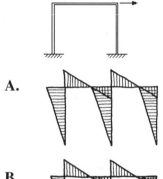

A.

B.

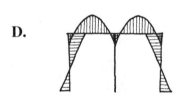

C.

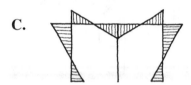

D.

247. Complete the following sentence. Eccentric braced frames

A. are no longer permitted, except in SDC A and B.

B. may be constructed of steel, concrete, or heavy timber.

C. may not be used in a dual system with moment-resisting frames.

D. are more ductile than concentric braced frames.

248. A rigid bar 20 feet long supports a load of 1,000 pounds at its end as shown. Which of the following sketches correctly represents the horizontal and vertical components of the forces acting on the bar?

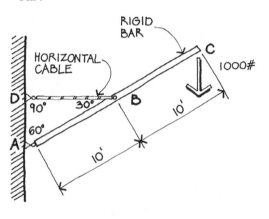

A.

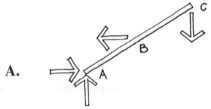

B.

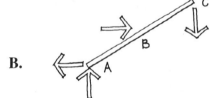

C.

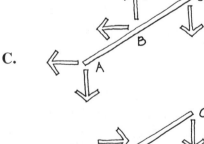

D.

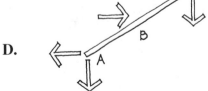

249. What is the internal force in the vertical member of the king post truss shown?

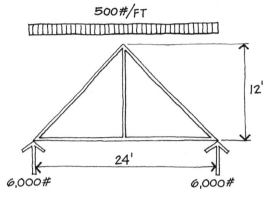

A. Zero

B. 3,000#

C. 6,000#

D. 12,000#

250. In the detail shown below, the wood members are loaded in

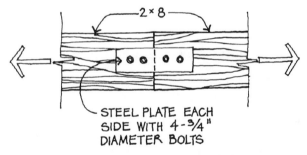

A. tension perpendicular to the grain.

B. tension parallel to the grain.

C. compression parallel to the grain.

D. horizontal shear.

251. The Imperial Hotel in Tokyo, designed by Frank Lloyd Wright, survived the great earthquake of 1923. What factors contributed to its survival?

I. It was founded on bedrock.

II. It was one of the first structures to utilize ductile steel frames to resist seismic forces.

III. It was divided by seismic separation joints into smaller separate units.

A. I and II

B. II and III

C. III only

D. I, II, and III

252. In designing buildings to resist lateral loads, how does the fundamental period of vibration of a building affect its seismic load?

A. The period is not related to the seismic load.

B. The longer the period, the greater the seismic load.

C. The longer the period, the smaller the seismic load.

D. Up to a period of two seconds, the seismic load increases as the period increases, and thereafter, the seismic load decreases as the period increases.

253. How much should two adjoining buildings assigned to Seismic Design Category D be separated?

 A. The sum of the two building displacements

 B. The greater of the two building displacements

 C. They are not required to be separated.

 D. They are not required to be separated, provided both buildings are designed and constructed in accordance with the same code provisions.

254. What system can resist both horizontal and vertical loads because the angle between its horizontal and vertical elements cannot change?

 A. Vierendeel truss

 B. Tapered girder

 C. Space frame

 D. Rigid frame

255. A rigid frame with hinged bases supports a uniformly distributed vertical load as shown above. Which of the following correctly shows the shape of the deflected frame?

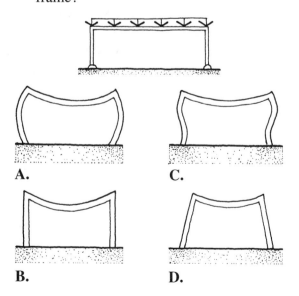

 A.

 B.

 C.

 D.

256. What system can have almost any configuration, so long as it is composed of triangles?

 A. Lamella

 B. Geodesic dome

 C. Truss

 D. Space frame

257. Which of the following statements about a circular dish roof are correct?

 I. The outer ring is in compression.

 II. The outer ring is in tension.

 III. The inner ring is in compression.

 IV. The inner ring is in tension.

 V. The inner ring is lower than the outer ring.

 VI. The inner ring is higher than the outer ring.

 A. II, III, and V

 B. II, III, and VI

 C. I, IV, and V

 D. I, IV, and VI

258. Which of the following statements about long-span roof trusses are correct? Check all that apply.

 A. Adequate lateral bracing should be provided.

 B. Secondary stresses caused by joint restraint should be considered.

 C. The trusses should be made up of triangles.

 D. The truss members are stressed primarily in tension, compression, or shear.

259. A beam of ASTM A992 steel supports a concentrated load of 10 kips at the center of a 30-foot span. Neglecting the weight of the beam, what is the required plastic section modulus?

   A. 75.0 in.^{3}

   B. 30.1 in.^{3}

   C. 25.0 in.^{3}

   D. 18.75 in.^{3}

260. Which of the following statements about the shear stress in wood beams is *INCORRECT*?

   A. The strength of wood beams in shear perpendicular to the grain should always be checked.

   B. The shear stress parallel to the grain at any point in a beam is equal to the shear stress perpendicular to the grain.

   C. The design shear value parallel to the grain is less than the allowable compressive or tensile value parallel to the grain.

   D. A notch on the tension face at the end of a beam greatly increases the shear stress.

261. The modulus of elasticity of concrete increases as

   I. its unit weight increases.

   II. its strength increases.

   III. the amount of reinforcing steel increases.

   IV. the depth of the member increases.

   A. I and II

   B. II and III

   C. III and IV

   D. I, II, III, and IV

262. What is concrete cover?

   A. The clear distance from the top of a concrete slab to the bottom reinforcing steel

   B. A covering placed over concrete during curing

   C. Protective wrapping over concrete members that are precast off-site

   D. The minimum thickness of concrete measured from the face of the concrete to the reinforcing steel

263. In the strength design method for reinforced concrete, the margin of safety is provided by two different factors: the load factor and ϕ, the strength reduction factor. In this regard, which of the following statements is *NOT* true?

   A. The load factor for dead and live loads is always greater than 1.

   B. ϕ is always greater than 1.

   C. The load factor is based on the possibility that the service loads may be exceeded.

   D. ϕ allows for variations in materials, dimensions, and calculation approximations.

264. The base plate under a steel column spreads the column load over a large area of the supporting foundation. The base plate must be thick enough to resist the resulting

   A. compression.

   B. tension.

   C. bending.

   D. shear.

265. Standardized lightweight steel trusses that are shop fabricated and have no fire resistance are called _____.

266. Which of the following is *NOT* a recommended seismic design practice?

    A. Buildings should be as regular and symmetrical as possible.

    B. Structural elements should be interconnected so that they move as a unit.

    C. Overturning effects should be minimized by designing buildings to have a high height-to-width ratio.

    D. Redundancy should be provided by secondary systems that can resist part of the lateral force if the primary system fails.

267. In areas of seismic risk, a structural separation is often provided between adjacent high-rise and low-rise portions of a building. What is the primary reason for this separation?

    A. To simplify the seismic design of a complex building by dividing it into simpler separate parts

    B. To allow for the differential settlement which would occur between the heavier high-rise portion and the lighter low-rise portion

    C. To permit the two portions to move independently

    D. To permit each of the two portions to resonate with the different frequency seismic waves

268. If the center of mass of a building coincides with the center of rigidity,

    A. torsion may be ignored.

    B. the design must provide for accidental torsion.

    C. the design must provide for accidental torsion if the diaphragm is rigid.

    D. the design must provide for accidental torsion if the diaphragm is flexible.

269. Four different girder arrangements are being considered to support three equal 60-foot spans, as shown below. Which arrangement will result in the *LEAST* deflection and moment in span 1-2?

A.

B.
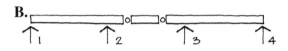

C.
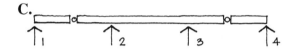

D.
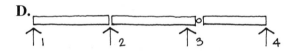

270. Loads applied to a truss chord between panel points result in

    A. local buckling of the chord.

    B. combined bending and axial stress in the chord.

    C. high shear stresses in the web members.

    D. compression in the chord.

271. Hooke's Law states that stress is proportional to strain. The constant ratio of stress to strain is termed

    A. the modulus of rupture.

    B. the modulus of elasticity.

    C. stiffness.

    D. the coefficient of expansion.

272. A truss is loaded as shown. Which sketch below correctly shows the reactions at A and B?

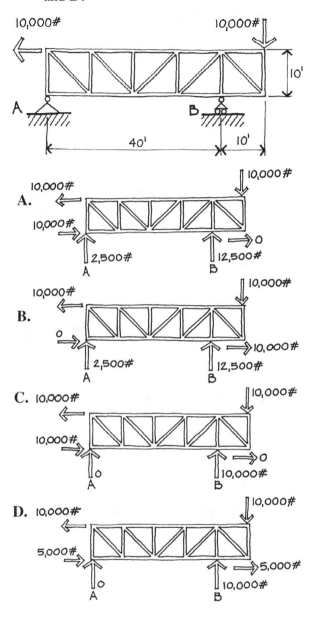

273. The braced frame shown resists a wind force of 10 kips as shown. Assuming that the braces can resist tension only, what are the internal forces in braces 1 and 2?

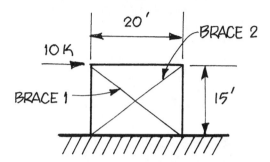

A. Brace 1 = zero, brace 2 = 10 kips tension

B. Brace 1 = 10 kips tension, brace 2 = zero

C. Brace 1 = zero, brace 2 = 12.5 kips tension

D. Brace 1 = 12.5 kips tension, brace 2 = zero

274. A shear wall has a dead load of 60,000 pounds and resists wind loads of 10,000 pounds and 20,000 pounds, as shown. What is the factor of safety against overturning?

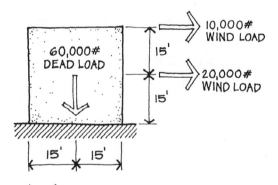

A. 1

B. 1.5

C. 2

D. 2.5

275. A load of 50 pounds per lineal foot is applied to the top rail as shown. What is the force in the upper bolt?

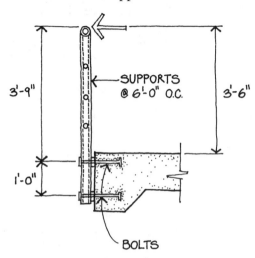

A. 238 lbs. tension

B. 1,125 lbs. tension

C. 1,425# tension

D. 1,425# compression

276. Select the *INCORRECT* statement about equilibrium.

A. If only two forces act on a body in equilibrium, they must be equal and opposite to each other.

B. If the vectorial sum of all the forces acting on a body in any direction equals zero, the body must be in equilibrium.

C. If three nonparallel forces acting on a body produce equilibrium, their lines of action must pass through a common point.

D. For equilibrium, the clockwise moments acting on a body must be equal to the counterclockwise moments.

277. A member in a testing machine elongates 0.03 inch when a tensile load of 75 kips is placed on it. The member is 12 inches long and one inch by one inch in cross section. What is the modulus of elasticity of the material?

A. 2,500 ksi

B. 3,000 ksi

C. 25,000 ksi

D. 30,000 ksi

278. An opening must be provided in a reinforced concrete beam. Which letter in the sketch shows the location that will *LEAST* affect the beam's load-carrying capacity?

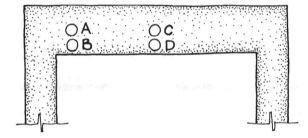

279. A post and beam system is able to resist which type of loads? Check all that apply.

A. Vertical live and dead loads

B. Lateral loads in its own plane

C. Lateral loads perpendicular to its own plane

280. A steel column supports a vertical load V and resists a horizontal shear H as shown. How is the horizontal shear transferred from the column to the footing?

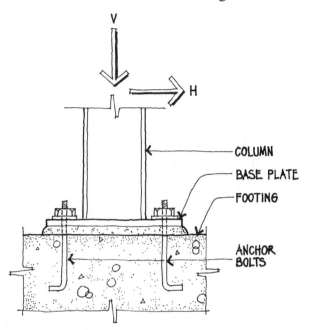

A. Bearing of the base plate on the footing

B. Friction between the base plate and the footing

C. Tension in the anchor bolts

D. Shear in the anchor bolts

281. Where is a wood beam most likely to fail in shear?

I. At midspan

II. Near the supports

III. Close to mid-depth of the beam

IV. Close to the top of the beam

A. I and IV

B. II and III

C. I and III

D. II and IV

282. Which of the following most closely represents the distribution of seismic forces used to design a building?

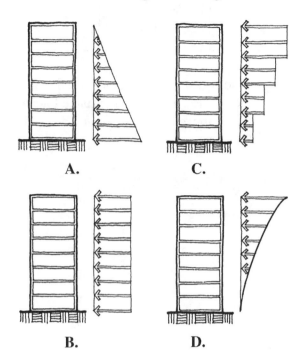

283. Which of the following statements about earthquake design is correct?

A. The earthquake regulations in the International Building Code are intended to limit damage caused by ground shaking, earth movement, or soil liquefaction.

B. Seismic design forces are not expected to be exceeded during the life of the structure.

C. Nonstructural elements must be rigidly connected to the structure in order to minimize damage to these elements.

D. Structures designed in accordance with the earthquake regulations in the International Building Code are expected to be able to resist a major earthquake without collapse, but possibly with structural and nonstructural damage.

284.

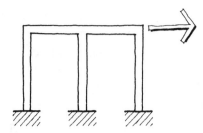

A moment-resisting frame with fixed bases resists a lateral earthquake load as shown above. Which diagram correctly shows the moment diagram for the frame?

A.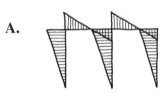

B.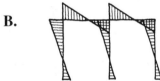

C.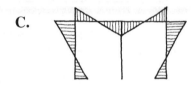

D.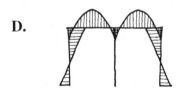

285. The factor R used for seismic design in the International Building Code depends on which of the following?

   A. The seismic risk for the area

   B. The soil characteristics at the site

   C. The lateral load resisting system of the building

   D. The building's fundamental period of vibration

286. How can the calculated deflection of a steel beam be reduced?

   A. Use steel with a greater yield strength.

   B. Use a beam with a greater moment of inertia.

   C. Use a beam with a greater section modulus.

   D. Use steel with a greater modulus of elasticity.

287. Which of the following statements about cable structures is correct? Check all that apply.

   A. When supporting loads that are uniformly distributed horizontally across its span, the shape of a cable is parabolic.

   B. When a cable is subject to changing loads, it changes its shape.

   C. The horizontal thrust at the ends of a cable is directly proportional to the sag of the cable.

288. The ratio of unit stress to unit strain is called the

   A. moment of inertia.

   B. elastic limit.

   C. modulus of elasticity.

   D. yield point.

289. The stiffness of a member refers to its resistance to

   A. deformation.

   B. applied loads.

   C. impact.

   D. abrasion.

290. Comparing the two beams shown, the two-span continuous beam and the simple beam, which of the following statements is *INCORRECT*?

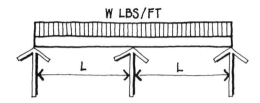

W LBS/FT

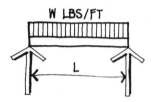

W LBS/FT

A. The maximum positive moment in the simple beam is greater than in the continuous beam.

B. The maximum shear in the simple beam is greater than in the continuous beam.

C. The maximum deflection of the simple beam is greater than that of the continuous beam.

D. The continuous beam has negative moment over the interior support, and the simple beam has no negative moment.

291. When a steel bar is subject to a tensile load, it increases in length. Up to a certain unit stress, the bar will return to its original length when the load is removed. This unit stress is called _____.

292. A retaining wall consisting of a vertical stem supported at intervals on the back side by triangular buttresses connected to the base is called a _____.

293. For the retaining wall shown, which faces are in tension (noted as T) and which are in compression (noted as C)?

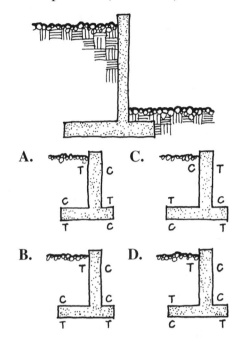

294. Two systems are being considered to support the roof of a fieldhouse, which has a column-free space 100 feet by 100 feet: a space frame and a system of parallel trusses. Select the *INCORRECT* statement in this regard.

A. The trusses will be about 10 feet deep, while the depth may be reduced to about five feet if the space frame is used.

B. The structural members spanning between the trusses are relatively flexible, so that the trusses act independently of each other.

C. The space frame is stiffer than the parallel trusses.

D. The space frame and the trusses are both statically determinate.

295. Four building plan shapes are shown below. Which of them should have greatest seismic resistance?

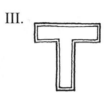

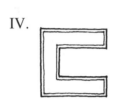

A. I only

B. II and III

C. II, III, and IV

D. I, II, III, and IV

296. The change of length that a member undergoes when loaded axially depends on which of the following?

I. The magnitude of the load

II. The length of the member

III. The moment of inertia of the member

IV. The cross-sectional area of the member

V. The modulus of elasticity of the material

A. II, III, and IV

B. I, II, IV, and V

C. I, III, and V

D. I, II, III, IV, and V

297. Which of the following correctly shows the variation of shear stress within the depth of a rectangular beam?

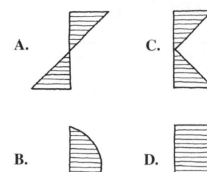

298. Which of the following statements about a three-hinged gabled frame is *INCORRECT*?

A. It is statically determinate.

B. Its supports permit rotation.

C. The moment at the center is zero.

D. The maximum moment occurs at the intersection of the column and the sloping beam and is generally greater than in a rectangular rigid frame.

299. Which of the diagrams shown best indicates the lateral seismic forces acting on a multistory building?

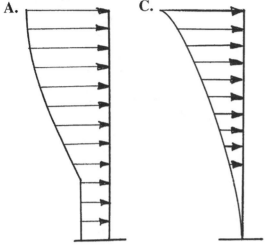

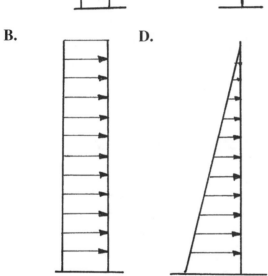

300. Structures must always be designed to resist seismic forces

A. only if they are assigned to SDC C and higher.

B. coming from any horizontal direction.

C. coming from any vertical direction.

D. acting concurrently in the direction of each principal axis of the structure.

301. In general, the internal forces in the web members of a parallel chord truss

A. decrease toward the center of the span.

B. increase toward the center of the span.

C. remain relatively constant across the span.

D. may increase or decrease toward the center of the span.

302. Which of the following statements is *INCORRECT*?

A. The cost of connections is a significant factor in selecting structural steel systems.

B. Fillet welds are usually more economical than full penetration welds.

C. Shop connections are usually more economical than field connections.

D. Welded connections are usually more economical than bolted connections.

303. A one-story steel rigid frame with fixed bases supports a uniformly distributed vertical load as shown. Which of the following correctly shows the shape of the deflected frame?

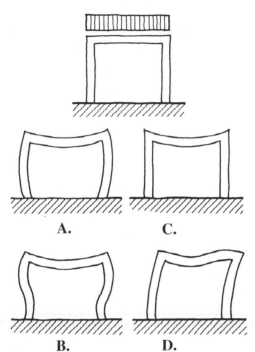

304. Which of the following retaining walls has the reinforcing steel *INCORRECTLY* placed?

A.

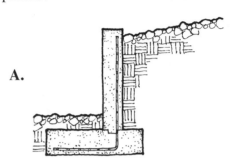

B.

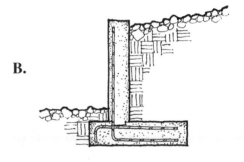

C.

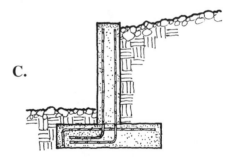

D.

305. Which of the following soils may be used to support building foundations?

    I. Sandy gravel

    II. Silty sand

    III. Sandy clay

    IV. Peat

    A. I only

    B. II and III

    C. I, II, and III

    D. I, II, III, and IV

306. For the retaining wall shown, which of the following correctly represents the pressure diagrams for the stem and base?

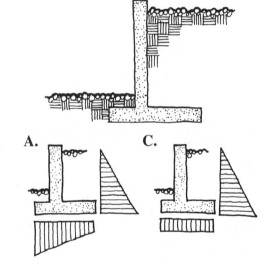

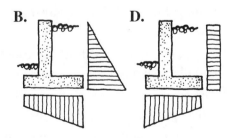

307. Wind pressures are usually assumed to act in which of the following directions? Check all that apply.

    A. Inward on windward walls

    B. Outward on windward walls

    C. Inward on leeward walls

    D. Outward on leeward walls

308. The wind design regulations in the International Building Code consider all of the following, *EXCEPT*

    A. exposure.

    B. gusting.

    C. hurricanes.

    D. tornadoes.

309. What is the design wind pressure on a windward wall 30 feet above the ground for a building with Exposure C, according to the International Building Code? $q = 17.3$ psf, $G = 0.85$, $C_p = 0.8$, and $I = 1.0$. Ignore internal pressure.

    A. 10.1 psf

    B. 11.8 psf

    C. 12.6 psf

    D. 15.5 psf

310. Select the *INCORRECT* statement. The wind pressures used in the design of buildings in accordance with the IBC

    A. account for the effects of hurricanes.

    B. are greater for buildings on flat, open terrain than on terrain with buildings or surface irregularities close to the site.

    C. increase with height.

    D. act inward on all wall surfaces.

311. In the reinforced concrete footing shown, the minimum concrete coverage for reinforcement is

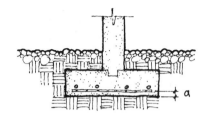

FOOTING

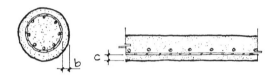

INTERIOR COLUMN   INTERIOR SLAB

    A. 1-1/2".

    B. 3".

    C. 6".

    D. 8".

312. Which of the following is *NOT* considered to be live load?

    I. Wind

    II. Earthquake

    III. Furniture

    IV. Snow

    A. II only

    B. I and IV

    C. I, II, and IV

    D. I, II, III, and IV

313. In the detail shown, the bolts conform to ASTM A325 in a bearing-type connection with threads excluded from the shear plane. Using Table 10-1 (p. 103) from the AISC Manual of Steel Construction, what is the allowable load of the connection? Assume A992 steel for the beam and column and A36 steel for the angles.

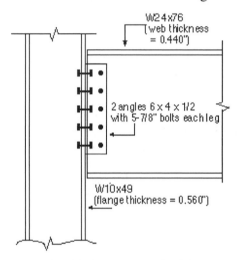

    A. 126.5 kips.

    B. 150 kips.

    C. 180.5 kips.

    D. 235.5 kips.

314. Select the correct statement concerning a change in the use or occupancy of an existing building.

    A. The building must comply with the live load requirements for the new use.

    B. The new use must be less hazardous than the existing use.

    C. The architect for the existing building must approve the change in use.

    D. The structural design of the building must be checked to verify that it will be safe for the new use.

315. The structural system shown below is called a

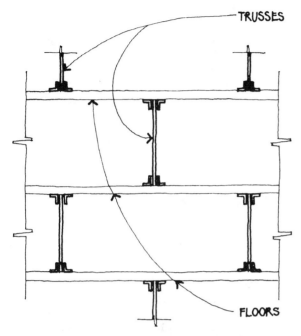

LONGITUDINAL SECTION

A. Vierendeel truss system.

B. staggered truss system.

C. space frame.

D. two-way truss system.

316. Which of the following statements about steel columns is correct?

A. The buckling tendency of a steel column depends on its yield point.

B. The maximum allowable slenderness ratio is 50.

C. Tubular sections have less tendency to buckle than wide flange sections.

D. If the value of r is different in each direction, the greater value is used to compute the Kl/r ratio.

317. What is the capacity of the connection shown? The beams are ASTM A992, and the connection parts are ASTM A36. Assume that the beam and connection angles are adequate, and use the tables on pages 100 and 101.

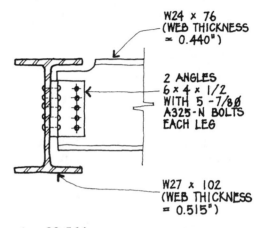

A. 82.5 kips

B. 104.3 kips

C. 165 kips

D. 330 kips

318. For the truss shown below, what is the internal axial force in member a?

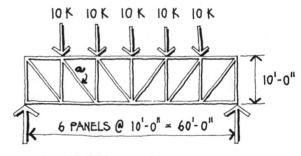

A. 10.6 kips tension

B. 14.1 kips tension

C. 15.0 kips tension

D. 21.2 kips tension

319. Wind design depends on the

    I. wind speed.

    II. occupancy category.

    III. terrain in which the building is located.

    IV. size and shape of the building.

    A. I and IV

    B. II, III, and IV

    C. I, II, III, and IV

    D. I and III

320. Considering the building shown, the total wind load in the north-south direction

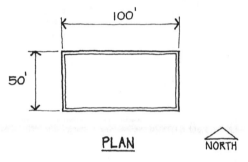

PLAN   NORTH

    A. is less than in the east-west direction.

    B. is the same as in the east-west direction.

    C. is greater than in the east-west direction.

    D. may be more or less than in the east-west direction, depending on the gust factor.

321. Wind load resistance for which building is provided by a bundle of nine tubes?

    A. John Hancock Building in Chicago

    B. First National Bank in Chicago

    C. Sears Tower

    D. CBS Building

322. A beam supports two 10-kip concentrated loads as shown. What are the values of R_1 and R_2?

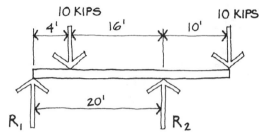

    A. R_1 = 17 kips, R_2 = 3 kips

    B. R_1 = 3 kips, R_2 = 17 kips

    C. R_1 = 13 kips, R_2 = 7 kips

    D. R_1 = 7 kips, R_2 = 13 kips

323. The section modulus of a beam is equal to its moment of inertia

    A. divided by the allowable flexural stress.

    B. multiplied by the allowable flexural stress.

    C. divided by the distance from the neutral axis to the outermost fiber.

    D. multiplied by the distance from the neutral axis to the outermost fiber.

324. Wide flange shapes are economical flexural members because

    A. the two flanges are equal in area.

    B. the flange width-to-thickness ratio is high.

    C. the web depth-to-thickness ratio is low.

    D. most of the beam's material is in the flanges.

325. What is the shear at section x-x of the beam shown?

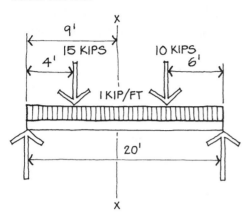

A. Zero   **C.** 4,000#

B. 1,000#   **D.** 5,000#

326. The shear diagram for a beam is shown. Which of the following is the corresponding moment diagram?

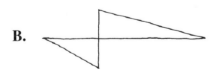

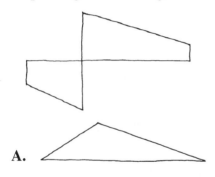

A.

B.

C.

D.

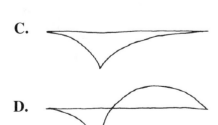

327. Which of the following systems is used by the John Hancock Center in Chicago to resist wind load?

   A. A combination of rigid frames and shear walls

   B. Tubular system

   C. Diagonal bracing

   D. Moment-resisting frames

328. The braced frame shown resists a wind force of 6 kips acting to the right. What is the internal force in rod a?

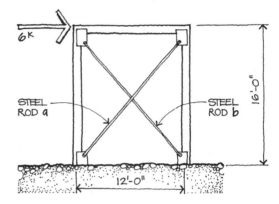

   A. Zero

   B. 6 kips tension

   C. 8 kips tension

   D. 10 kips tension

329. A 5 foot by 15 foot sign is located 20 feet above the ground and receives a wind pressure equal to 12.74 pounds per square foot. What is the overturning moment at the ground caused by wind forces?

   A. 4,300 ft.-lbs.

   B. 19,110 ft.-lbs.

   C. 21,499 ft.-lbs.

   D. 23,888 ft.-lbs.

330. A braced frame resists a horizontal wind load of 10 kips acting to the right, as shown. The diagonal brace can resist either tension or compression. What is the internal force in the brace?

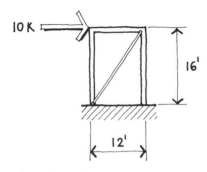

    A. 10 kips tension

    B. 10 kips compression

    C. 13.3 kips tension

    D. 16.7 kips tension

331. A 10-foot by 30-foot sign is mounted on top of a building. Design wind pressure on the sign is 16.8 psf. What is the total wind force on the sign?

    A. 1,676#

    B. 2,514#

    C. 3,591#

    D. 5,040#

332. The wind pressure on a building is dependent on which of the following factors?

    I.   Surrounding terrain

    II. The building's proximity to large bodies of water

    III. The size and shape of the building

    IV. The height of the building

    A. I and II

    B. I, II, and III

    C. I and IV

    D. I, II, III, and IV

333. For the three-hinged arch shown, the horizontal thrust is equal to H. If the span length (L) is doubled, while the rise (h) and the load per lineal foot (w) remain the same, what will be the magnitude of the horizontal thrust?

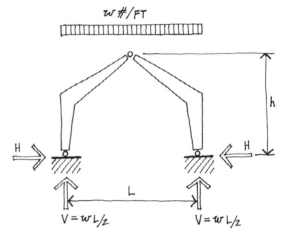

    A. H

    B. 2H

    C. 3H

    D. 4H

334. Which of the following diagrams correctly shows the variation in shear stress in a rectangular homogeneous beam?

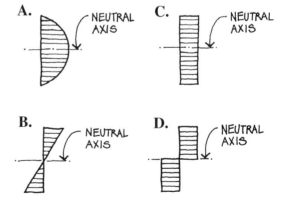

335. How do the seismic forces used in the design of a fire or police station compare with those used for a standard occupancy structure?

   A. The seismic forces are greater.

   B. The seismic forces are less.

   C. The seismic forces are the same.

   D. The seismic forces are not considered in the design of standard occupancy structures.

336. Open-front buildings are subject to high torsional stresses under earthquake loading. Which of the following are solutions to this problem?

   I. Provide braced frames of approximately equal stiffness for both side walls

   II. Provide a shear wall at the front, whose stiffness approaches that of the rear shear wall

   III. Use moment-resisting frames of approximately equal stiffness for both front and rear walls

   A. I only

   B. I and II

   C. II and III

   D. I, II, and III

337. In existing buildings, which of the following are most vulnerable to damage or collapse as a result of an earthquake?

   A. Unreinforced masonry walls

   B. Wood frame walls

   C. Reinforced concrete floor diaphragms

   D. Reinforced concrete walls

338. In comparing the two trusses shown below, which of the following statements is correct?

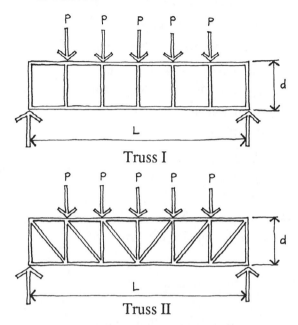

Truss I

Truss II

   A. The chords in truss I have greater axial tension and compression than those in truss II.

   B. Because of the absence of diagonals, truss I is unstable.

   C. The chords and verticals of truss I are subject to bending stress.

   D. Truss II will deflect more than truss I.

339. Which of the following are advantages of Vierendeel trusses?

   I. Unencumbered webs

   II. Simple joints

   III. Low deflection

   IV. Economy

   A. I and II

   B. II, III, and IV

   C. I and III

   D. I, II, III, and IV

340. Which of the following are advantages of the stub girder framing system?

   I. Reduced weight of steel

   II. Reduced story height

   III. Simplified steel erection

   IV. Ease of providing simulated continuity for floor beams

   A. I and II

   B. II and III

   C. I and III

   D. I, II, III, and IV

341. Why are drop panels and column capitals used in flat slab construction?

   I. To reduce shear stress in the slab near the columns

   II. To provide greater effective depth for negative bending moment

   III. To provide greater effective depth for positive bending moment

   IV. To provide increased bond resistance

   A. I and II

   B. I and III

   C. I, II, and IV

   D. II and IV

342. The staggered truss system is usually economical for

   I. spans greater than 45 feet.

   II. buildings under 8 stories in height.

   III. hotel and residential occupancies.

   A. I and II

   B. II and III

   C. I and III

   D. I, II, and III

343. Which of the four steel column sections shown below can support the greatest amount of vertical load, assuming they have the same cross-sectional area?

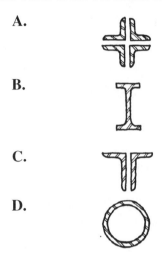

   A.

   B.

   C.

   D.

344. Two angles 6 × 4 × 3/8 are connected to a 3/8″ gusset plate at a truss joint as shown. The angles resist a tensile force of 50 kips. How many 3/4″ A325-N bolts are required? Assume bolt spacing and edge distance are such that full bearing strength can be achieved. Use the tables on pages 100 and 101.

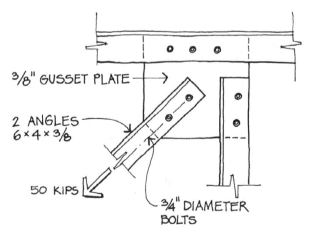

   A. 2

   B. 3

   C. 4

   D. 5

345. What is the maximum allowable height for a building assigned to SDC D?

    A. 160 feet

    B. 240 feet

    C. 320 feet

    D. No limit

346. What factor in the International Building Code accounts for the short-period design acceleration at a site?

    A. S_{DS}

    B. S_{DI}

    C. I

    D. R_L

347. Select the correct statement about design for lateral forces.

    A. Buildings assigned to SDC D and higher are designed only for earthquake forces, not wind.

    B. Buildings assigned to SDC D and higher are designed only for wind forces, not earthquake.

    C. Buildings assigned to SDC D and higher are designed for wind or earthquake forces, but not both acting at the same time.

    D. Buildings assigned to SDC D and higher must be provided with special moment-resisting frames.

348. You are designing a building assigned to SDC D that is not a high occupancy, essential, or hazardous facility. $S_{DS} = 0.45g$, $S_{DI} = 0.27g$, T = 2.0, R = 6, and the total dead load = 5,000 kips. What is the base shear?

    A. 50 kips

    B. 115 kips

    C. 137 kips

    D. 287 kips

349. A beam fixed at both ends supports a concentrated load at the center of the span, as shown. Neglecting the weight of the beam, which of the following diagrams correctly shows the deflected shape of the beam?

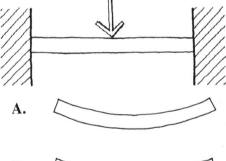

    A.

    B.

    C.

    D.

350. Complete the following statement. A three-hinged arch is

    A. stiffer than a fixed arch.

    B. statically determinate.

    C. unstable when subject to horizontal loads.

    D. generally semicircular in profile.

351. In historic architecture, the transition from a round dome or drum to the pillars at the corners of a square space below was achieved by

A. a lantern.

B. a drum.

C. pendentives.

D. a vault.

352. Select the correct statements about the Leaning Tower of Pisa.

I. It began to tilt during construction.

II. The leaning was caused by differential settlement of the underlying soil.

III. The top of the tower is out of plumb by 16 inches.

IV. The leaning was caused by the unbalanced structure of the tower.

A. II and III

B. I and IV

C. I, II, and III

D. I and II

353. Pier Luigi Nervi is associated with all of the following design techniques or materials, *EXCEPT*

A. ferrocement.

B. tubular frames.

C. concrete lamella roofs.

D. suspension roofs.

354. A one-story reinforced building is shown below in plan. The roof framing system consists of concrete slabs and beams. For seismic loads acting in the north-south direction, which of the vertical elements will resist the greatest amount of load?

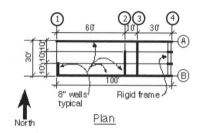

A. Shear wall on line A

B. Shear wall on line 2

C. Shear wall on line 3

D. Rigid frame on line 4

355. Nonstructural building components and the attachments of permanent equipment must be properly designed to resist seismic forces. In this regard, which of the following may be used to resist seismic forces?

I. Anchor bolts

II. Bracing

III. Friction resulting from gravity loads

A. I and II

B. I only

C. II and III

D. I, II, and III

356. Which of the following statements about moment-resisting frames are correct? Check all that apply.

   A. They are generally more ductile than other systems.

   B. They tend to deflect less under lateral loads than other systems.

   C. They absorb seismic energy by deformation.

   D. They are generally designed for smaller seismic loads than other systems.

357. A wall weighing 100 pounds per square foot extends four feet above the roof of an office building assigned to SDC C. What is the magnitude of the horizontal seismic force acting on the parapet wall, per foot of length? $S_{DS} = 0.29g$.

   A. 35 pounds

   B. 70 pounds

   C. 140 pounds

   D. 175 pounds

358. Which of the following statements concerning the economy of structural steel framing is correct?

   I. Moment connections should be used in preference to simple connections.

   II. Built-up sections should be used instead of rolled sections, to save weight.

   III. High-strength low-alloy steel should be used instead of ASTM A36 steel in connection members, because of its greater strength.

   IV. Composite steel deck should be used, rather than non-composite steel deck.

   A. III and IV

   B. I and III

   C. II and III

   D. IV only

359. Comparing the post-and-beam and the rigid frame shown below, which of the following statements are correct?

   I. The maximum moment in columns D is greater than in columns B.

   II. The maximum moment in beam C is less than in beam A.

   III. The axial force in columns D is the same as in columns B.

   IV. The horizontal reaction at the base of columns D is greater than at columns B.

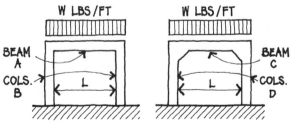

A. I and II   **C.** I and III

B. III and IV   **D.** I, II, III, and IV

360. What happens to a reinforced concrete dome when the exterior temperature rises?

    A. The top of the dome moves up.

    B. The top of the dome moves down.

    C. The dome develops internal compressive stresses.

    D. The dome develops internal tensile stresses.

361. Which of the structural steel framing plans below is usually the most economical?

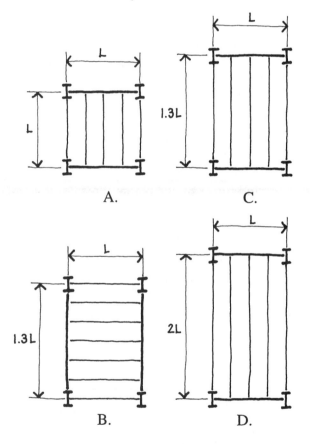

362. A steel or concrete frame that has bases fixed against rotation is called a _____.

363. A lateral seismic load acts on the reinforced concrete wall shown. Which of the following statements is correct?

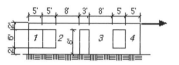

    A. Piers 1 and 4 resist more lateral load than piers 2 and 3.

    B. Each pier resists an equal amount of lateral load.

    C. The wall cannot resist any lateral load because of the size and location of the openings.

    D. Piers 2 and 3 resist more lateral load than piers 1 and 4.

364. What is meant by redundancy in connection with seismic design?

    A. The ability of a structure to redistribute seismic loads to other elements, if a particular element fails or is damaged

    B. The use of two systems, such as shear walls and moment-resisting frames, to resist seismic loads

    C. Providing excessive seismic resistance, thereby attracting an excessive amount of seismic load

    D. Providing seismic resistance for buildings located in non-seismic areas

365. The Richter scale measures

    A. the intensity of an earthquake, that is, its effects on people and buildings.

    B. the duration of an earthquake.

    C. the frequency of seismic waves.

    D. the amount of energy released in an earthquake.

366. A moment-resisting frame resists a lateral seismic load of 24 kips, as shown. Both columns are pinned at the base and have the same cross section. What is the maximum column moment and the vertical force in each column caused by the lateral load?

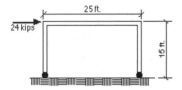

A. Column moment = 180 ft.-kips, vertical force = 12 kips

B. Column moment = 180 ft.-kips, vertical force = 14.4 kips

C. Column moment = 360 ft.-kips, vertical force = 12 kips

D. Column moment = 360 ft.-kips, vertical force = 14.4 kips

367. Which of the following statements is correct?

A. Buildings designed in accordance with the earthquake regulations in the IBC are expected to have no drift during a major earthquake.

B. The actual displacement of a structure subject to a major earthquake can be calculated using design seismic forces and assuming that the structure remains elastic.

C. Because ductile shear-resisting elements tend to have large displacements, the amount of drift is not limited.

D. Drift is limited to insure structural integrity, minimize discomfort, and limit nonstructural damage.

368. In glued laminated construction, it is often necessary to join pieces of lumber end to end to produce laminations of sufficient length. Which of the following joints are acceptable for this purpose?

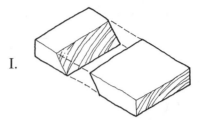

I.

PLAIN SCARF JOINT

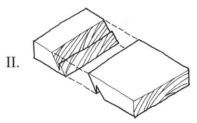

II.

HOOKED SCARF JOINT

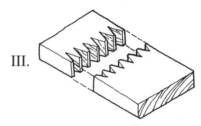

III.

FINGER JOINT

A. I and II

B. I and III

C. II and III

D. I, II, and III

369. Which of the following statements is *INCORRECT*? The flat slab floor system

A. spans simultaneously in two directions.

B. is economical in reinforcing steel.

C. is appropriate for heavy live loads.

D. generally has no beams or girders.

370. What is the maximum moment in the beam shown?

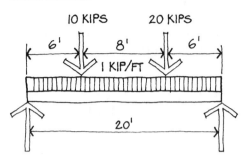

A. 50.0 ft.-kips

B. 110.0 ft.-kips

C. 144.5 ft.-kips

D. 170.0 ft.-kips

371. What is the moment of inertia of the section shown below about its *x-x* axis? $I = bd^3/12$.

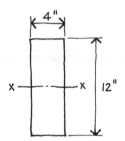

A. 48 in.^{4}

B. 64 in.^{4}

C. 96 in.^{4}

D. 576 in.^{4}

372. Building structures must be designed to resist

A. dead load plus half the live load.

B. live load plus half the dead load.

C. dead load plus live load.

D. dead load or live load, whichever is greater.

373. A beam of A36 steel with a span of 24 feet is installed at 40°F. It has unyielding supports. If the temperature rises to 100°F, what is the resulting stress in the beam? E = 29,000 ksi and the coefficient of expansion is 6.5×10^{-6}.

A. 11,310 psi compression

B. 11,310 psi tension

C. 13,572 psi compression

D. 18,850 psi compression

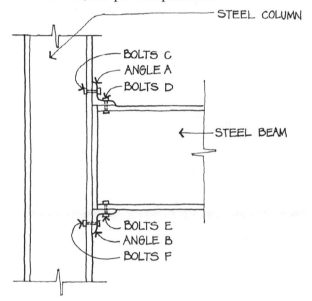

374. In the beam connection shown above, the beam reaction is transferred to the column through

A. angle A and bolts C and D.

B. angle B and bolts F.

C. angles A and B and bolts C and F.

D. angle B and bolts E.

375. In the connection shown,

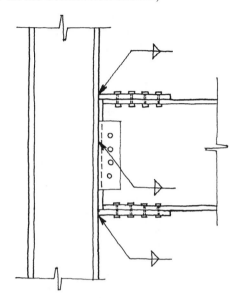

A. the web plate resists the shear and the flange plates resist the moment.

B. the web plate resists the moment and the flange plates resist the shear.

C. the web plate and flange plates resist the shear and there is no moment resistance.

D. the web plate and flange plates resist both the shear and moment.

376. In general, which of the following will help reduce the cost of structural steel framing? Check all that apply.

A. Use moment connections in preference to nonmoment connections.

B. Use rolled sections rather than built-up sections.

C. Restrict the number of members to a practical minimum.

D. Use high-strength steel for all members.

377. A long period is associated with which of the following?

I.   Flexibility
II. Stiffness
III. High seismic forces
IV. Low seismic forces

A. I and III
B. I and IV
C. II and III
D. II and IV

378. A structural system that has an essentially complete frame that supports gravity loads and shear walls or braced frames that resist lateral seismic loads is called a

A. dual system.
B. bearing wall system.
C. moment-resisting frame system.
D. building frame system.

379. An earthquake with a magnitude of 8.0 on the Richter scale releases how much more energy than a 4.0 magnitude earthquake?

A. 400 times
B. 10,000 times
C. 100,000 times
D. 1,000,000 times

380. Select the correct statement about drift.

A. Drift is limited to insure structural integrity, minimize discomfort, and restrict nonstructural damage.

B. Earthquake regulations in most codes do not permit any drift.

C. Drift refers to the strain of a material when it is stressed to the yield point.

D. Misalignment of adjoining fabricated elements is known as drift.

381. Wherever a hinge or pin exists in a structure, there can be no

    A. shear.

    B. moment.

    C. tension.

    D. compression.

382. What is the internal axial force in member *a* of the truss below?

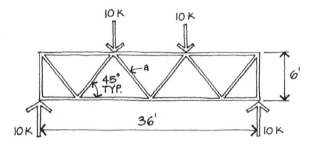

    A. Zero

    B. 5 kips compression

    C. 7.07 kips compression

    D. 10 kips compression

383. Complete the following statement. A cable supports load by

    A. compression.

    B. tension.

    C. bending.

    D. a combination of tension and bending.

384. For a simply supported glued laminated beam subject to vertical loads, where is the bending stress maximum?

    A. At the outermost laminations near midspan

    B. At the outermost laminations near the supports

    C. At the neutral axis near midspan

    D. At the neutral axis near the supports

385. Which of the following is the resultant of the two forces shown?

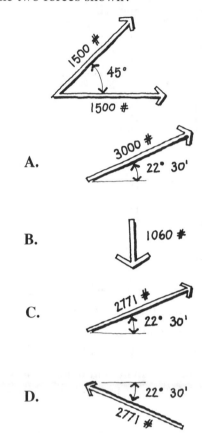

386. When seismic forces cause a building to deflect laterally, the vertical load acting on a deflected column results in increased moments. This effect is called _____.

387. Seismic forces are generally considered to act

    A. in a vertical or horizontal direction, whichever is more critical.

    B. in one horizontal direction parallel to the short axis of a building.

    C. in the two horizontal directions parallel to the axes of a building, but not necessarily simultaneously.

    D. at the same time as wind forces.

388. The additional cost to provide seismic resistance for a building to conform to the IBC regulations for Seismic Design Category D would be roughly what percentage of the total cost of construction?

 A. 5 percent or less

 B. 10 percent

 C. 25 percent

 D. 50 percent

389. Reduced bearing capacity of loose, saturated sand as a result of earthquake ground motion is known as

_____.

390. Which of the following are intended purposes of seismic isolation? Check all that apply.

 A. To separate adjacent buildings to prevent pounding

 B. To reduce the total displacement of a building caused by earthquake

 C. To reduce story drift

 D. To reduce a building's acceleration from earthquake ground motion

391. Comparing the fundamental period of vibration of a building with that of the ground shaking because of an earthquake, which of the following is most desirable?

 A. The period of the building is close to that of the ground shaking.

 B. The period of the building is double that of the ground shaking.

 C. The period of the building is very different from that of the ground shaking.

 D. The period of the building is half that of the ground shaking.

392. Unbraced parapet walls must be designed to resist seismic forces that

 A. are smaller than the forces used for the building's design.

 B. are the same as the forces used for the building's design.

 C. are greater than the forces used for the building's design.

 D. may be either smaller or greater than the forces used for the building's design.

393. The calculated deflection of a single reinforced concrete beam is excessive, making it necessary to redesign the beam. Assuming no other structural elements are affected, and the load supported cannot be reduced, what is the most efficient way to reduce the beam's calculated deflection?

 A. Make the beam wider.

 B. Add reinforcing steel.

 C. Specify higher strength concrete.

 D. Make the beam deeper.

394. What is the maximum moment in the beam shown below?

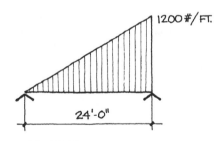

 A. 88,681'#

 B. 29,560'#

 C. 44,340'#

 D. 36,950'#

395. The nominal diameter and yield strength of the bar shown are as follows:

    A. Diameter = 0.40 inch, yield strength = 60 ksi

    B. Diameter = 1/2 inch, yield strength = 60 ksi

    C. Diameter = 0.60 inch, yield strength = 40 ksi

    D. The markings shown designate only the producer of the bar and the chemical content.

396. In the stress-strain diagram for steel shown below, the point labeled A is called _____.

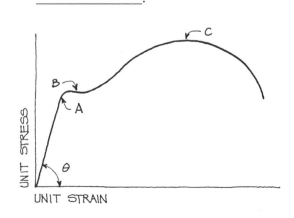

397. What is the internal force in member BD of the truss shown?

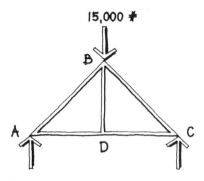

    A. Zero

    B. 5 kips

    C. 7.5 kips

    D. 15 kips

398. Select the correct statement about composite design.

    A. Connectors welded to the steel beam and embedded in the concrete resist flexural stresses.

    B. Composite design is most efficient with light loads and short spans.

    C. The concrete slab resists compressive bending stresses.

    D. Because a composite beam is stiffer than a noncomposite beam, it is usually unnecessary to check deflections.

399. Why are stirrups used in reinforced concrete construction?

    A. To provide compressive reinforcement

    B. To provide web reinforcement where the concrete is overstressed in shear

    C. To anchor the tensile reinforcement

    D. To prevent lateral buckling of compressive reinforcement

400. How do the wind forces used in the design of a fire or police station compare with those used for a standard occupancy structure?

A. The wind forces are greater.

B. The wind forces are less.

C. The wind forces are the same.

D. Wind forces are not considered in the design of standard occupancy structures.

401. According to the International Building Code, the magnitude of the design wind pressures on a building is influenced by which of the following?

I. The building's occupancy category

II. The height of the building

III. The exposure of the building

IV. The wind speed

A. I and IV

B. II, III, and IV

C. I, II, and III

D. I, II, III, and IV

402. The wind pressures used in the design of buildings in accordance with the International Building Code are

A. those caused by tornadoes.

B. increased when the amount and height of ground surface irregularities increase in an area within one mile of the site.

C. greater in the middle of a wall than at the corners.

D. required to act in both inward and outward directions on wall surfaces.

403. A steel beam spans 30 feet and supports a load of 1,800 pounds per foot including the weight of the beam. What is the lightest steel section that can support the load? Assume A992 steel and full lateral support. Use the table on page 105.

A. W16 × 45

B. W12 × 58

C. W16 × 50

D. W21 × 44

404. What is a stub girder system?

A. A steel beam-and-girder system in which floor beams pass over the main girders and stub girders are welded over the main girders along the same axis

B. Short lengths of steel girders shop-welded to steel columns to simplify field erection

C. Wood or steel girders designed and detailed for simulated continuity

D. Steel girders used at the base of a steel column to spread the column load

405. Select the correct statements.

I. The modulus of elasticity of concrete varies with the strength and weight of the concrete.

II. The deflection of a reinforced concrete beam increases over time, even if the load is not increased.

III. Adding compressive reinforcement has no effect on the deflection of a reinforced concrete beam.

A. I and II

B. II and III

C. I and III

D. I, II, and III

406. Four building plan shapes are shown. Which is best able to withstand earthquakes?

A.

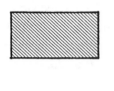

B.

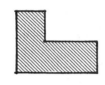

C.

D.

407. A building assigned to SDC E has a special steel moment-resisting frame capable of resisting the total required lateral force. Its total dead weight is 15,000 kips. Its fundamental period of vibration is 0.4 seconds. What is the maximum allowable height of the building?

   A. 120 feet

   B. 60 feet

   C. 240 feet

   D. No limit

408. A load of 1,000 pounds is supported by cables A and B as shown. What is the tension in each cable?

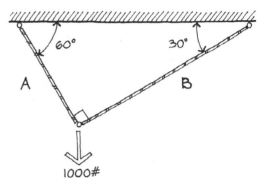

   A. A = 500#, B = 500#

   B. A = 500#, B = 866#

   C. A = 866#, B = 500#

   D. A = 866#, B = 866#

409. A 10-foot-deep tank is filled with water. The magnitude of the pressure exerted by the water against the sides of the tank depends on which of the following?

   I.   The unit weight of the water

   II. The depth of the water

   III. The width of the tank

   A. I and II

   B. II and III

   C. I and III

   D. I, II, and III

410. Complete the following statement. An arch supports load by

   A. compression.

   B. tension.

   C. bending.

   D. a combination of compression and bending.

411. What is the moment about point O of the three forces shown below?

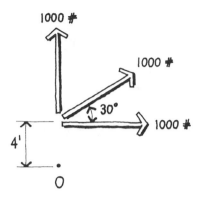

A. Zero

B. 4,000 ft.-lbs.

C. 7,464 ft.-lbs.

D. 12,000 ft.-lbs.

412. A 16-ft.-long steel column supports an axial load of 300 kips and is welded to a 20″ × 20″ base plate. What is the bearing pressure under the base plate?

A. 1,500 psi

B. 1,200 psi

C. 750 psi

D. 469 psi

413. A parabolic arch supports a uniformly distributed vertical load. What is the nature of the stress in the arch at any point along its length?

A. Pure compression, no bending moment

B. Pure bending moment, no compression

C. Combined compression and bending moment

D. Pure tension, no bending moment

414. Which of the live load arrangements shown below will result in the greatest positive moment in span 1-2?

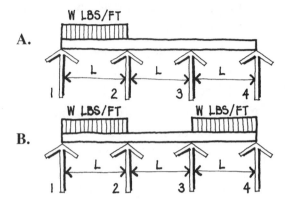

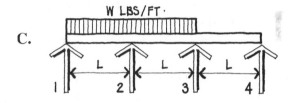

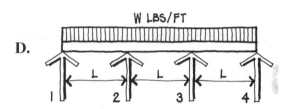

415. The radius of gyration r of a steel section is a function of which items? Check all that apply.

A. Modulus of elasticity

B. Moment of inertia of the section

C. Cross-sectional area of the section

D. Section modulus of the section

416. In earthquake-prone areas, adjacent buildings, or portions of a building, are often separated by a seismic joint. Which of the following statements about seismic joints is correct?

   A. The separation must extend from the roof through and including the foundation.

   B. The dimension of the separation should be one inch for each 10 feet of building height.

   C. Using properly designed joints effectively limits the drift to a safe value.

   D. The amount of separation should be at least equal to the sum of the drifts of the two adjacent buildings or portions.

417. The location on the earth's surface directly above the point where an earthquake fault slippage begins is called the _____.

418. A braced frame resists earthquake forces as shown. Its behavior is closest to that of a

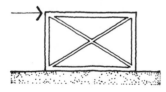

   A. special moment-resisting space frame.

   B. ordinary moment-resisting space frame.

   C. appendage.

   D. shear wall.

419. In the stress-strain diagram for steel shown below, what is B called?

   A. Elastic limit

   B. Modulus of elasticity

   C. Yield point

   D. Ultimate strength

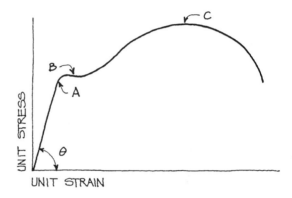

420. In the stress-strain diagram for steel shown above, what is C called?

   A. Elastic limit

   B. Modulus of elasticity

   C. Yield point

   D. Ultimate strength

421. In the stress-strain diagram for steel shown above, what is the tangent of angle θ called?

   A. Elastic limit

   B. Modulus of elasticity

   C. Yield point

   D. Ultimate strength

422. A building is spanned with 62-foot-long 32LH06 steel joists placed at 6 feet on center. Using the table provided on page 104, how many lines of bridging are required for the joists?

    A. 4

    B. 5

    C. 6

    D. 7

423. Select the correct statements about trusses. Check all that apply.

    A. Although trusses are efficient in supporting loads, they are deep and slender and therefore require adequate lateral bracing.

    B. When purlins are connected to trusses at the panel points, the top chord members are subject to axial stress only.

    C. Trusses are generally economical for spans between 60 and 200 feet.

    D. The optimum depth to span ratio of a truss is about 1/24.

    E. Increasing the depth of a truss decreases the stress in the web members.

424. Select the correct statement.

    A. A trussed steel arch is generally used where the span is less than 100 feet.

    B. Steel arches are trussed in order to increase their bending resistance.

    C. Trussing a steel arch minimizes the horizontal thrust at the base.

    D. Using a trussed steel arch eliminates the need for a center hinge.

425. Seismic loads are resisted by a two-story moment-resisting frame as shown below. Which of the choices below correctly shows the internal forces in the members at the beam-column joint circled? (T = tension, C = compression)

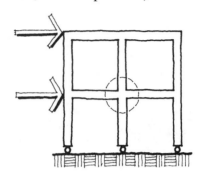

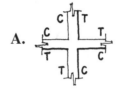 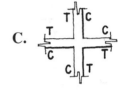

A.   C.

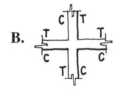 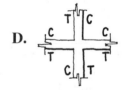

B.   D.

426. Drift caused by earthquake is limited for which of the following reasons? Check all that apply.

    A. To assure that the building will not undergo inelastic deformation during a major earthquake

    B. To insure structural integrity

    C. To minimize discomfort to the building's occupants

    D. To restrict damage to brittle nonstructural elements

427. Which of the following plans are considered plan irregularities in earthquake design?

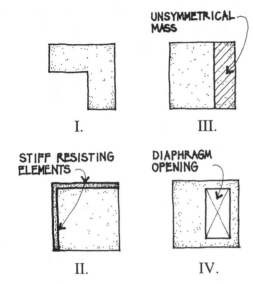

I.

UNSYMMETRICAL MASS

III.

STIFF RESISTING ELEMENTS

II.

DIAPHRAGM OPENING

IV.

A. I and II

B. II and IV

C. I and III

D. I, II, III, and IV

428. About how much does the cost of construction increase if seismic resistance is provided in the design of a building?

A. Under 5 percent

B. 5 to 10 percent

C. 10 to 20 percent

D. 25 percent

429. An unbraced parapet must be designed to resist a horizontal seismic force equal to what percentage of its weight? The building is assigned to SDC D and S_{DS} = 1.0g.

A. 10 percent

B. 50 percent

C. 100 percent

D. 120 percent

430. Which of the following systems provides maximum flexibility for a hospital without interruption of service?

A. Interstitial trusses

B. Staggered trusses

C. Space frame

D. Flat slab

431. Which of the following statements about Allowable Stress Design (ASD) and Load and Resistance Factor Design (LRFD) are correct?

I.   ASD uses unfactored working loads and a single factor of safety.

II. LRFD uses separate factors for each load and for the resistance.

III. ASD provides uniform reliability for all steel structures under various loading conditions.

A. I and II

B. II and III

C. I and III

D. I, II, and III

432. Which of the following 19th-century buildings is considered to be the first true skyscraper?

A. Monadnock Building

B. Home Insurance Building

C. Carson Pirie Scott Store

D. Marshall Field Warehouse

433. All of the following are tubular steel buildings, *EXCEPT* the

A. Water Tower Building in Chicago.

B. Bank of China Tower in Hong Kong.

C. Sears Tower in Chicago.

D. John Hancock Building in Chicago.

434. The work of Pier Luigi Nervi is associated with which of the following?

   I. Ferrocement

   II. Prefabricated concrete domes

   III. Prefabricated concrete lamella roofs

   IV. Suspension bridge roof

   A. II and III

   B. I and IV

   C. III and IV

   D. I, II, III, and IV

435. The shape that a cable assumes when the only load acting on it is its own weight is called a _____.

436. A thin shell structure is able to resist which of the following?

   I. Shear

   II. Tension

   III. Compression

   IV. Bending moment

   A. II only

   B. III only

   C. I, II, and III

   D. II, III, and IV

437. Section modulus is a measure of a beam's

   A. resistance to deflection.

   B. stiffness.

   C. elasticity.

   D. bending strength.

438. Steel decking and a concrete slab, which act together to span between beams, is called a _____.

439. The nominal diameter and yield strength of the reinforcing bar shown below are as follows:

   A. Diameter = 5/8 inch, yield strength = 60 ks

   B. Diameter = 1 inch, yield strength = 60 ksi

   C. Diameter = 0.60 inch, yield strength = 100 ksi

   D. Diameter = 1-1/4 inch, yield strength = 60 ksi

440. I-shaped wood joists consist of lumber flanges and a strand board web inserted and glued into a groove in each flange. What type of stress does the glue resist?

   A. Flexural tension or compression

   B. Axial tension or compression

   C. Bending moment

   D. Horizontal shear

441. Select the correct statement about earthquake design.

- **A.** A soft first story isolates the structure from the ground, thereby reducing the building's acceleration and potential earthquake damage.

- **B.** Wood frame buildings generally perform poorly in an earthquake and pose a significant threat to life.

- **C.** Adjacent buildings should be adequately separated to minimize the possibility of pounding.

- **D.** Wood stud walls should preferably have no mechanical connection to the foundation, but bear on a neoprene pad, in order to minimize the building's distortion.

442. Which of the following statements concerning the earthquake design of buildings is true?

- **A.** In an earthquake, the ground moves horizontally and vertically, but the effects of the vertical motion are usually neglected in the design.

- **B.** The acceleration of the ground beneath the building and the acceleration of the building usually have the same value.

- **C.** Special moment-resisting space frames have less ability to resist earthquakes without major damage than shear walls.

- **D.** The overturning moment due to seismic forces need not be considered in design, since earthquakes reverse direction and thus buildings cannot overturn.

443. Two trusses having the same load and span are shown. Which of the following statements are true?

- **I.** The axial tension and compression forces in the chords are greater in truss A than in truss B.

- **II.** The diagonals in truss B have greater axial tension forces than those in truss A.

- **III.** The verticals in truss A have the same axial compression forces as those in truss B.

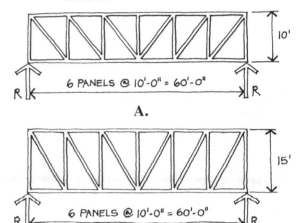

A.

B.

- **A.** I and II
- **B.** II and III
- **C.** I and III
- **D.** I, II, and III

444. A two-story warehouse has 40-foot by 40-foot bays. Which of the following reinforced concrete systems is likely to be the most economical?

- **A.** Flat plate
- **B.** Flat slab
- **C.** Waffle slab
- **D.** Pan joist

445. Which of the following statements about prestressed concrete is *INCORRECT*?

   A. Prestressed members have no tension cracks because they are completely in compression.

   B. Prestressed concrete has greater material and labor costs than conventional reinforced concrete.

   C. Posttensioned members are usually produced at a casting yard away from the building site.

   D. Smaller sizes may be used with prestressed concrete, because the entire section is effective in resisting applied loads.

446. The maximum deflection of the cantilevered steel beam shown is limited to 0.67 inch. What is the minimum required moment of inertia? $E = 29 \times 10^6$ psi. Use the beam diagrams on page 109 and neglect the weight of the beam.

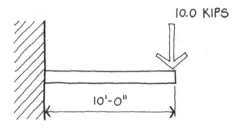

   A. 24.7 in.^{4}
   B. 171.6 in.^{4}
   C. 205.9 in.^{4}
   D. 296.4 in.^{4}

447. Two different framing schemes are being considered, as shown below. Scheme A consists of three simple beams of equal span. In scheme B, the middle beam is hung from the outer beams. What are the advantages of scheme B?

   I. Reduced positive moment in the end spans

   II. Reduced positive moment in the center span

   III. Reduced column loads

   A. I only
   B. I and II
   C. II only
   D. I, II, and III

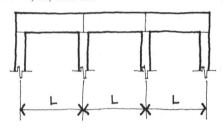

448. The soil boring log for a level building site shows that the top six feet of subsurface material consists of a loose fill, below which is a thick layer of dense sand. Which of the following foundation systems could be used on this site?

   I.   Mat foundation

   II. Pile foundation

  III. Shallow footings placed after removal and recompaction of the fill

  IV. Footings extending through the fill into the dense sand

   A. I only

   B. II and III

   C. I, II, and IV

   D. I, II, III, and IV

449. The load applied to a retaining wall by the retained earth and the resulting soil pressure under its footing are most closely approximated by which of the following diagrams?

A.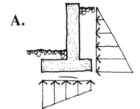

C.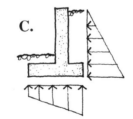

B.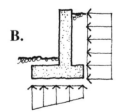

D.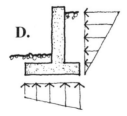

450. Which of the following describes ductility? Check all that apply.

   A. The resilience of a structural system

   B. The stiffness of a structural system

   C. The ability of a structural system to accommodate seismic loads by redistributing them to other elements, without collapse

   D. The ability of a structural system to accommodate seismic loads by inelastic yielding, without collapse

451. For the building shown in the plan, the relative rigidities of the shear walls are noted as R = . How far is the center of rigidity from the north wall?

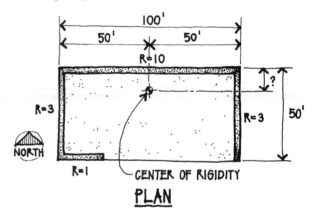

PLAN

   A. 2.5 feet

   B. 4.5 feet

   C. 5 feet

   D. 10 feet

452. You are the architect for a gymnasium that is 120 feet by 120 feet in plan and has no interior columns. Two systems are being considered: a space frame and a system of one-way parallel trusses spaced 30 feet apart. Which of the following are advantages of the space frame over the parallel trusses?

   I. Economy through the use of many identical members and connections

   II. Greater stiffness

   III. Less depth

   IV. Simpler analysis

   A. II and III

   B. I and III

   C. I, II, and IV

   D. I, II, and III

453. What is the purpose of belling a caisson?

   A. To increase the caisson's frictional resistance

   B. To stabilize the soil around the caisson

   C. To increase the caisson's bearing capacity

   D. To make the excavation watertight

454. Which of the following factors affects the shear capacity of a reinforced concrete beam?

   A. The cross-sectional area of the longitudinal tension reinforcing

   B. The span of the beam

   C. The ultimate 28-day strength of the concrete

   D. The load on the beam

455. What is the maximum bending moment that can be resisted by a 6 × 12 wood beam, if $F_b = 1{,}600$ psi, $A = 63.25$ in.^{2}, $S = 121.229$ in.^{3}, and $I = 697.068$ in.^{4}?

   A. 10,120 ft.-lbs.

   B. 11,153 ft.-lbs.

   C. 16,164 ft.-lbs.

   D. 19,397 ft.-lbs.

456. Long-span steel joists with a clear span of 72 feet are used to support a roof. The joists are six feet apart, the dead load is 20 pounds per square foot (including the joist weight), the live load is 30 pounds per square foot, and the live load deflection is limited to 1/360 of the span. What is the lightest joist that can be used? Use the table on page 105.

   A. 36LH10

   B. 36LH11

   C. 36LH12

   D. 36LH13

457. Which of the following statements concerning strength design of reinforced concrete is correct? Check all that apply.

   A. The amount of reinforcing steel used ensures that yielding of the steel will occur before failure of the concrete.

   B. The reinforcing steel is generally assumed to resist all the tensile stresses, while the concrete is assumed to resist all the compressive stresses.

   C. The amount of reinforcing steel used must be at least equal to that which would produce a balanced design.

   D. The ultimate load factors are greater for live load than for dead load.

458. In Mies van der Rohe's Lake Shore Drive Apartments, lateral displacement under wind loads is reduced by the use of

   A. steel plate cladding bonded to the concrete fireproofing.

   B. special concrete moment-resisting frames.

   C. perimeter shear walls.

   D. perimeter Vierendeel trusses.

459. Which of the following structures has a form that best reflects the structural concepts of wind resistance?

   A. Empire State Building

   B. Eiffel Tower

   C. Stonehenge

   D. Chrysler Building

460. What is the allowable shear force that can be resisted by a ⅜-inch thick structural I blocked horizontal diaphragm with 8d nails spaced at 6 inches at all panel edges and 3-inch thick framing members at the edges and boundaries?

   A. 200 pounds per foot

   B. 300 pounds per foot

   C. 400 pounds per foot

   D. 450 pounds per foot

461. For a shear wall consisting of wood studs with plywood sheathing, which of the following statements is most correct?

   A. The minimum width of the shear wall is determined by its height.

   B. The minimum width of the shear wall is two feet.

   C. There is no minimum width of the shear wall.

   D. The minimum width of the shear wall is determined by dividing the total shear force by the allowable shear per foot.

462. Which of the diagrams below represents the flexural stresses in a reinforced concrete beam at failure?

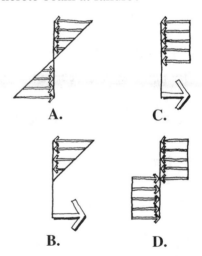

   A.   **C.**

   B.   **D.**

463. What is the internal force in member a of the cantilever truss shown?

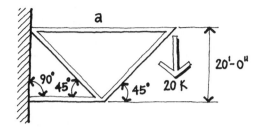

A. 20 kips tension

B. 20 kips compression

C. 40 kips tension

D. 40 kips compression

464. Which type of arch is statically determinate when subject to a uniformly distributed load across the entire span?

A. A two-hinged arch

B. A three-hinged arch

C. A fixed arch

D. Any arch

465. The ponding of water on a flat roof supported by long-span open web joists can be a problem. In this regard, which of the following statements are correct?

I. The most economical way to prevent ponding is to build pitch into the joist top chords.

II. An effective way to minimize ponding is to provide sufficient camber for the joists.

III. A slope of 1/8 inch per foot will prevent ponding.

IV. Using parallel chord joists with end supports at different elevations is an economical way to provide slope.

A. I and II

B. II and III

C. II, III, and IV

D. I and III

466. What is the horizontal thrust at each end of the three-hinged arch shown below?

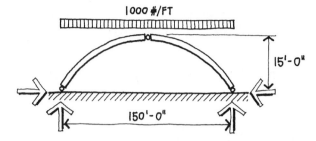

A. Not determinable from the information given

B. 75 kips

C. 187.5 kips

D. 375 kips

467. What is the maximum load P that can be transferred by the splice detail shown below? The members are Douglas Fir-Larch. Use the table on page 107.

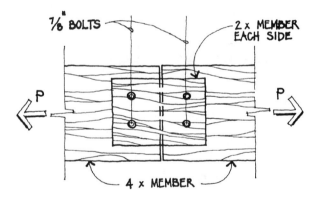

A. 2,520#

B. 2,780#

C. 5,600#

D. 6,360#

468. What property is practically constant for all structural steels?

A. Yield point

B. Ultimate strength

C. Weldability

D. Modulus of elasticity

469. What is a lamella roof?

   A. A series of parallel arches, skewed with respect to the axes of a building, which intersect another series of skewed arches

   B. A two-way truss system in which the trusses are inclined, rather than in a vertical plane

   C. A series of radial cables stabilized by another series of cables

   D. A system consisting of two intersecting arches placed along the diagonals of a building

470. Which of the following statements are correct concerning an air-supported fabric structure that encloses an occupied space?

   I. Fans are required to pressurize the space.

   II. People and equipment must pass through airlocks or special doors to get into and out of the facility.

   III. Long spans require steel cable reinforcement.

   IV. Loss of pressure can cause the roof to deflate and possibly fail.

   A. I and III

   B. II and IV

   C. I, II, and IV

   D. I, II, III, and IV

471. Two angles placed as shown are to be used for the top chord of a truss whose panel points are 10 feet apart. To determine the required size of the angles, the value of the radius of gyration r should be with respect to which axis?

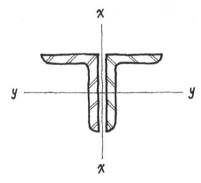

   A. x-x

   B. y-y

   C. x-x or y-y, whichever results in the lower value of r

   D. x-x or y-y, whichever results in the higher value of r

REFERENCE MATERIAL

The Architect Registration Examination (ARE) is closed book; no reference material is permitted for any part of the exam. Any reference material required for the test will be provided when you take the exam.

We suggest that, prior to the exam, you obtain some of the reference books that may be excerpted, in order to become familiar with them and thereby save valuable time at the exam.

The reference books that have often had sections reproduced for reference during the test include the *AISC Manual*, the *International Building Code*, and the *Standard Specifications for Steel Joists*.

Many architectural and engineering offices have these references in their library, which you may be able to borrow during your exam preparation.

Once you have the reference books, you should try to become generally familiar with the scope and format of each book, how its charts and tables are organized, and so forth, rather than trying to memorize anything.

On the following pages, we have reproduced the charts and tables needed to answer several of the questions in this book.

Table 7–1
Available Shear
Strength of Bolts, kips

Nominal Bolt Diameter d_b, in.					\(5/8\)		\(3/4\)		\(7/8\)		1	
Nominal Bolt Area, in.²					0.307		0.442		0.601		0.785	
ASTM Desig.	**Thread Cond.**	F_{nv}/Ω (ksi)	ϕF_{nv} (ksi)	**Load-ing**	r_n/Ω_v	$\phi_v r_n$	r_n/Ω_v	$\phi_v r_n$	r_n/Ω_v	$\phi_v r_n$	r_n/Ω_v	$\phi_v r_n$
		ASD	**LRFD**		**ASD**	**LRFD**	**ASD**	**LRFD**	**ASD**	**LRFD**	**ASD**	**LRFD**
A325 F1852	N	24.0	36.0	S	7.36	11.0	10.6	15.9	14.4	21.6	18.8	28.3
				D	14.7	22.1	21.2	31.8	28.9	43.3	37.7	56.5
	X	30.0	45.0	S	9.20	13.8	13.3	19.9	18.0	27.1	23.6	35.3
				D	18.4	27.6	26.5	39.8	36.1	54.1	47.1	70.7
A490	N	30.0	45.0	S	9.20	13.8	13.3	19.9	18.0	27.1	23.6	35.3
				D	18.4	27.6	26.5	39.8	36.1	54.1	47.1	70.7
	X	37.5	56.3	S	11.5	17.3	16.6	24.9	22.5	33.8	29.5	44.2
				D	23.0	34.5	33.1	49.7	45.1	67.6	58.9	88.4
A307	–	12.0	18.0	S	3.68	5.52	5.30	7.95	7.22	10.8	9.42	14.1
				D	7.36	11.0	10.6	15.9	14.4	21.6	18.8	28.3

Nominal Bolt Diameter d_b, in.					\(1 1/8\)		\(1 1/4\)		\(1 3/8\)		\(1 1/2\)	
Nominal Bolt Area, in.²					0.994		1.23		1.48		1.77	
ASTM Desig.	**Thread Cond.**	F_{nv}/Ω (ksi)	ϕF_{nv} (ksi)	**Load-ing**	r_n/Ω_v	$\phi_v r_n$	r_n/Ω_v	$\phi_v r_n$	r_n/Ω_v	$\phi_v r_n$	r_n/Ω_v	$\phi_v r_n$
		ASD	**LRFD**		**ASD**	**LRFD**	**ASD**	**LRFD**	**ASD**	**LRFD**	**ASD**	**LRFD**
A325 F1852	N	24.0	36.0	S	23.9	35.8	29.5	44.2	35.6	53.5	42.4	63.6
				D	47.7	71.6	58.9	88.4	71.3	107	84.8	127
	X	30.0	45.0	S	29.8	44.7	36.8	55.2	44.5	66.8	53.0	79.5
				D	59.6	89.5	73.6	110	89.1	134	106	159
A490	N	30.0	45.0	S	29.8	44.7	36.8	55.2	44.5	66.8	53.0	79.5
				D	59.6	89.5	73.6	110	89.1	134	106	159
	X	37.5	56.3	S	37.3	55.9	46.0	69.0	55.7	83.5	66.3	99.4
				D	74.6	112	92.0	138	111	167	133	199
A307	–	12.0	18.0	S	11.9	17.9	14.7	22.1	17.8	26.7	21.2	31.8
				D	23.9	35.8	29.5	44.2	35.6	53.5	42.4	63.6

ASD	LRFD
$\Omega_v = 2.00$	$\phi_v = 0.75$

Table 7–5
Available Bearing Strength at Bolt Holes Based on Bolt Spacing
kips/in. thickness

Hole Type	Bolt Spacing, s, in.	F_u, ksi	Nominal Bolt Diameter d_b, in.							
			5/8		3/4		7/8		1	
			r_n/Ω_v	$\phi_v r_n$	r_n/Ω_v	$\phi_v r_n$	r_n/Ω_v	$\phi_v r_n$	r_n/Ω_v	$\phi_v r_n$
			ASD	LRFD	ASD	LRFD	ASD	LRFD	ASD	LRFD
STD SSLT	$2^2/_3 d_b$	58	34.1	51.1	41.3	62.0	48.6	72.9	55.8	83.7
		65	38.2	57.3	46.3	69.5	54.4	81.7	62.6	93.8
	3 in.	58	43.5	65.3	52.2	78.3	60.9	91.4	67.4	101
		65	48.8	73.1	58.5	87.8	68.3	102	75.6	113
SSLP	$2^2/_3 d_b$	58	27.6	41.3	34.8	52.2	42.1	63.1	47.1	70.7
		65	30.9	46.3	39.0	58.5	47.1	70.7	52.8	79.2
	3 in.	58	43.5	65.3	52.2	78.3	60.9	91.4	58.7	88.1
		65	48.8	73.1	58.5	87.8	68.3	102	65.8	98.7
OVS	$2^2/_3 d_b$	58	29.7	44.6	37.0	55.5	44.2	66.3	49.3	74.0
		65	33.3	50.0	41.4	62.2	49.6	74.3	55.3	82.9
	3 in.	58	43.5	65.3	52.2	78.3	60.9	91.4	60.9	91.4
		65	48.8	73.1	58.5	87.8	68.3	102	68.3	102
LSLP	$2^2/_3 d_b$	58	3.62	5.44	4.35	6.53	5.08	7.61	5.80	8.70
		65	4.06	6.09	4.88	7.31	5.69	8.53	6.50	9.75
	3 in.	58	43.5	65.3	39.2	58.7	28.3	42.4	17.4	26.1
		65	48.8	73.1	43.9	65.8	31.7	47.5	19.5	29.3
LSLT	$2^2/_3 d_b$	58	28.4	42.6	34.4	51.7	40.5	60.7	46.5	69.8
		65	31.8	47.7	38.6	57.9	45.4	68.0	52.1	78.2
	3 in.	58	36.3	54.4	43.5	65.3	50.8	76.1	56.2	84.3
		65	40.6	60.9	48.8	73.1	56.9	85.3	63.0	94.5
STD, SSLT, SSLP, OVS, LSLP	$s \geq s_{full}$	58	43.5	65.3	52.2	78.3	60.9	91.4	69.6	104
		65	48.8	73.1	58.5	87.8	68.3	102	78.0	117
LSLT	$s \geq s_{full}$	58	36.3	54.4	43.5	65.3	50.8	76.1	58.0	87.0
		65	40.6	60.9	48.8	73.1	56.9	85.3	65.0	97.5
Spacing for full bearing strength s_{full}[a], in.	STD, SSLT, LSLT		$1^{15}/_{16}$		$2^5/_{16}$		$2^{11}/_{16}$		$3^1/_{16}$	
	OVS		$2^1/_{16}$		$2^7/_{16}$		$2^{13}/_{16}$		$3^1/_4$	
	SSLP		$2^1/_8$		$2^1/_2$		$2^7/_8$		$3^5/_{16}$	
	LSLP		$2^{13}/_{16}$		$3^3/_8$		$3^{15}/_{16}$		$4^1/_2$	
Minimum Spacing[a] = $2^2/_3 d_b$, in.			$1^{11}/_{16}$		2		$2^5/_{16}$		$2^{11}/_{16}$	

STD = Standard Hole
SSLT = Short-Slotted Hole oriented transverse to the line of force
SSLP = Short-Slotted Hole oriented parallel to the line of force
OVS = Oversized Hole
LSLP = Long-Slotted Hole oriented parallel to the line of force
LSLT = Long-Slotted Hole oriented transverse to the line of force

ASD	LRFD	Note: Spacing indicated is from the center of the hole or slot to the center of the adjacent hole or slot in the line of force. Hole deformation is considered. When hole deformation is not considered, see AISC Specification Section J3.10.
$\Omega_v = 2.00$	$\phi_v = 0.75$	[a] Decimal value has been rounded to the nearest sixteenth of an inch.

Table 7–6
Available Bearing Strength at Bolt Holes Based on Edge Distance
kips/in. thickness

Hole Type	Edge Distance L_e, in.	F_u, ksi	5/8 r_n/Ω_v ASD	5/8 $\phi_v r_n$ LRFD	3/4 r_n/Ω_v ASD	3/4 $\phi_v r_n$ LRFD	7/8 r_n/Ω_v ASD	7/8 $\phi_v r_n$ LRFD	1 r_n/Ω_v ASD	1 $\phi_v r_n$ LRFD
STD SSLT	1 1/4	58	31.5	47.3	29.4	44.0	27.2	40.8	25.0	37.5
		65	35.3	53.0	32.9	49.4	30.5	45.7	28.0	42.0
	2	58	43.5	65.3	52.2	78.3	53.3	79.9	51.1	76.7
		65	48.8	73.1	58.5	87.8	59.7	89.6	57.3	85.9
SSLP	1 1/4	58	28.3	42.4	26.1	39.2	23.9	35.9	20.7	31.0
		65	31.7	47.5	29.3	43.9	26.8	40.2	23.2	34.7
	2	58	43.5	65.3	52.2	78.3	50.0	75.0	46.8	70.1
		65	48.8	73.1	58.5	87.8	56.1	84.1	52.4	78.6
OVS	1 1/4	58	29.4	44.0	27.2	40.8	25.0	37.5	21.8	32.6
		65	32.9	49.4	30.5	45.7	28.0	42.0	24.4	36.6
	2	58	43.5	65.3	52.2	78.3	51.1	76.7	47.9	71.8
		65	48.8	73.1	58.5	87.8	57.3	85.9	53.6	80.4
LSLP	1 1/4	58	16.3	24.5	10.9	16.3	5.44	8.16	—	—
		65	18.3	27.4	12.2	18.3	6.09	9.14	—	—
	2	58	42.4	63.6	37.0	55.5	31.5	47.3	26.1	39.2
		65	47.5	71.3	41.4	62.2	35.3	53.0	29.3	43.9
LSLT	1 1/4	58	26.3	39.4	24.5	36.7	22.7	34.0	20.8	31.3
		65	29.5	44.2	27.4	41.1	25.4	38.1	23.4	35.0
	2	58	36.3	54.4	43.5	65.3	44.4	66.6	42.6	63.9
		65	40.6	60.9	48.8	73.1	49.8	74.6	47.7	71.6
STD, SSLT, SSLP, OVS, LSLP	$L_e \geq L_{e\,full}$	58	43.5	65.3	52.2	78.3	60.9	91.4	69.6	104
		65	48.8	73.1	58.5	87.8	68.3	102	78.0	117
LSLT	$L_e \geq L_{e\,full}$	58	36.3	54.4	43.5	65.3	50.8	76.1	58.0	87.0
		65	40.6	60.9	48.8	73.1	56.9	85.3	65.0	97.5

Edge distance for full bearing strength $L_e \geq L_{e\,full}$[a], in.

	STD, SSLT, LSLT	OVS	SSLP	LSLP
5/8	1 5/8	1 11/16	1 11/16	2 1/16
3/4	1 15/16	2	2	2 7/16
7/8	2 1/4	2 5/16	2 5/16	2 7/8
1	2 9/16	2 5/8	2 11/16	3 1/4

STD = Standard Hole
SSLT = Short-Slotted Hole oriented transverse to the line of force
SSLP = Short-Slotted Hole oriented parallel to the line of force
OVS = Oversized Hole
LSLP = Long-Slotted Hole oriented parallel to the line of force
LSLT = Long-Slotted Hole oriented transverse to the line of force

ASD	LRFD	
$\Omega_v = 2.00$	$\phi_v = 0.75$	— indicates spacing less than minimum spacing required per AISC Specification Section J3.3.

Note: Spacing indicated is from the center of the hole or slot to the center of the adjacent hole or slot in the line of force. Hole deformation is considered. When hole deformation is not considered, see AISC Specification Section J3.10.

[a] Decimal value has been rounded to the nearest sixteenth of an inch.

Beam	F_y = 50 ksi F_u = 65 ksi
Angle	F_y = 36 ksi F_u = 58 ksi

Table 10–1 (continued)
All-Bolted Double-Angle Connections
$7/8$-in. Bolts

Bolt and Angle Available Strength, kips

5 Rows	ASTM Desig.	Thread Cond.	Hole Type	Angle Thickness							
				1/4		5/16		3/8		1/2	
W30, 27, 24, 21, 18				ASD	LRFD	ASD	LRFD	ASD	LRFD	ASD	LRFD
	A325/ F1852	N	—	82.4	124	103	155	124	185	144	216
		X	—	82.4	124	103	155	124	185	165	247
		SC Class A	STD	82.4	124	103	154	103	154	103	154
			OVS	74.3	111	74.3	111	74.3	111	74.3	111
			SSLT	81.1	122	87.4	131	87.4	131	87.4	131
		SC Class B	STD	82.4	124	103	155	124	185	144	216
			OVS	77.2	116	96.5	145	106	159	106	159
			SSLT	81.1	122	101	152	122	182	125	187
	A490	N	—	82.4	124	103	155	124	185	165	247
		X	—	82.4	124	103	155	124	185	165	247
		SC Class A	STD	82.4	124	103	155	124	185	129	194
			OVS	77.2	116	93.3	140	93.3	140	93.3	140
			SSLT	81.1	122	101	152	110	165	110	165
		SC Class B	STD	82.4	124	103	155	124	185	165	247
			OVS	77.2	116	96.5	145	116	174	133	200
			SSLT	81.1	122	101	152	122	182	157	235

Beam Web Available Strength per Inch Thickness, kips/in.

Hole Type		STD				OVS				SSLT			
		L_{eh}*											
L_{ev}, in.		1 1/2		1 3/4		1 1/2		1 3/4		1 1/2		1 3/4	
		ASD	LRFD	ASD	LRFD	ASD	LRFD	ASD	LRFD	ASD	LRFD	ASD	LRFD
Coped at Top Flange Only	1 1/4	195	293	203	305	182	273	190	285	192	288	200	300
	1 3/8	197	296	206	308	184	277	193	289	194	292	203	304
	1 1/2	200	300	208	312	187	280	195	293	197	295	205	307
	1 5/8	202	303	210	316	189	284	197	296	199	299	207	311
	2	210	314	218	327	197	295	205	307	207	310	215	322
	3	229	344	237	356	216	324	224	336	226	339	234	351
Coped at Both Flanges	1 1/4	185	278	185	278	173	260	173	260	185	278	185	278
	1 3/8	190	285	190	285	178	267	178	267	190	285	190	285
	1 1/2	195	293	195	293	183	274	183	274	195	293	195	293
	1 5/8	200	300	200	300	188	282	188	282	199	299	200	300
	2	210	314	215	322	197	295	202	303	207	310	215	322
	3	229	344	237	356	216	324	224	336	226	339	234	351
Uncoped		341	512	341	512	341	512	341	512	341	512	341	512

Support Available Strength per Inch Thickness, kips/in.

Notes:
STD = Standard holes
OVS = Oversized holes
SSLT = Short-slotted holes transverse to direction of load

N = Threads included
X = Threads excluded
SC = Slip critical

Hole Type	ASD	LRFD
STD/ OVS/ SSLT	683	1020

* Tabulated values include 1/4-in. reduction in end distance L_{eh} to account for possible underrun in beam length.

ASD

STANDARD LOAD TABLE FOR LONGSPAN STEEL JOISTS, LH-SERIES
Based on a 50 ksi Maximum Yield Strength - Loads Shown in Pounds per Linear Foot (plf)

CLEAR SPAN IN FEET

Joist Designation	Approx. Wt in Lbs. Per Linear Ft. (Joists only)	Depth in inches	SAFELOAD* in Lbs. Between 28-32	33	34	35	36	37	38	39	40	41	42	43	44	45	46	47	48
24LH03	11	24	11500	342	339	336	323	307	293	279	267	255	244	234	224	215	207	199	191
24LH04	12	24	14100	419	398	379	360	343	327	312	298	285	273	262	251	241	231	222	214
24LH05	13	24	15100	449	446	440	419	399	380	363	347	331	317	304	291	280	269	258	248
24LH06	16	24	20300	604	579	555	530	504	480	457	437	417	399	381	364	348	334	320	307
24LH07	17	24	22300	665	638	613	588	565	541	516	491	468	446	426	407	389	373	357	343
24LH08	18	24	23800	707	677	649	622	597	572	545	520	497	475	455	435	417	400	384	369
24LH09	21	24	28000	832	808	785	764	731	696	663	632	602	574	548	524	501	480	460	441
24LH10	23	24	29600	882	856	832	809	788	768	737	702	668	637	608	582	556	533	511	490
24LH11	25	24	31200	927	900	875	851	829	807	787	768	734	701	671	642	616	590	567	544

Joist Designation	Wt	Depth	SAFELOAD 33-40	41	42	43	44	45	46	47	48	49	50	51	52	53	54	55	56
28LH05	13	28	14000	337	323	310	297	286	275	265	255	245	237	228	220	213	206	199	193
28LH06	16	28	18600	448	429	412	395	379	364	350	337	324	313	301	291	281	271	262	253
28LH07	17	28	21000	505	484	464	445	427	410	394	379	365	352	339	327	316	305	295	285
28LH08	18	28	22500	540	517	496	475	456	438	420	403	387	371	357	344	331	319	308	297
28LH09	21	28	27700	667	639	612	586	563	540	519	499	481	463	446	430	415	401	387	374
28LH10	23	28	30300	729	704	679	651	625	600	576	554	533	513	495	477	460	444	429	415
28LH11	25	28	32500	780	762	736	711	682	655	629	605	582	561	540	521	502	485	468	453
28LH12	27	28	35700	857	837	818	800	782	766	737	709	682	656	632	609	587	566	546	527
28LH13	30	28	37200	895	874	854	835	816	799	782	766	751	722	694	668	643	620	598	577

Joist Designation	Wt	Depth	SAFELOAD 38-46	SAFELOAD 47-48	49	50	51	52	53	54	55	56	57	58	59	60	61	62	63	64
32LH06	14	32	16700	16700	338	326	315	304	294	284	275	266	257	249	242	234	227	220	214	208
32LH07	16	32	18800	18800	379	366	353	341	329	318	308	298	288	279	271	262	254	247	240	233
32LH08	17	32	20400	20400	411	397	383	369	357	345	333	322	312	302	293	284	275	267	259	252
32LH09	21	32	25600	25600	516	498	480	463	447	432	418	404	391	379	367	356	345	335	325	315
32LH10	21	32	28300	28300	571	550	531	512	495	478	462	445	430	416	402	389	376	364	353	342
32LH11	24	32	31000	31000	625	602	580	560	541	522	505	488	473	458	443	429	416	403	390	378
32LH12	27	32	36400	36400	734	712	688	664	641	619	598	578	559	541	524	508	492	477	463	449
32LH13	30	32	40600	40600	817	801	785	771	742	715	690	666	643	621	600	581	562	544	527	511
32LH14	33	32	41800	41800	843	826	810	795	780	766	738	713	688	665	643	622	602	583	564	547
32LH15	35	32	43200	43200	870	853	837	821	805	791	776	763	750	725	701	678	656	635	616	597

Joist Designation	Wt	Depth	SAFELOAD 42-46	SAFELOAD 47-56	57	58	59	60	61	62	63	64	65	66	67	68	69	70	71	72
36LH07	16	36	16800	16800	292	283	274	266	258	251	244	237	230	224	218	212	207	201	196	191
36LH08	18	36	18500	18500	321	311	302	293	284	276	268	260	253	246	239	233	227	221	215	209
36LH09	21	36	23700	23700	411	398	386	374	363	352	342	333	323	314	306	297	289	282	275	267
36LH10	21	36	26100	26100	454	440	426	413	401	389	378	367	357	347	338	328	320	311	303	295
36LH11	23	36	28500	28500	495	480	465	451	438	425	412	401	389	378	368	358	348	339	330	322
36LH12	25	36	34100	34100	593	575	557	540	523	508	493	478	464	450	437	424	412	400	389	378
36LH13	30	36	40100	40100	697	675	654	634	615	596	579	562	546	531	516	502	488	475	463	451
36LH14	36	36	44200	44200	768	755	729	706	683	661	641	621	602	584	567	551	535	520	505	492
36LH15	36	36	46600	46600	809	795	781	769	744	721	698	677	656	637	618	600	583	567	551	536

Table 104.5-1			
LH-DLH SECTION* NUMBER	**MAX. SPACING OF LINES OF TOP CHORD BRIDGING**	**NOMINAL** HORIZONTAL BRACING FORCE**	
		lbs	**(N)**
02,03,04	11'-0" (3352 mm)	400	(1779)
05,06	12'-0" (3657 mm)	500	(2224)
07,08	13'-0" (3962 mm)	650	(2891)
09,10	14'-0" (4267 mm)	800	(3558)
11,12	16'-0" (4876 mm)	1000	(4448)
13,14	16'-0" (4876 mm)	1200	(5337)
15,16	21'-0" (6400 mm)	1600	(7117)
17	21'-0" (6400 mm)	1800	(8006)
18,19	26'-0" (7924 mm)	2000	(8896)

Number of lines of bridging is based on joist clear span dimensions
* Last two digits of joist designation shown in load table.
** Nominal bracing force is unfactored.

Table 3–2 (continued)
W Shapes
Selection by Z_x

F_y = 50 ksi

Z_x

Shape	Z_x	M_{px}/Ω_b	$\phi_b M_{px}$	M_{rx}/Ω_b	$\phi_b M_{rx}$	BF		L_p	L_r	I_x	V_{nx}/Ω_v	$\phi_v V_{nx}$
		kip-ft	kip-ft	kip-ft	kip-ft	kips	kips	ft	ft	in.⁴	kips	kips
	in.³	ASD	LRFD	ASD	LRFD	ASD	LRFD	ft	ft	in.⁴	ASD	LRFD
W21×55	126	314	473	192	289	10.8	16.3	6.11	17.4	1140	156	234
W14×74	126	314	473	196	294	5.34	8.03	8.76	31.0	795	128	191
W18×60	123	307	461	189	284	9.64	14.5	5.93	18.2	984	151	227
W12×79	119	297	446	187	281	3.77	5.67	10.8	39.9	662	116	175
W14×68	115	287	431	180	270	5.20	7.81	8.69	29.3	722	117	175
W10×88	113	282	424	172	259	2.63	3.95	9.29	51.1	534	131	197
W18×55	112	279	420	172	258	9.26	13.9	5.90	17.5	890	141	212
W21×50	110	274	413	165	248	12.2	18.3	4.59	13.6	984	158	237
W12×72	108	269	405	170	256	3.72	5.59	10.7	37.4	597	105	158
W21×48ᶠ	107	265	398	162	244	9.78	14.7	6.09	16.6	959	144	217
W16×57	105	262	394	161	242	7.98	12.0	5.65	18.3	758	141	212
W14×61	102	254	383	161	242	4.96	7.46	8.65	27.5	640	104	156
W18×50	101	252	379	155	233	8.69	13.1	5.83	17.0	800	128	192
W10×77	97.6	244	366	150	225	2.59	3.90	9.18	45.2	455	112	169
W12×65ᶠ	96.8	237	356	154	231	3.60	5.41	11.9	35.1	533	94.5	142
W21×44	95.4	238	358	143	214	11.2	16.8	4.45	13.0	843	145	217
W16×50	92.0	230	345	141	213	7.59	11.4	5.62	17.2	659	124	185
W18×46	90.7	226	340	138	207	9.71	14.6	4.56	13.7	712	130	195
W14×53	87.1	217	327	136	204	5.27	7.93	6.78	22.2	541	103	155
W12×58	86.4	216	324	136	205	3.76	5.66	8.87	29.9	475	87.8	132
W10×68	85.3	213	320	132	199	2.57	3.86	9.15	40.6	394	97.8	147
W16×45	82.3	205	309	127	191	7.16	10.8	5.55	16.5	586	111	167
W18×40	78.4	196	294	119	180	8.86	13.3	4.49	13.1	612	113	169
W14×48	78.4	196	294	123	184	5.10	7.66	6.75	21.1	484	93.8	141
W12×53	77.9	194	292	123	185	3.65	5.48	8.76	28.2	425	83.2	125
W10×60	74.6	186	280	116	175	2.53	3.80	9.08	36.6	341	85.8	129
W16×40	73.0	182	274	113	170	6.69	10.1	5.55	15.9	518	97.7	146
W12×50	71.9	179	270	112	169	3.97	5.97	6.92	23.9	391	90.2	135
W8×67	70.1	175	263	105	159	1.73	2.60	7.49	47.7	272	103	154
W14×43	69.6	174	261	109	164	4.82	7.24	6.68	20.0	428	83.3	125
W10×54	66.6	166	250	105	158	2.49	3.74	9.04	33.7	303	74.7	112

ASD	LRFD	ᶠ Shape exceeds compact limit for flexure with F_y = 50 ksi.
Ω_b = 1.67	ϕ_b = 0.90	
Ω_v = 1.50	ϕ_v = 1.00	

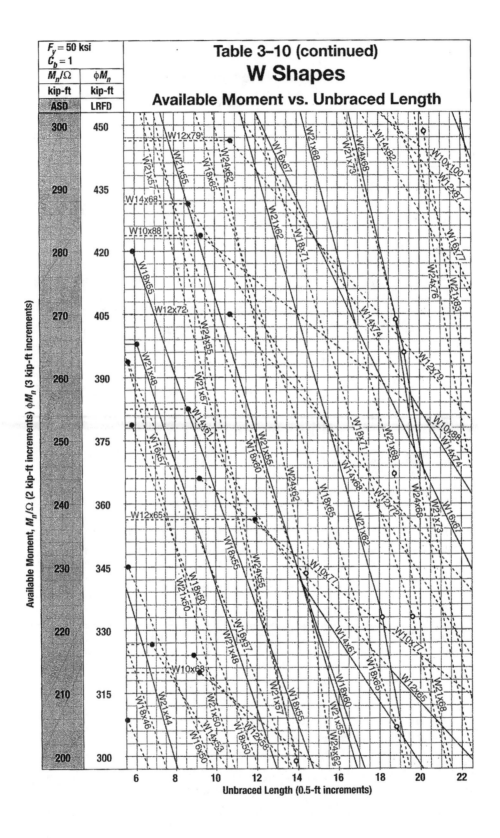

$F_y = 50$ ksi $C_b = 1$	
M_n/Ω	ϕM_n
kip-ft	kip-ft
ASD	LRFD

Table 3–10 (continued)
W Shapes
Available Moment vs. Unbraced Length

Available Moment, M_n/Ω (2 kip-ft increments) ϕM_n (3 kip-ft increments)

Unbraced Length (0.5-ft increments)

Table 11F BOLTS: Reference Lateral Design Values (Z) for Double Shear (three member) Connections[1,2]

for sawn lumber or SCL with all members of identical specific gravity

t_m in.	t_s in.	D in.	$Z_\parallel$ lbs.	$Z_{s\perp}$ lbs.	$Z_{m\perp}$ lbs.	$Z_\parallel$ lbs.	$Z_{s\perp}$ lbs.	$Z_{m\perp}$ lbs.	$Z_\parallel$ lbs.	$Z_{s\perp}$ lbs.	$Z_{m\perp}$ lbs.	$Z_\parallel$ lbs.	$Z_{s\perp}$ lbs.	$Z_{m\perp}$ lbs.	$Z_\parallel$ lbs.	$Z_{s\perp}$ lbs.	$Z_{m\perp}$ lbs.
			G=0.67 Red Oak			G=0.55 Mixed Maple Southern Pine			G=0.50 Douglas Fir-Larch			G=0.49 Douglas Fir-Larch(N)			G=0.46 Douglas Fir(S) Hem-Fir(N)		
1-1/2	1-1/2	1/2	1410	960	730	1150	800	550	1050	730	470	1030	720	460	970	680	420
		5/8	1760	1310	810	1440	1130	610	1310	1040	530	1290	1030	520	1210	940	470
		3/4	2110	1690	890	1730	1330	660	1580	1170	590	1550	1130	560	1450	1040	520
		7/8	2460	1920	960	2020	1440	720	1840	1260	630	1800	1210	600	1690	1100	550
		1	2810	2040	1020	2310	1530	770	2100	1350	680	2060	1290	650	1930	1200	600
1-3/4	1-3/4	1/2	1640	1030	850	1350	850	640	1230	770	550	1200	750	530	1130	710	490
		5/8	2050	1370	940	1680	1160	710	1530	1070	610	1500	1060	600	1410	1000	550
		3/4	2460	1810	1040	2020	1550	770	1840	1370	680	1800	1310	660	1690	1210	600
		7/8	2870	2240	1120	2350	1680	840	2140	1470	740	2110	1410	700	1970	1290	640
		1	3280	2380	1190	2690	1790	890	2450	1580	790	2410	1510	750	2250	1400	700
2-1/2	1-1/2	1/2	1530	960	1120	1320	800	910	1230	730	790	1210	720	760	1160	680	700
		5/8	2150	1310	1340	1870	1130	1020	1760	1040	880	1740	1030	860	1660	940	780
		3/4	2890	1770	1480	2550	1330	1110	2400	1170	980	2380	1130	940	2280	1040	860
		7/8	3780	1920	1600	3360	1440	1200	3060	1260	1050	3010	1210	1010	2820	1100	920
		1	4690	2040	1700	3840	1530	1280	3500	1350	1130	3440	1290	1080	3220	1200	1000
3-1/2	1-1/2	1/2	1530	960	1120	1320	800	940	1230	730	860	1210	720	850	1160	680	810
		5/8	2150	1310	1510	1870	1130	1290	1760	1040	1190	1740	1030	1170	1660	940	1090
		3/4	2890	1770	1980	2550	1330	1550	2400	1170	1370	2380	1130	1310	2280	1040	1210
		7/8	3780	1920	2240	3360	1440	1680	3180	1260	1470	3150	1210	1410	3030	1100	1290
		1	4820	2040	2380	4310	1530	1790	4090	1350	1580	4050	1290	1510	3860	1200	1400
	1-3/4	1/2	1660	1030	1180	1430	850	1030	1330	770	940	1310	750	920	1250	710	870
		5/8	2310	1370	1630	1990	1160	1380	1860	1070	1230	1840	1060	1200	1760	1000	1090
		3/4	3060	1810	2070	2670	1550	1550	2510	1370	1370	2480	1310	1310	2370	1210	1210
		7/8	3940	2240	2240	3470	1680	1680	3270	1470	1470	3240	1410	1410	3110	1290	1290
		1	4960	2380	2380	4400	1790	1790	4170	1580	1580	4120	1510	1510	3970	1400	1400
	3-1/2	1/2	1660	1180	1180	1500	1040	1040	1430	970	970	1420	960	960	1370	920	920
		5/8	2590	1770	1770	2340	1560	1420	2240	1410	1230	2220	1390	1200	2150	1290	1090
		3/4	3730	2380	2070	3380	1910	1550	3220	1750	1370	3190	1700	1310	3090	1610	1210
		7/8	5080	2820	2240	4600	2330	1680	4290	2130	1470	4210	2070	1410	3940	1960	1290
		1	6560	3340	2380	5380	2780	1790	4900	2580	1580	4810	2520	1510	4510	2410	1400
5-1/4	1-1/2	5/8	2150	1310	1510	1870	1130	1290	1760	1040	1190	1740	1030	1170	1660	940	1110
		3/4	2890	1770	1980	2550	1330	1690	2400	1170	1580	2380	1130	1550	2280	1040	1480
		7/8	3780	1920	2520	3360	1440	2170	3180	1260	2030	3150	1210	1990	3030	1100	1900
		1	4820	2040	3120	4310	1530	2680	4090	1350	2360	4050	1290	2260	3860	1200	2100
	1-3/4	5/8	2310	1370	1630	1990	1160	1380	1860	1070	1270	1840	1060	1250	1760	1000	1180
		3/4	3060	1810	2110	2670	1550	1790	2510	1370	1660	2480	1310	1630	2370	1210	1550
		7/8	3940	2240	2640	3470	1680	2260	3270	1470	2100	3240	1410	2060	3110	1290	1930
		1	4960	2380	3240	4400	1790	2680	4170	1580	2360	4120	1510	2260	3970	1400	2100
	3-1/2	5/8	2590	1770	1770	2340	1560	1560	2240	1410	1460	2220	1390	1450	2150	1290	1390
		3/4	3730	2380	2480	3380	1910	2180	3220	1750	2050	3190	1700	1970	3090	1610	1810
		7/8	5080	2820	3290	4600	2330	2530	4390	2130	2210	4350	2070	2110	4130	1960	1930
		1	6630	3340	3570	5740	2780	2680	5330	2580	2360	5250	2520	2260	4990	2410	2100
5-1/2	1-1/2	5/8	2150	1310	1510	1870	1130	1290	1760	1040	1190	1740	1030	1170	1660	940	1110
		3/4	2890	1770	1980	2550	1330	1690	2400	1170	1580	2380	1130	1550	2280	1040	1480
		7/8	3780	1920	2520	3360	1440	2170	3180	1260	2030	3150	1210	1990	3030	1100	1900
		1	4820	2040	3120	4310	1530	2700	4090	1350	2480	4050	1290	2370	3860	1200	2200
	3-1/2	5/8	2590	1770	1770	2340	1560	1560	2240	1410	1460	2220	1390	1450	2150	1290	1390
		3/4	3730	2380	2480	3380	1910	2180	3220	1750	2050	3190	1700	2020	3090	1610	1900
		7/8	5080	2820	3290	4600	2330	2650	4390	2130	2310	4350	2070	2210	4130	1960	2020
		1	6630	3340	3740	5740	2780	2810	5330	2580	2480	5250	2520	2370	4990	2410	2200
7-1/2	1-1/2	5/8	2150	1310	1510	1870	1130	1290	1760	1040	1190	1740	1030	1170	1660	940	1110
		3/4	2890	1770	1980	2550	1330	1690	2400	1170	1580	2380	1130	1550	2280	1040	1480
		7/8	3780	1920	2520	3360	1440	2170	3180	1260	2030	3150	1210	1990	3030	1100	1900
		1	4820	2040	3120	4310	1530	2700	4090	1350	2530	4050	1290	2480	3860	1200	2390
	3-1/2	5/8	2590	1770	1770	2340	1560	1560	2240	1410	1460	2220	1390	1450	2150	1290	1390
		3/4	3730	2380	2480	3380	1910	2180	3220	1750	2050	3190	1700	2020	3090	1610	1940
		7/8	5080	2820	3290	4600	2330	2890	4390	2130	2720	4350	2070	2670	4130	1960	2560
		1	6630	3340	4190	5740	2780	3680	5330	2580	3380	5250	2520	3230	4990	2410	3000

1. Tabulated lateral design values (Z) for bolted connections shall be multiplied by all applicable adjustment factors (see Table 10.3.1).
2. Tabulated lateral design values (Z) are for "full diameter" bolts (see Appendix L) with bending yield strength (F_{yb}) of 45,000 psi.

I

W10

Table 4–1 (continued)
Available Strength in
Axial Compression, kips
W Shapes

$F_y = 50$ ksi

Shape		W10×									
Wt/ft		54		49		45		39		33	
Design		P_n/Ω_c	$\phi_c P_n$	P_n/Ω_c	$\phi_c P_n$	P_n/Ω_c	$\phi_c P_n$	P_n/Ω_c	$\phi_c P_n$	P_n/Ω_c	$\phi_c P_n$
		ASD	LRFD	ASD	LRFD	ASD	LRFD	ASD	LRFD	ASD	LRFD
Effective length KL (ft) with respect to least radius of gyration r_y	0	474	712	432	649	397	597	343	516	291	437
	6	447	672	407	612	361	543	312	469	263	395
	7	438	658	399	599	349	525	301	452	253	381
	8	428	643	389	585	336	505	289	435	243	365
	9	416	625	378	569	321	483	276	415	232	348
	10	404	607	367	551	306	460	263	395	220	330
	11	390	586	355	533	290	435	248	373	207	311
	12	376	565	341	513	273	410	233	351	194	292
	13	361	543	328	493	256	384	218	328	181	272
	14	346	520	314	471	238	358	203	305	168	253
	15	330	496	299	450	221	332	188	282	155	233
	16	314	472	284	428	204	306	173	260	142	213
	17	298	448	270	405	187	281	158	238	130	195
	18	282	423	255	383	171	256	144	216	117	177
	19	265	399	240	360	155	233	130	195	106	159
	20	249	375	225	338	140	210	117	176	95.4	143
	22	218	327	196	295	116	174	97.0	146	78.8	118
	24	188	282	169	254	97.1	146	81.5	122	66.2	99.5
	26	160	241	144	216	82.7	124	69.4	104	56.4	84.8
	28	138	208	124	186	71.3	107	59.9	90.0	48.7	73.1
	30	120	181	108	162	62.1	93.4	52.2	78.4	42.4	63.7
	32	106	159	94.9	143	54.6	82.1	45.8	68.9	37.2	56.0
	34	93.7	141	84.0	126						
	36	83.6	126	75.0	113						
	38	75.0	113	67.3	101						
	40	67.7	102	60.7	91.3						

Properties											
P_{wo} (kips)		68.8	103	60.1	90.1	65.3	98.0	54.1	81.1	45.2	67.8
P_{wi} (kips/in.)		12.3	18.5	11.3	17.0	11.7	17.5	10.5	15.8	9.67	14.5
P_{wb} (kips)		112	168	86.5	130	94.4	142	68.8	103	53.7	80.7
P_{fb} (kips)		70.8	106	58.7	88.2	71.9	108	52.6	79.0	35.4	53.2
L_p (ft)		9.04		8.97		7.10		6.99		6.85	
L_r (ft)		33.7		31.6		26.9		24.2		21.8	
A_g (in.²)		15.8		14.4		13.3		11.5		9.71	
I_x (in.⁴)		303		272		248		209		171	
I_y (in.⁴)		103		93.4		53.4		45.0		36.6	
r_y (in.)		2.56		2.54		2.01		1.98		1.94	
Ratio r_x/r_y		1.71		1.71		2.15		2.16		2.16	
$P_{ex}(KL^2)/10^4$ (k-in.²)		8670		7790		7100		5980		4890	
$P_{ey}(KL^2)/10^4$ (k-in.²)		2950		2670		1530		1290		1050	

ASD	LRFD	Note: Heavy line indicates Kl/r equal to or greater than 200.
$\Omega_c = 1.67$	$\phi_c = 0.90$	

BEAM DIAGRAMS AND FORMULAS
For various static loading conditions

For meaning of symbols, see page **2 - 293**

1. SIMPLE BEAM—UNIFORMLY DISTRIBUTED LOAD

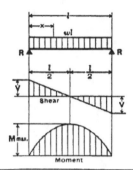

Total Equiv. Uniform Load $\dots = wl$

$R = V \ \dots \dots \dots \dots = \dfrac{wl}{2}$

$V_x \ \dots \dots \dots \dots \dots = w\left(\dfrac{l}{2} - x\right)$

M max. $\left(\text{at center}\right) \ \dots \dots = \dfrac{wl^2}{8}$

$M_x \ \dots \dots \dots \dots \dots = \dfrac{wx}{2}(l - x)$

Δmax. $\left(\text{at center}\right) \ \dots \dots = \dfrac{5\,wl^4}{384\,EI}$

$\Delta_x \ \dots \dots \dots \dots \dots = \dfrac{wx}{24EI}(l^3 - 2lx^2 + x^3)$

7. SIMPLE BEAM—CONCENTRATED LOAD AT CENTER

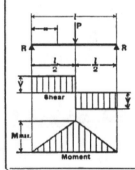

Total Equiv. Uniform Load $\dots \dots = 2P$

$R = V \ \dots \dots \dots \dots = \dfrac{P}{2}$

M max. $\left(\text{at point of load}\right) \ \dots \dots = \dfrac{Pl}{4}$

$M_x \ \left(\text{when } x < \dfrac{l}{2}\right) \ \dots \dots = \dfrac{Px}{2}$

Δmax. $\left(\text{at point of load}\right) \ \dots \dots = \dfrac{Pl^3}{48EI}$

$\Delta_x \ \left(\text{when } x < \dfrac{l}{2}\right) \ \dots \dots = \dfrac{Px}{48EI}(3l^2 - 4x^2)$

22. CANTILEVER BEAM—CONCENTRATED LOAD AT FREE END

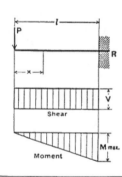

Total Equiv. Uniform Load $\dots \dots = 8P$

$R = V \ \dots \dots \dots \dots = P$

M max. $\left(\text{at fixed end}\right) \ \dots \dots = Pl$

$M_x \ \dots \dots \dots \dots \dots = Px$

Δmax. $\left(\text{at free end}\right) \ \dots \dots = \dfrac{Pl^3}{3EI}$

$\Delta_x \ \dots \dots \dots \dots \dots = \dfrac{P}{6EI}(2l^3 - 3l^2x + x^3)$

1. **A.** The flexural stress in a homogeneous rectangular beam varies from zero at the neutral axis to a maximum value at the top and bottom fibers, as shown in correct answer A. C indicates the variation of shear stress, and D shows the stress in a reinforced concrete beam at failure.

2. **A, B, and C.** The three conditions described in A, B, and C will cause bending in truss members. The members of a truss without diagonals (A), known as a Vierendeel truss, are subject to bending moment in addition to axial forces. The use of closely spaced joists (B) loads the trusses between panel points, which results in bending moment in the truss chord members that are loaded. In truss analysis, the joints are generally assumed to be hinged. In actual practice, however, the joints are not hinged; the truss members are restrained against rotation by the gusset plates to which they are connected. This restraint introduces small bending stresses, known as secondary stresses (C). Application of a load to a truss member would also cause bending in that member, however, application of loads to truss joints will only increase axial stresses within truss members, not bending (D).

3. **B.** It is not necessary to memorize any deflection formulas in order to answer this question. But, at least, you should know that deflection formulas generally are in this form: Deflection = KWL^3/EI, where K depends on the loading, W is the total load, L is the length, E is the modulus of elasticity, and I is the moment of inertia. Therefore, to decrease the deflection by 20 percent (0.90/0.75 = 1.20), one would increase the moment of inertia (I) by 20 percent (correct answer B).

4. **D.** While many of the questions on the test usually involve wind or earthquake forces, some questions may relate to other lateral forces, such as earth pressure against retaining walls. In this question, all four factors are considered in designing a cantilever retaining wall (correct answer D). A retaining wall can fail by overturning (I), and this can be prevented by making the base sufficiently wide. The resistance of a retaining wall to sliding (II) is provided by friction between the base and the underlying soil and by earth pressure in front of the toe. The maximum soil pressure under the footing (III) must be less than the allowable soil bearing pressure. And finally, the bending moment in the stem (IV) is resisted by the wall itself, which is usually reinforced concrete or reinforced masonry.

5. **A, C, and E.** Tall buildings have relatively large overturning moments from wind or earthquake, and slender buildings have relatively small dead load resisting moments. Therefore, overturning effects are most critical for buildings that are tall and slender, that is, those with a high height-to-width ratio (A and C are correct, B and D are incorrect). And top-heavy buildings have a greater tendency to overturn than pyramidal buildings (E is correct, F is incorrect).

6. **B.** Let's look at each statement in this question. A shear wall does resist lateral wind or earthquake forces by developing shear in its own plane (A), shear walls may be used with moment-resisting frames to form a dual system (C), and a shear wall is analogous to a vertical beam which cantilevers from its base (D). Answer B is incorrect and therefore the answer to this question; a shear wall

may be made of reinforced concrete or structural steel, but it may also be made of masonry or plywood.

7. **C.** Let's look at the four choices. A is the loading diagram for a uniform load. B is the shear diagram, as it starts at zero and increases at a uniform rate; that is, the diagram is a straight line. As the slope of the moment diagram is equal to the value of the shear diagram, the slope varies from zero at the free end to a maximum value at the fixed end as shown in correct choice C. In choice D, the slope varies from maximum at the free end to zero at the fixed end, which is the reverse of what it should be.

8. **Yield point.** The yield point of a material is correctly defined in the question. In contrast, the elastic limit is the maximum unit stress that can be developed in a material without causing permanent deformation. The ultimate strength is the maximum unit stress that can be developed in a material. The modulus of elasticity is the constant ratio of the unit stress in a material to the accompanying unit strain, when the material is stressed below the elastic limit.

9. **B.** Beams whose reactions can be determined from the equations of equilibrium only are statically determinate. These include simple beams, cantilever beams (I), and overhanging beams with two supports (III). Beams whose reactions cannot be found from the equations of equilibrium only, but require additional equations, are called statically indeterminate beams. Continuous (IV) and fixed end beams (II) are statically indeterminate.

10. **B.** The best definition of redundancy is that in choice B. Long span structures generally have little redundancy; if overload or failure occurs, there is often no way for the system to redistribute loads to other parts of the structure. Consequently, there is greater potential for sudden failure of the entire structure. For seismic design, redundancy is often provided by secondary systems that can resist part of the lateral force if the primary system fails or is damaged.

11. **C.** To solve this problem, you need to know the formula for the base shear $V = C_S W$ where $C_S = S_{DS} I/R$. S_{DS} is given as 1.0g. The importance factor I is equal to 1.0 since this is not a high-occupancy, essential, or hazardous facility, and $R = 6$, as given. Thus, $C_S = 1.0 \times 1.0/6 = 0.167$. Also, C_S need not exceed $S_{D1} I/TR$, where S_{D1} is given as 0.55g. T is the fundamental period of the building, and is equal to 0.4 seconds, as given. Thus, $C_S = (0.55 \times 1.0)/(0.4 \times 6) = 0.229$. Minimum $C_S = 0.01$. Therefore, $V = 0.167 \times 1,000,000 = 167,000$ lbs. $= 167$ kips.

12. **D.** Tall buildings have longer periods than short buildings, and therefore answers B and C can be ruled out. But the period does not vary directly with the height, but rather with the 0.8 power of the height for steel moment-resisting frames; therefore, even without using a calculator, you can see that choice A is incorrect, leaving D as the only possible answer. To calculate the answer, you compute the value of $(240)^{0.8} = 80.2$ and $(120)^{0.8} = 46.1$, since the period varies with the 0.8 power of the height. The ratio of 80.2 to 46.1 is 1.74; thus, the period of the 240-foot building is 74 percent greater than that of the 120-foot building. Incidentally, the seismic design

category is irrelevant, as is the actual value of the period.

13. **C.**   Nonstructural elements must be designed to resist seismic forces that are usually greater than those used for the design of the building (correct answer C). For example, if the seismic force on a building is 15 percent of the dead load of the building, the seismic force on a given nonstructural element might be 30 percent of the weight of that element.

14. **A.**   Openings in beams have the least effect on the beam's load-carrying capacity if they are located in areas of low stress. The two main types of stress in beams are shear stress and bending, or flexural, stress. The shear stress is usually greatest near the supports and least near midspan. Thus, an opening in an area of low shear stress would be near the center of the span (A, B, or C). For a simply supported beam, the bending stresses are greatest near the middle of the span and least near the supports. Within the beam depth, the bending stresses are greatest near the top (compression in the concrete) and bottom (tension in the reinforcing steel) and least at about the mid-depth of the beam. Therefore, an opening in an area of low bending stress would be near the supports (D) or at the mid-depth of the beam (A). The only location in an area of both low shear stress and low bending stress is A.

15. **A.**   Prestressing of concrete is done by either pretensioning or posttensioning. In pretensioning, high-strength steel is tensioned before the concrete is cast. After the concrete hardens, the prestress wires are cut and the prestress force is applied to the concrete through bond. Therefore, no end anchorages are required (B is correct). Most precast, prestressed members are pretensioned and, again, no end anchorages are required. A is therefore the untrue statement we are looking for. In posttensioning, the steel tendons are stressed after the concrete is cast on the site, by jacking against anchorages at the ends of the member (D is correct). Whether pretensioned or posttensioned, prestressing results in more efficient use of the material, making smaller sections possible (C is correct).

16. **C.**   The overturning moment is equal to the seismic load multiplied by the distance from that load to the base of the structure = (0.30×30) kips $\times$ (12 ft. + 12 ft. + 4 ft.) = 9 kips $\times$ 28 ft. = 252 ft.-kips.

17. **B.**   The allowable shear in a plywood diaphragm depends on the plywood grade and thickness, the nail size and spacing, and the width of framing members (A, C, and D). The direction of framing (B) generally does not affect the allowable shear in a plywood diaphragm.

18. **B.**   Reinforced concrete buildings are generally heavier than steel frame buildings (III), which results in greater seismic load (I), because the seismic load is proportional to a building's weight. However, the wind load is not affected by the type of construction (II is incorrect).

19. **A.**   The frame shown is an example of an eccentric braced frame, in which at least one end of each brace is eccentric to the beam-column joint or the opposing brace. The intent is to make the braced frame more ductile and therefore able to absorb a significant amount of energy without buckling the braces.

20. **B.**   The basic seismic formula is $V = C_s W$ where C_s is equal to $S_{DS}I/R$, not to exceed $S_{D1}I/TR$. Because the problem states that all other factors are the same, the only variable is R. The lateral force (V) resisted by the special moment-resisting frame is proportional to $\frac{1}{8}$, while the force resisted by the shear wall is proportional to $\frac{1}{5}$. Thus, the moment-resisting frame resists $\frac{5}{8}$ of that resisted by the shear wall, which is $\frac{3}{8}$ (or 37.5 percent) less. Even if you don't know the formula, you should understand that a special moment-resisting frame is much more ductile than a shear wall—it can absorb much more energy without failure. Therefore, the code allows such a frame to resist less seismic load than a shear wall.

21. **A, B, and C.**   Three types of stress that are important in building design are tension, compression, and shear (A, B, and C). Strain (D) is not a type of stress; it is the deformation, or change in size, of a body caused by external loads.

22. **D.**   Structural steel columns tend to fail by buckling. The slenderness ratio Kl/r is a measure of the buckling tendency of a steel column; the larger the value of Kl/r, the greater the tendency of the column to buckle, resulting in a lower column capacity. In this ratio, K is a constant determined by the end conditions of the column; that is, whether the column is free to translate (move laterally). The unbraced length of the column (A) is l, and the moment of inertia and area of the column (B) determine its radius of gyration r. The grade of steel (B) does not affect the value of K.

23. **D.**   All four methods will strengthen the beam; what we are looking for is the most effective method. How do we approach this problem? As no information is given about loads, span, or beam size, the only fact we know for sure is that we want to increase the beam's flexural strength. To accomplish this, we must increase its section modulus $S(= I/c)$. To increase the section modulus efficiently, we must provide as much material as possible the maximum distance away from the neutral axis. Of the four choices offered, D most effectively satisfies this concept.

24. **D.**   Remember the basic formula for unit stress $f = P/A$? Similarly, unit foundation pressure $f = P/A$, where P is the total load on the foundation and A is the area of the footing. Transposing, required footing area A = foundation load P ÷ allowable soil bearing pressure $f = (120,000\# + 150,000\#) \div 4,000\#/\text{ft.}^2 = 67.5$ sq. ft. Most column pads are square, as are the four choices in this question. To determine the required side dimension of the square pad, we calculate $\sqrt{67.5} = 8.22$ feet, and we therefore select answer D, $8'-3'' \times 8'-3''$.

25. **C.**   The pressure varies linearly from zero at the top to a value at the bottom equal to 30 pounds per cubic foot times the depth of 10 feet, or 300 pounds per foot, per lineal foot of wall, as shown below. The total lateral force is equal to the area of the pressure diagram = $10 \times 300/2 = 1,500\#$.

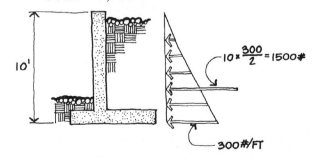

26. D. The resistance of a retaining wall to sliding is provided by friction between the footing and the underlying soil and by earth pressure in front of the toe. Where these are insufficient, additional sliding resistance may be obtained by constructing the footing with an integral key (A), or by making the footing wider (B) or deeper (C). Increasing the amount of reinforcing steel in the footing has no effect on sliding resistance. D is therefore the correct answer.

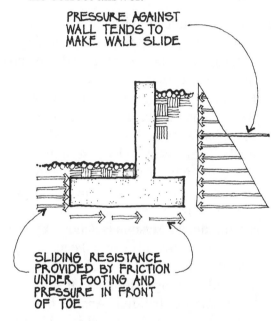

PRESSURE AGAINST WALL TENDS TO MAKE WALL SLIDE

SLIDING RESISTANCE PROVIDED BY FRICTION UNDER FOOTING AND PRESSURE IN FRONT OF TOE

27. D. For concentrated columns loads, the most common type of footing is a square pad centered under the column, which results in a uniform soil pressure acting upward on the footing. However, if the column is located close to a property line, the footing cannot be centered under the column, and the resulting eccentricity between the center of the column and the center of the footing would cause the soil pressure distribution to be nonuniform. This could result in undesirable footing settlement, or an uneconomically large footing. To avoid these problems, a combined footing, as shown in the sketch, is often used, in which the resultant of the column loads coincides with the centroid of the combined footing. D is correct.

28. B. If the upper soils were strong enough to support the building loads, then footings at a shallow depth could be used. However, because the upper soils consist of loose fill, we must penetrate through the fill to bear on the dense sand below. Choices III and IV are therefore likely to be appropriate foundation systems (correct answer B). What about choices I and II? Wouldn't they also be appropriate? Not very likely; removal and recompaction of fill is usually economical up to a depth of about six feet, not 15 feet. And footings extending through the fill into the dense sand might be economical up to several feet in depth, but not 15 feet as in this question.

29. A and C. Wood frame buildings generally perform well in an earthquake and do not pose a significant threat to life (A is correct). Wood cripple walls below the first floor should be braced, to prevent the structure from falling onto the foundation (C is correct). B is incorrect, because plywood is much stronger as a diaphragm than straight sheathing. D is also incorrect; wood stud walls should be adequately bolted to the foundation, to prevent the structure from sliding off the foundation.

30. B. The answer is *14.1 psf.* The wind pressure in psf varies as the square of the wind velocity in mph. In other words, the wind pressure in psf is equal to the square of the wind velocity in mph times a constant. At any site, $p = KV^2$, where p is the wind pressure, K is a constant, and V is the wind velocity.

At site 1, $p_1 = K(V_1)^2$

$12.6 = K(85)^2$

$K = 12.6 / (85)^2$

At site 2, $p_2 = K(V_2)^2 = (12.6 / 85^2) \times 90^2$
$= 14.1$ psf

31. **C.** An earthquake causes the ground to shake erratically, both vertically and horizontally (D is incorrect). The vertical motions are usually neglected in design since they are generally smaller than the horizontal (A is incorrect). Only in certain cases are seismic forces required to act simultaneously in the two horizontal directions parallel to the axes of the building, so B is incorrect. C is correct because seismic forces may or may not act simultaneously in the two horizontal directions.

32. **C.** A number of skyscrapers behave essentially as steel tubes that cantilever from the base when subject to wind loads. These include some of the tallest buildings in the world, such as the Sears Tower and the John Hancock Building. But of these, only the John Hancock Building is trussed by enormous exposed X-braces.

33. **C.** You may believe that this is such a simple, basic problem that there must be a trick to it. No, there is no trick; this is just a straightforward problem, like most exam problems. The unit stress in the bar is simply P/A, where P is the load of 50,000 pounds and A is the cross-sectional area of the two-inch-diameter bar = $\pi(2)^2/4 = 3.14$ square inches. So the unit stress is equal to 50,000 lbs. ÷ 3.14 square inches = 15,915 psi (answer C). The length of the bar is irrelevant.

34. **A.** A statically determinate beam is one whose reactions can be determined by using the basic equations of static equilibrium ($\Sigma H = 0, \Sigma V = 0, \Sigma M = 0$). Examples include simple beams and overhanging beams on two supports (IV). Beams whose reactions cannot be determined from the equations of equilibrium only, but require additional equations, are called statically indeterminate beams. These include beams fixed at both ends (I); beams fixed at one end and simply supported at the other end (II); and continuous beams (III). A is the correct answer.

35. **C.** In seismic base isolation, the structure is isolated from the ground by specially-designed bearings and dampers that absorb earthquake forces. Most of the building's displacement occurs at the isolators, which are located below the columns at the lowest level. This method effectively reduces seismic forces (correct answer C). Answer A is incorrect; separating adjacent buildings to prevent pounding is called seismic separation, not seismic isolation. Answer B is also incorrect because the total lateral displacement of a seismically isolated building is similar to that of a conventional building. Answer D is incorrect; a major earthquake causes a building to respond inelastically.

36. **D.** All of the statements are incorrect except D. Soft ground, not firm ground, tends to amplify earthquake motion (A). Steel structures are generally more flexible than concrete structures and therefore tend to sway more (B). If the period of ground motion waves coincides with the natural period of the building, large amplifications may result, that is, the building's acceleration will be much greater than the ground acceleration (C). Answer D is correct: by placing infill walls between columns, the columns effectively become

shorter and stiffer, thereby attracting much greater seismic forces.

37. **C.** The maximum moment of the girders in either plan equals $wL^2/8$, where w is the uniform load, which is the same for both plans, and L is the girder span. Thus, the maximum moment in the plan A girders $= wL^2/8 = 72w$, and the maximum moment in the plan B girders $= wL^2/8 = 288w$, or four times as great ($288/72 = 4$). As the required section modulus is equal to the maximum moment divided by the allowable flexural stress ($S = M/F_b$), the required section modulus of the plan B girders is four times as great as that of the plan A girders.

38. **A.** Questions involving shear and moment diagrams often appear on the exam. Among the concepts that should be understood are: (1) the slope of the moment diagram is equal to the value of the shear at that point and (2) the bending moment is maximum where the shear passes through zero. In this case, the slope of the moment diagram is constant and positive between points 1 and 2, and therefore the shear is constant and positive between 1 and 2. From 2 to 3, the slope of the moment diagram is also constant and positive, but less than the slope between 1 and 2. Therefore, the shear has a constant positive value between 2 and 3, which is less than that between 1 and 2. At point 3, the moment is maximum, and therefore the shear passes through zero at point 3. Between 3 and 4, the slope of the moment diagram is constant and negative, and therefore the shear is constant and negative between 3 and 4. The only shear diagram that meets all these criteria is shown in correct choice A.

39. **B.** If a deflection question should appear on the exam, it is likely that the necessary deflection formula will be provided. In this case, we are given the formula $\Delta = 5wL^4/384EI$. As $wL = W$, the total load on the beam, the formula becomes $\Delta = 5WL^3/384EI$.

Δ = 1.0 inch

W = 1,500#/ft. × 28 feet = 42,000#

L^3 = (28 feet × 12 in./ft.)^3

    = 37,933,056 in.^{3}

E = 29,000,000 psi

Thus

$$1.0 = \frac{5(42,000)(37,933,056)}{384(29,000,000)(I)}$$

$$I = \frac{5(42,000)(37,933,056)}{384(29,000,000)(1.0)}$$

$$= 715.3 \text{ in.}^4 \text{ (answer B)}$$

40. **B.** A soft story is defined as one in which the lateral stiffness is less than 70 percent of the stiffness of the story above, as in this case, where the moment-resisting frames in the first story are much more flexible than the shear walls above. This abrupt change of stiffness, called a stiffness irregularity, is undesirable in seismic design and should therefore be avoided if possible. Thus, the sketch illustrates soft story (I) and stiffness irregularity (IV). The other two terms, re-entrant corner (II) and torsional irregularity (III), are not illustrated in the sketch. Both are plan structural irregularities that should also be avoided if possible.

41. **B.** All elements of a building are vulnerable to earthquake damage; however, those that have historically been among the most vulnerable are

unreinforced masonry chimneys and parapets (B is correct).

42. **D.** Rigid frames are widely used in building construction, and candidates should therefore understand their basic behavior. The rigid beam-column joints restrain the ends of the beam, resulting in negative moment in the beam at the columns and reduced positive moment between the columns. There is moment in each column, which varies from zero at the hinged base to a maximum value at the beam. D is therefore correct. Choice A shows the moment diagram if the beam were simply supported and not part of a rigid frame, B is the moment diagram if a concentrated horizontal load acted on the frame, and C correctly shows the beam's moment diagram but omits the moment diagram for the columns.

43. **Ductility.** Ductility is especially desirable for systems that resist earthquake loads. Strength, in contrast, refers to the ability to resist load. Yielding is deformation that a material undergoes at a certain level of stress, with no increase of load. Stiffness means resistance to deformation.

44. **C.** In the detail shown, the joists are hung from the ledger by the joist hangers (not anchors), and the ledger, in turn, is supported from the wall by the bolts (A and D are incorrect). The diaphragm shear, which is parallel to the wall, is transferred from the diaphragm to the ledger by the boundary nails, and from the ledger to the wall by the bolts (B is incorrect). The anchors, which are embedded in the wall and usually spaced at 48 inches on center, anchor the wall to the joists, which in turn are connected to the diaphragm, for wind or seismic forces acting perpendicular to the wall (correct

answer C). If the wall were not properly anchored, it could separate from the framing and possibly collapse.

45. **B.** The ultimate tensile capacity of a reinforcing bar is the product of its area and yield strength ($T_u = A_s f_y$). Grade 40 reinforcing steel has a yield strength of 40 ksi, while grade 60 has a yield strength of 60 ksi. For 2-#6, using the table given in the problem,

$A_s = 0.44$ in.$^2 \times 2$ bars $= 0.88$ in.^{2}

$T_u = 0.88$ in.$^2 \times 40$ kips/in.$^2 = 35.2$ kips

For 1-#8,

$A_s = 0.79$ in.^{2}

$T_u = 0.79$ in.$^2 \times 60$ kips/in.$^2 = 47.4$ kips

Therefore B is correct. D is incorrect; although one must know the concrete strength to determine the capacity of a beam, the tensile capacity of the bars themselves is independent of the concrete strength.

46. **A.** A flat slab floor is a two-way reinforced concrete system in which the supporting beams are eliminated and the slab is supported directly on the columns. A flat plate floor is a special type of flat slab that does not have a thickened slab at the columns or an enlarged section at the tops of the columns. The floor slab of uniform thickness is thus supported directly by columns of uniform cross section. Statement IV is therefore incorrect. Flat plate floors are often economical where the spans are moderate and the loads relatively light (statement V is incorrect). Construction depth for each floor is minimum (correct statement I). Some problems inherent in the flat plate system include high shear stresses in the slab near the columns (correct statement

II), and high deflection of the relatively thin slab (incorrect statement III). To sum up, only statements I and II are correct (correct choice A).

47. **D.** Continuous beams (those that rest on more than two supports) offer certain advantages over simple beams. The maximum positive bending moment in a continuous beam is less (A), and the maximum deflection is also less (incorrect statement D). However, a continuous beam is subject to negative bending moment over its supports, while a simple beam never has negative moment (B). C is also correct: for equal spans and loads, the maximum positive bending moment is greater in the end spans of a continuous beam than in the center span.

48. **B.** This question tests your understanding of beam behavior. In a simple beam subject to downward vertical loads, the upper beam fibers (1) shorten and are in compression, while the lower beam fibers (3) lengthen and are in tension. The fibers at mid-depth of the beam (2) do not change in length. The correct answer is therefore B.

49. **A.** Although ground motions in an earthquake are both horizontal and vertical, seismic design usually accounts for the horizontal motions only, but not the vertical effects (A is correct). The acceleration of a building and that of the ground beneath are not usually the same, and thus B is incorrect. A special moment-resisting frame has the greatest ability to withstand earthquakes without failure, while a shear wall system usually does not perform as well in earthquakes (C is incorrect). The overturning moment is considered in earthquake design, and thus statement D is also false.

50. **A.** The natural or fundamental period of vibration of a building is the time it takes for it to go through one complete back-and-forth motion when subject to a lateral load. Buildings with long periods, such as building II, have relatively low accelerations and low seismic forces. Conversely, buildings with shorter periods, such as building I, have relatively high accelerations and high seismic forces (A is correct).

51. **B.** Torsion is the rotation caused in a rigid diaphragm when the center of mass does not coincide with the center of rigidity, as in this problem.

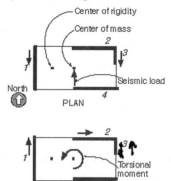

The seismic load acting to the north is resisted by forces in walls 1 and 3 acting to the south, as shown in the first plan. The seismic load causes a torsional moment that is counterclockwise, as shown in the second plan, resulting in forces in all the walls. For wall 1, the shear caused by torsional moment is in the opposite direction from that caused by the seismic load. However, for wall 3, the shear caused by torsional moment is in the same direction as that caused by the seismic load, resulting in increased shear in wall 3 (B is correct).

52. **B.** The natural or fundamental period of vibration of a building is the time it takes for it to go through one complete back-and-

forth motion when the subject to a lateral load. A number of different factors affect the period, but height (B) is the primary factor. Flexible buildings, such as tall steel frame buildings, have long natural periods and relatively low accelerations and seismic forces. Conversely, stiff buildings, such as low masonry buildings, have short natural periods and relatively high accelerations and seismic forces.

53. **D.**   The total horizontal seismic force V acting on a building is equal to the product of C_s and W, where W is the total dead load of the building. The quanity C_s is equal to $S_{DS}/(R/I)$, and it need not exceed $S_{D1}/T(R/I)$. S_{DS} and S_{D1} are the design accelerations, which depend on the location of the building site; I is the importance factor, accounting for the occupancy of the building; R is the response modification factor, related to the type of structural system employed; T is the fundamental period of vibration of the building, and is a function of building height. In general, C_s can depend on all of these quantities, so D is the correct answer.

54. **B.**   It is important for exam candidates to be familiar with shear and moment diagrams. Looking at the four choices in this question, A is the moment diagram for a simple beam with a concentrated load at the center; B is the moment diagram for a beam fixed at both ends with a concentrated load at the center, which is the case in this question; C is the shear diagram for a beam (simple or fixed at both ends) with a concentrated load at the center; and D is the moment diagram for a beam fixed at both ends with a uniformly distributed load.

55. **D.**   The shear stress in a column pad is essentially a function of the column load, the column size, and the thickness

of the pad. It is not at all related to the reinforcing steel (B and C), and only slightly affected by the pad size (A). Increasing the pad thickness (correct answer D) provides more area of concrete to resist the shear load, and hence decreases the shear stress.

56. **D.**   The code requires that both structural and nonstructural elements be designed for lateral seismic forces (I is incorrect). The lateral seismic force on a part or component is equal to

$$\frac{0.4a_p S_{DS} W_p}{\left(\dfrac{R_p}{I_p}\right)}\left(1+2\frac{z}{h}\right)$$

where S_{DS} is the same value used for the building; a_p is the component amplification factor that varies from 1.0 to 2.5; W_p is the weight of the part; R_p is the component response modification factor, varying from 1.0 to 3.5 for architectural components; I_p is the component importance factor, varying from 1.0 to 1.5; z is the height above ground where the component is attached to the structure; and, h is the average roof height of the structure with respect to the base. The seismic factor

$$\frac{0.4a_p S_{DS}}{\left(\dfrac{R_p}{I_p}\right)}\left(1+2\frac{z}{h}\right)$$

has a greater than value than the seismic factor used to determine the base shear. In other words, the seismic factor used in designing the bracing for the part is greater than that used for the building as a whole (II is incorrect, III is correct). IV is also correct; all seismic design is based on seismic forces coming from any horizontal direction. The correct statements (III and IV) are given in choice D.

57. **D.** Dynamic analysis is always acceptable for design. The static lateral force procedure is allowed only under certain conditions of regularity, occupancy, and height. Therefore, choice D is correct.

58. **B.** This problem tests candidates' understanding of continuous beams and may be approached nonmathematically as follows: beam AB deflects downward under load, and if there were no reaction at C, the beam would lift off of C as shown.

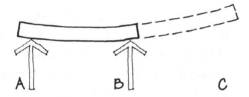

But because the beam is connected to C, the reaction at C pulls *downward* on the beam to prevent it from lifting off.

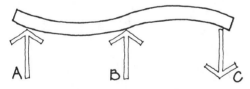

One can also solve this problem analytically. There is negative moment at support B (tension at the top, compression at the bottom), since B is an interior support of a continuous beam. We isolate span BC and take moments about B, assuming that the reaction at C is downward.

$$\sum M_B = 0$$

$$- M + R_C(L) = 0$$

$$R_C = +M/L$$

Because R_C comes out positive, our assumption that it acts downward is correct.

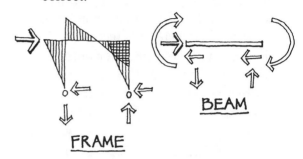

FRAME   BEAM

59. **C.** Questions of this type can be frustrating because the differences among the deflected shapes are subtle. As the column bases are hinged, they provide no restraint against rotation. A and C correctly show the column base condition. If the column bases were fixed, they would be restrained against rotation, as shown in B and D. The lateral load causes moment in the frame members as shown. The beam therefore distorts as shown in C and D. Only choice C correctly shows both the column and beam conditions.

60. **D.** A diaphragm is the horizontal floor or roof system that distributes lateral wind or earthquake forces to the vertical resisting elements. A flexible diaphragm, such as plywood, acts as a simple beam between the vertical resisting elements (III is correct), while a rigid diaphragm, such as concrete, distributes horizontal forces to the vertical resisting elements in proportion to their relative rigidities (IV is incorrect). I is not correct: plywood diaphragms are permitted in buildings with concrete or masonry shear walls. Finally, II is correct, since

torsional moments only occur with rigid diaphragms. In summary, II and III are the correct statements (answer D).

61. D. The overturning caused by the lateral loads is resisted by uplift in columns 1 and 2 and compression in columns 3 and 4 (correct answer D). Because the bases of the frame are hinged, no moments can be developed there (A is incorrect). There is shear in the columns, but it doesn't resist the overturning (B is incorrect), and there is no torsion in the columns (C is incorrect).

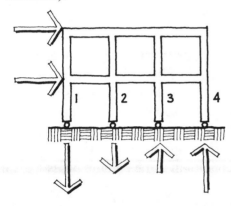

62. C. A three-hinged arch is statically determinate (I); that is, its reactions can be determined using only the equations of equilibrium. II is also correct. However, III is incorrect; the hinge at the center does not allow any moment to be developed. C is therefore the correct answer.

63. Inelastic. If no strain remains when the stress is removed, it is called elastic action. However, if some strain remains, the action is termed inelastic. Steel is elastic up to the elastic limit and inelastic at stresses above the elastic limit. Concrete and wood are nearly elastic at low stresses, but inelastic at higher stresses.

64. B. If a question like this were to appear on the exam, it is likely that the dimensions of the column would be found in tables reproduced from the AISC Manual, rather than in the question itself. In any event, one should know which information is relevant and which is not. In this case, the compressive stress is simply the load P divided by the area A. All the other information given is irrelevant. Therefore, the compressive stress = P/A = 200 kips/14.1 in.^{2} = 14.2 ksi.

65. C. In this problem, the diagonal braces can only resist tension. Therefore, when the wind load acts to the right, brace 1 will be in tension while brace 2 will have zero stress, since it cannot resist compression. When the wind reverses direction and acts to the left, brace two will be in tension. Let's draw a free body diagram of the upper right joint with the wind load acting to the right.

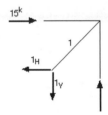

$\Sigma H = 0$

$+ 15$ kips $- 1_x = 0$

$1_x = 15$ kips

Brace 1 is at 45° (horizontal projection = vertical projection = 12 feet).

Therefore, $1_v = 1_x = 15$ kips

The tension in brace $1 = \sqrt{15^2 + 15^2}$ = 21.2 kips.

66. The overturning moment is equal to the sum of each wind load multiplied by its distance above the base = (20 kips × 15 ft.) + 10 kips × (15 + 15)ft. = 300 + 300 = 600 ft.-kips. The dead load resisting moment is equal to the sum of each dead load multiplied by its distance from the edge of the wall = (20 kips × 20 ft.) + (20 kips × 0) = 400 ft.-kips. Because the dead load resisting moment must be at least 1.67 times the overturning moment, the ends of the wall in this case would have to be tied down to a heavy foundation in order to increase the dead load resisting moment.

67. A. On the test, you can expect to see a number of problems involving beams of various types (simple, cantilever overhanging) supporting various loadings. You may be asked to determine the beam reactions, shears, or moments. The best preparation for this kind of problem is to practice solving a number of beams, such as this one. First, what is the resultant of the triangular load?

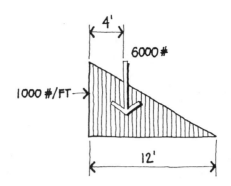

It is simply the area of the triangle, which is (1,000#/ft. ÷ 2) × 12 ft. = 6,000#, applied at the centroid of the triangle, which is 12 ft. ÷ 3 = 4 ft. from the left end.

$$\Sigma V = 0$$

$$+ V - 6,000\# - 5,000\# = 0$$

$$V = 11,000\#$$

$$\Sigma M = 0$$

$$(6,000\# \times 4 \text{ ft.}) + (5,000\# \times 12 \text{ ft.}) - M = 0$$

$$M = 24,000 + 60,000 = 84,000 \text{ ft.-lbs.}$$

Therefore, choice A is correct.

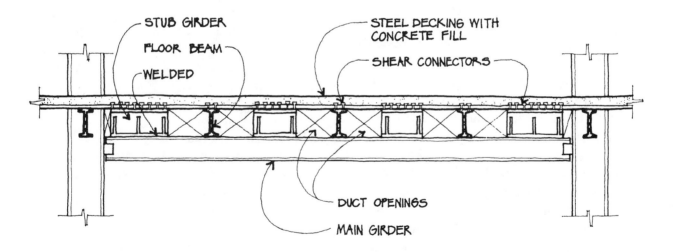

STUB GIRDER SYSTEM

68. A, B, and C. The load-carrying capacity of a wood column is determined by several factors: the modulus of elasticity E of the wood, which in turn depends on its species and grade; the design compressive stress F_c, which also depends on the species and grade of the wood; the ratio 1/d, where 1 is the unbraced height of the column and d is the least lateral dimension of the column; and the cross-sectional area of the column. Therefore A, B, and C are all correct. D is incorrect; the load-carrying capacity is not affected by the applied load. The applied load cannot exceed the load-carrying capacity.

69. C. A groove weld is placed between two butting plates or members and is usually stressed in direct compression or tension. A complete penetration groove weld is one whose depth is the same as the thickness of the member. The strength of a complete penetration groove weld is considered to be the same as that of the connected material (correct answer C).

70. D. The maximum size of coarse aggregate that may be used depends on the size of concrete members and the spacing of reinforcing bars. In general, the maximum size of coarse aggregate should not exceed 1/5 of the narrowest dimension between sides of forms (A) or 3/4 of the clear spacing between reinforcing bars (B). Usually, more water is required for smaller size coarse aggregates than for larger maximum sizes (C). For a given water-cement ratio, then, the amount of cement required increases as the maximum size of coarse aggregate decreases. Therefore, for economy, the maximum size of coarse aggregate should be as large as possible. D is the incorrect statement and therefore the answer to this question.

71. C. The stub girder system consists of main steel girders framed between columns, above which short lengths of stub girders are welded. They are typically about five feet long and spaced about five feet apart. Shear connectors are welded to the tops of the stub girders to provide composite action with the concrete slab. Transverse to the stub girders are floor beams of the same depth, with shear connectors welded to their top flanges. The concrete slab above the stub girders acts with the main girder to form a sort of Vierendeel truss, in which the main girder is the bottom chord, the slab is the top chord, and the stub girders are the verticals. Note that the concrete floor slab may be either a structural concrete slab or a composite steel deck with concrete fill. C is therefore correct.

72. C. This question tests your ability to use a table from the AISC Manual, which is on page 108, to select the most economical column section. We read down the left column to a length of 16 feet and then read across to the allowable axial load in kips for each column section. For the W10 × 49, we read 284 kips; for the W10 × 45, we read 204 kips; for the W10 × 39, we read 173 kips; and for the W10 × 33, we read 142 kips. We select the W10 × 45 (choice C), as it is the lightest W10 column with a capacity of at least 200 kips.

73. B. This problem may be solved either analytically or graphically. In the analytical solution, we first determine the truss reactions.

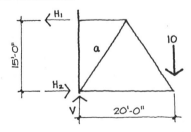

$\sum M = 0$

$10(20) - H_1(15) = 0$

$H_1 = \dfrac{10(20)}{15} = 13.33$ kips

$\sum H = 0 \quad H_2 - H_1 = 0$

$H_1 = H_2$

$H_2 = 13.33$ kips

$\sum V = 0$

$V - 10 = 0$

$V = 10.0$ kips

Next we isolate the truss joint at the lower reaction.

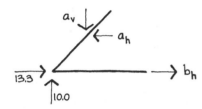

$\sum V = 0 \quad 10 - a_v = 0 \quad a_v = 10.0$ kips

Because the horizontal projection of member *a* is 10 feet and its vertical projection is 15 feet,

$a_h = \dfrac{10}{15} \times a_v = \dfrac{2}{3} \times 10.0 = 6.67$ kips

The total force in member *a* is

$$\sqrt{\left(a_v\right)^2 + \left(a_h\right)^2} = \sqrt{\left(10.0\right)^2 + \left(6.67\right)^2}$$

$= 12.02$ kips

Because the stress acts *toward* the joint, the stress is *compressive*. The correct answer is therefore B.

74. B. Standardized weld symbols are used to convey information about the required welding. The weld symbol approximates the shape of the weld; in this case $\nwarrow$ indicates a fillet weld. If a bevel weld (B) were specified, the symbol $\nwarrow$ would have been shown. The number to the left of the weld symbol indicates the size of the weld, in this case ¼ inch. The number to the right of the weld symbol indicates the length of the weld if one number is shown, or the length and spacing if two numbers are shown, in this case 2-inch long welds at 12 inches on center. The darkened flag indicates that the weld is to be made in the field, as opposed to the shop. Information on weld testing and electrodes is not usually shown on the weld symbol.

75. D. Formwork represents a large portion of the cost of any reinforced concrete building, and therefore the use of repetitive and reusable forms is one of the most important steps in achieving an economical concrete building. In addition, having a simple and repetitive reinforcing steel layout is also economical (D is correct). The amount of reinforcing steel is important, but not so much that the concrete sizes are increased disproportionately (A), as this adds to the weight of the building, increases footing sizes, and may have adverse seismic implications. In general, for low-rise buildings, vertical and lateral loads are economically resisted by bearing/shear walls, whereas in high-rise buildings, rigid frames are often more economical. Hence, B is not correct. While C correctly describes the advantages of waffle slab construction, this is not always the most economical system, and thus C is not the correct answer.

76. A. To solve for the left reaction, we take moments about the right reaction.

$\Sigma M = 0$

$-5{,}000\ (24 + 8)\ (16) - 12{,}000\ (24 - 8)$

$-5{,}000\ (32) + 24R_L = 0$

$$R_L =$$

$$\frac{5,000(32)(16)+12,000(16)+5,000(32)}{24}$$

25,333# (answer A)

77. D.   All of the terms in this question are associated with Roman architecture, except *stoa* (correct answer D). *Thermae* were Roman public bathing establishments, a *basilica* was a rectangular building used as a hall of justice and public meeting place, and an *amphitheater* was an oval arena surrounded by tiers of seats and used in Rome for gladiatorial contests and other events. A *stoa* was a colonnade used by the ancient Greeks to provide access to law courts, gymnasiums, and so forth.

78. A.   When a building resists seismic or wind load, it deflects horizontally, which is called drift. The amount of drift between adjacent stories is known as the story drift, or delta (Δ). If the vertical load in a column is P, then the bending moments in the story are increased by an amount equal to P times Δ, or P-delta. This effect must be taken into account unless it is very low relative to the primary story bending moments.

79. B, C, and D.   Although there are many exceptions, old buildings usually have simple configurations and regular, direct paths of load resistance (A and E are incorrect). However, their connections are often inadequate to resist lateral loads (C). Old masonry walls may be strong enough to support vertical loads, but weak in resisting lateral loads because they are unreinforced (B) and often have low mortar strength (D).

80. B.   In seismic design, redundancy should be provided by secondary, or

back-up, systems that can resist part of the lateral load if the primary system fails or is damaged (B is correct). Rigidity refers to resistance to deformation (A is incorrect). Elasticity is the property of a material that returns to its original shape after load is removed (C is incorrect). Ductility is the ability of a structural material or system to deform and absorb energy without failure or collapse (D is incorrect).

81. A.   This question illustrates several seismic design concepts: regularity, torsion, and redundancy. Plans C and D are structurally irregular; in C, the perimeter shear wall is much more rigid than the moment-resisting frame on the opposite wall, which would cause severe torsional effects. The core shear walls in D, particularly since they are not at the center of the building, would also result in torsion. That leaves A and B as possible choices. Answer B is a good arrangement, since it is structurally regular with moment-resisting frames at the perimeter. But A is even better, since it has redundancy; the multiple frames that provide lateral resistance are preferable to the perimeter resistance only of plan B.

82. B. The answer is *1661 ft.-lbs.* A parapet must be designed to resist a seismic force (F_p) perpendicular to its face equal to

$$\frac{0.4a_p S_{DS} W_p \left(1+2\frac{z}{h}\right)}{\left(\frac{R_p}{I_p}\right)}$$

where (from ASCE 7 Table 13.5-1) $a_p =$ 2.5 and $R_p = 2.5$ for a cantilevered parapet wall that is braced to the structural frame below its center of mass. Also, I_p is the importance factor and is equal to 1.0 since this is not a high occupancy, essential, or hazardous facility. Since the parapet is at the roof of the building, $z/h = 1.0$. The weight of the parapet (W_p) is given as 100 pounds per square foot. Thus, with $S_{DS} = 1.37g$, $F_p =$

$$\frac{0.4 \times 2.5 \times 1.37 \times 100}{\left(\dfrac{2.5}{1.0}\right)}(1+2) = 164$$

pounds per square foot. Maximum $F_p = 1.6 S_{DS} I_p W_p = 1.6 \times 1.37 \times 1.0 \times 100 = 219$ pounds per square foot, and minimum $F_p = 0.3 S_{DS} I_p W_p = 0.3 \times 1.37 \times 1.0 \times 100 = 41$ pounds per square foot. Therefore, the resultant parapet force is equal to 164 pounds per square foot times the hight of $4'6'' = 738\#$ per linear foot. This force acts at the mid-height of the parapet wall as shown. The moment is equal to $738 \times (4.5/2) = 1661$ ft.-lbs.

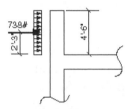

83. **D.** The floor framing system described in choice A (concrete fill, steel deck, composite beams, girders) is very widely used for a number of reasons, including economy, stiffness, simplicity, and ease of providing fire protection. The open web joist system (B) is also economical, but has less stiffness and is sometimes more difficult to fire protect than choice A. The concrete plank system described in C is often economical, quite stiff, and easily fire protected. The flat plate system (D), although economical in formwork, is not generally economical for spans longer than 25 feet.

84. **Tension.** The water in the tank exerts hydrostatic pressure against the tank wall, as shown in the horizontal section in the next column.

This pressure tends to increase the diameter of the tank, or to lengthen its circumference. Any force that tends to stretch a member is tension. Another approach is to isolate one half of a horizontal section through the tank, as shown below.

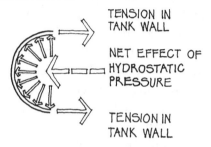

The net effect of the hydrostatic pressure is a horizontal force acting to the left. For equilibrium, the internal force in the tank wall must act to the right, *away* from the cut section. A force that acts away from a section is tension.

85. **C.** In this problem, all you need to know is that the wind pressure in psf varies as the square of the wind velocity in mph. If we call the wind pressure at 85 mph p, then the wind pressure at 120 mph = $(120^2/85^2) \times p = 1.99$ p, which represents an increase of $(1.99 - 1) \times 100 = 99$ percent (answer C).

86. **B.** Buildings respond to wind forces in various ways. The most obvious is the inward pressure on windward walls (A). The wind also creates an outward (upward) pressure on flat roofs (C). Windward roofs may be subject to inward or outward pressure, depending on the slope (D). Answer B is incorrect, and is therefore the correct answer to this

question, because the wind pressure on leeward roofs is outward, not inward.

87. **A.**   The wind pressures depicted in I are obtained from ASCE 7 Method II, the Analytical Procedure. The windward wall is subjected to pressure toward the surface, while the leeward wall and roof are subjected to pressure away from the surface (suction). Note that the windward portion of the roof is subjected to pressure toward the surface when the angle of the roof is larger. The wind pressures depicted in II are obtained from Method I, Simplified Procedure. Wind pressures in the horizontal direction are projected on a vertical plane. These pressures are the sum of the windward and leeward pressures on the building and are shown acting towards the surface on one side. Note that the horizontal pressure on the roof may also act away from the roof surface. Wind pressures on the roof are projected on a horiztonal plane and are shown to act away from the surface. The pressures on the windward roof may also act in the other direction. III is incorrect because the horizontal pressure on the roof is too large and the direction of the vertical pressure on the leeward roof is incorrect. Because I and II correctly represent the wind pressures, A is the correct answer.

88. **D.**   An arch is a long-span structure whose internal stresses are essentially compressive. A three-hinged arch has hinges at each support and at the top, or crown. The horizontal thrust at each support is directly proportional to the load (I) and the span (II), and inversely proportional to the rise (III is incorrect). A three-hinged arch rotates when the temperature changes, rather than undergoing any change in the horizontal

thrust (IV is incorrect). The correct answer is therefore D.

89. **C.**   The behavior of long-span structures is not exactly the same as that of conventional structures. Secondary effects may become critical, and consequently safety factors may need to be increased (A). Because the levels of quality control of site and factory assembly are not the same, the architect should consider using different factors of safety (B). The effects of temperature are more pronounced in long-span structures because of the greater length of members (D). However, C is incorrect, and therefore the answer to this question. Building codes establish minimum criteria for design, but the architect may choose to use higher factors of safety for a particular structure.

90. **Tensile.**   A membrane is a thin, flexible sheet that can only resist tension. Examples include circus tents, umbrellas, and trampolines. Some permanent structures, too, have spanned great distances with the use of membranes, most notably the Haj Terminal in Saudi Arabia.

91. **B.**   Lateral wind forces are unrelated to a building's dead load (II is incorrect, IV is correct). However, lateral earthquake forces are directly proportional to the dead load: the greater the dead load, the greater the seismic force (I is correct, III is incorrect).

92. **A.**   The lateral load resisted by each column is in proportion to its stiffness, or resistance to deformation. The stiffness of a column is inversely proportional to the cube of its length; in other words, long columns are flexible and attract less lateral load, while short columns are stiff

and attract more lateral load. Answer A is therefore correct. A number of freeway bridge failures caused by earthquakes are believed to be the direct result of this type of action: short, stiff columns attracted large seismic loads, but were not strong enough to resist those loads and consequently failed.

93. **A.** Because the load decreases uniformly, the slope of the shear diagram also decreases, and the shear at the left support is greater than at the right support. These conditions are correctly shown in diagram A.

94. **C.** This question tests your knowledge concerning one of the great structures of the Renaissance. All of the statements are correct, except C. The dome contains a number of circular compression rings, which made it stable during construction without the use of any temporary shoring, an incredible achievement for its time.

95. **D.** The Pantheon, built in the year 123, remains to this day one of the greatest achievements of Roman architecture. Its immense concrete dome is so thick at its bottom that tensile hoop stresses are resisted by the concrete, without any need for iron reinforcing. The opening at the crown of the dome was designed and built to act as a compression hoop.

96. **D.** All of the men in this question, with the exception of Maillart, were important figures in the development of the skyscraper. Otis (I) invented the first safe elevator, which made tall buildings practical. Khan (II) was a brilliant structural engineer responsible for the design of two of the most important skyscrapers of modern times: the John Hancock Building and the Sears Tower, both in Chicago. Jenney (III) designed

the first skyscraper, the Home Insurance Co. Building of 1883. Maillart (IV), a Swiss engineer, was noted for his arched concrete bridges.

97. **B.** The roof of the Dulles Airport terminal is supported by a series of steel cables suspended between huge concrete piers. The concept of leaning these piers outward may have been inspired by aesthetic considerations, or to express the idea of flight (A), but the main purpose was to counteract the inward pull of the cables (B).

98. **A.** When the outside temperature goes up, the dome naturally tends to expand. As its supports are generally unyielding, the only way the dome can become longer is to move up (correct answer A).

99. **B.** The total wind load on the sign is 13 psf × (10 ft. × 20 ft.) = 2,600#. Each column resists one-half of the total wind load = 2,600 ÷ 2 = 1,300#, which effectively acts at the midheight of the sign, as shown. Since the braces can only resist tension, the right brace is ineffective when the wind acts to the right. We take moments about the column base. (See figure on next page.)

$\Sigma M = 0$

$+ 1,300\# (10 \text{ ft.} + 5 \text{ ft.}) - H (10 \text{ ft.}) = 0$

$H = 1,300 (15/10) = 1,950\#$

Because the brace is at 45°, V = H = 1,950#, and the force in the brace = $\sqrt{1,950^2 + 1,950^2} = 2,758\#$ tension (answer B).

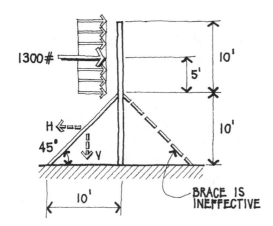

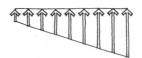

100. **B, C, and D.**   A diaphragm is a horizontal system that transmits lateral wind or earthquake forces to the vertical resisting elements, which may be shear walls, braced frames, or moment-resisting frames (D is correct). These vertical resisting elements, not the diaphragm, transfer the lateral loads to the foundation (A is incorrect). A diaphragm is analogous to a horizontal beam, which resists shear in its own plane and tension and compression in chords at the diaphragm edges (B is correct). A rigid diaphragm can transfer forces by torsion, while a flexible diaphragm cannot (C is correct).

101. **C.**   The vertical load on the wall results in uniform soil pressure under the footing:

The overturning results in varying soil pressure:

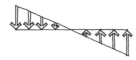

Therefore, the soil pressure from combined vertical load and overturning is as shown in the next column (C is correct):

Answer A is incorrect because the lateral load acting to the right causes the soil pressure to increase under the right end and decrease under the left end. If the lateral load acted to the left, then A would be correct. Answers B and D cannot be correct because they show the soil pressure acting downward at the left, which would mean that the soil is in tension, which is not possible.

102. **C.**   SOM's Hancock Building and Sears Tower are tubular buildings, in which the perimeter walls form an immense hollow tube that cantilevers out of the ground under the action of wind loads. The Sears Tower is actually a bundle of nine such tubes, which terminate at varying heights. Both buildings, among the tallest in the world, are framed in structural steel. As I and II are both correct, C is the correct answer.

103. **B.**   The correct definition of live load is given in answer B. There is no relationship between dead and live load (A); live load may not be neglected unless specifically permitted by the building code (C); and although long-span structures are often more vulnerable to failure than conventional structures, there is no requirement that they be designed for a greater live load (D).

104. **C.**   Certain types of structures obtain their strength by their shape. Such form-resistant structures include membranes, which resist loads by tension, and thin shells, which develop compression, shear, and tension.

105. C.   The overturning moment is equal to the seismic load multiplied by the distance from that load to the base of the structure = 15 kips × (12 ft. + 12 ft. + 5 ft.) = 435 ft.-kips.

106. A, B, C, and D.   The nature of long-span construction requires a comprehensive quality control program, including proper field inspection and testing (A). Snow drifts, partial snow loads, and the effects of wind and earthquake demand special attention in long-span structures (B). The effects of temperature, creep, and shrinkage are more pronounced in long-span structures (C). And long-span structures are sensitive to secondary stresses caused by deflection and the interaction of building elements (D).

107. A.   The moment over the interior supports of a continuous beam is always negative when the beam supports downward loads (B is correct). We isolate span 1-2.

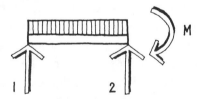

The moment at 1 is zero, the moment at 2 is negative (tension at the top, compression at the bottom), and the moment diagram is parabolic because the load is uniform. The moment diagram for span 1-2 is therefore as shown.

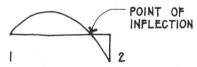

There is positive moment from 1 to the point of inflection and negative moment from there to 2. A is therefore the incorrect statement we are looking for. We

now isolate span 2-3 and take moments about 2, assuming that the reaction at 3 is downward.

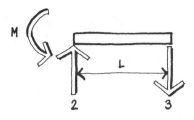

$$\sum M_2 = 0$$

$$- M + (R_3 \times L) = 0$$

$$R_3 = +M/L$$

Because R_3 comes out positive, our assumption that it acts downward is correct (C is correct). The moment in span 2-3 is always negative and varies from zero at 3 to M at 2 (D is correct).

108. B.   One of the most fundamental concepts in structures is that of equilibrium. For an object to be in equilibrium, it must have no unbalanced force acting on it (A and D are correct). It must also have no unbalanced moment acting on it (C is correct). B is incorrect and is therefore the answer to this question, because if there is a resultant force on an object, it will not be in equilibrium.

109. A, B, and D.   Long-span structures are used for a variety of reasons and a variety of buildings. For maximum flexibility, columns in exhibition halls (A) should be spaced as far apart as possible. Basketball pavilions (B), auditoriums (D), and other places of public entertainment and assembly require large column-free areas for optimum visibility and flexibility. The other building types (library, university science building, and municipal administration building) generally do not require large column-free flexible spaces, and therefore are not likely candidates for long-span construction.

110. **A.**   A hyperbolic paraboloid is a saddle-shaped surface formed by moving a parabola with downward curvature along a perpendicular parabola that is curved upward. Although its surface is doubly curved, it can be formed using a series of straight timber planks.

111. **B.**   Where two vaults perpendicular to each other intersect in Gothic cathedrals, the resulting form is called a groined vault. The diagonal lines of intersection, called groins, transmit the load to piers at the four corners.

112. **C.**   All suspension structures have a cable as their essential structural element. Cables can resist only tension, and are always curved upward.

113. **D.**   This question tests familiarity with the provisions of the International Building Code relating to wind and earthquake forces. Statement I, modifying the seismic overturning moment, is false. Earlier editions of the IBC did have a factor that effectively reduced the calculated seismic overturning moment. In recent earthquakes, however, overturning moments have sometimes been greater than expected, and as a result, this factor was eliminated. Statement II is true. Statement III is not true. Statement IV is also false. Except for single-story and two-story buildings, the distribution of the lateral force V in the height of the structure is essentially parabolic, varying from zero at the bottom to a maximum value at the top. Finally, statement V is also untrue. While symmetrical buildings have generally performed well in earthquakes, the IBC requires that all buildings provide for horizontal torsional moments, even when there is no

eccentricity between the center of mass and the center of rigidity. Only statement II is true, and the correct answer is therefore D.

114. **A, C, and D.**   The total lateral earthquake force on a structure is equal to $C_S W$. In this formula, W is the total dead load and C_S is the seismic response coefficient, which is equal to $S_{DS}/(R/I)$. Also, C_S need not exceed $S_{D1}/T(R/I)$. S_{DS} and S_{D1} are the short-period and one-second design accelerations that account for the seismic risk for the area and the soil characteristics at the site. I is the importance factor and is related to the occupancy of the building, and T is the building's fundamental period of vibration. R is the response modification factor determined by the type of lateral load resisting system used. The building's live load (B) does not affect the lateral earthquake force, making it the correct answer.

115. **Base plate.**   The principal purpose of a base plate under a steel column is to spread the column load over a relatively large area of the concrete foundation, so that the bearing pressure on the concrete is not excessive. The thickness of the base plate is determined by assuming the bearing pressure to be uniform and considering the portions of the plate outside of the column to cantilever from the column edges.

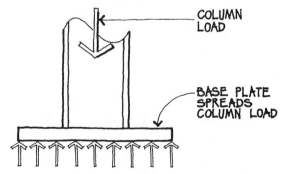

116. A.   A Vierendeel truss has no diagonals. Therefore, large openings, such as doors and windows, may be made within the depth of a Vierendeel truss without conflicting with diagonal members (III is incorrect). A conventional triangulated truss tends to have less deflection and use less material than a comparable Vierendeel truss (I and II are correct). Both conventional and Vierendeel trusses can have loads applied between panel points (IV is incorrect), although this results in bending stress in the chord member. A is therefore the correct answer.

117. D.   To transfer the flexural tensile and compressive forces in the beam flanges to the columns of a rigid frame, the flanges may be attached directly with full penetration groove welds (II) or with cover plates welded to the columns and bolted (III) or welded to the beam flanges. Two clip angles bolted to the beam web may be adequate to transfer shear, but are not adequate to transfer moment (I is incorrect). Likewise, a seat angle may transfer shear, but is inadequate to transfer moment (IV is incorrect). Therefore, the correct choices are II and III (answer D).

118. C.   Determining the design compressive strength of a wood column is very complicated. Fortunately, the design stress in compression parallel to the grain has been determined for us. The required column area is determined by dividing the axial load by the design value: 40,000#/732 psi = 54.6 square inches.

119. Joist anchor.   Walls must be anchored to all floors and roofs that provide lateral support for the wall. The anchorage for masonry or concrete walls must resist a force equal to either the design wind or the seismic forces perpendicular to the wall, whichever is greater. The minimum seismic force is the greater of the following: $0.4_{DS}I$ times the weight of the wall; 10 percent of the weight of the wall; $400S_{DS}I$ pounds per linear foot of wall; or 280 pounds per linear foot of wall. The joist anchors in the detail serve this function.

120. C.   In the moment-resisting frame in this question, each column resists one-half of the lateral load, since the columns are identical, or 60 kips × 1/2 = 30 kips. The moment at the beam-column intersection is equal to 30 kips multiplied by the column height of 15 feet, or 450 ft.-kips (C).

121. A.   An air-supported roof is a membrane pretensioned by internal air pressure, enabling it to resist downward loads without wrinkling or buckling. In this case, the uplift from the wind increases the tension in the membrane. The pull of the tensed membrane on the concrete foundation ring is tangent to the surface of the membrane; its components therefore act upward and inward. The upward component is resisted by the weight of the concrete ring, while the inward component tends to shorten the concrete ring, thus stressing it in compression (correct answer A).

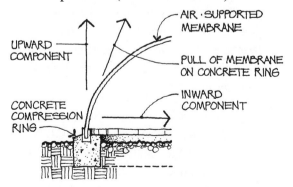

122. **B.** Candidates should be conversant with some of the terminology of long-span structural systems. The groined vault (A) is a structure devised by the ancient Romans in which two barrel vaults intersect at right angles. The Schwedler dome (C) is a type of steel-framed dome, comprising meridional ribs and circular hoops. The hyperbolic paraboloid (D) is a type of thin shell structure whose surface shape is determined by moving a parabola with downward curvature along a perpendicular parabola that is curved upward. The correct answer is lamella (B).

123. **D.** A shell, or thin shell, structure has a curved surface and supports load by tension, compression, and shear in its own plane (II is correct, IV is incorrect). However, it is too thin to resist bending stresses (III is correct), which makes it unable to support any substantial concentrated loads (I is incorrect). The correct statements are II and III (answer D).

124. **A.** An arch (A) is primarily a compression structure, although it may also be subject to some bending stress. The horizontal members of a rectangular rigid frame (B) are stressed principally in bending, plus some axial compression, while the vertical members are stressed primarily in compression, with some bending. When supporting vertical loads, all the members of a gabled frame (C) are subject to combined bending and compression. Finally, a cable (D) is able to resist only tension. A is therefore the correct answer.

125. **C.** A space frame is essentially a series of trusses of equal depth that intersect each other in a consistent grid pattern and are connected at their points of intersection. Loads are supported by the trusses in both directions, and the entire system works as a unit. Sometimes, the top and bottom chords in both directions are offset by half a module, creating inclined, rather than vertical, trusses.

126. **B.** Solving this kind of problem is very easy if you know how to use the tables. The total load supported by each joist is equal to $(20 + 20)6 = 240$ pounds per linear foot. The live load per joist is equal to $20 \times 6 = 120$ pounds per linear foot. We enter the table with a span of 60 feet, and read the figures "266" and "153" corresponding to the joist designation 36LH07. This means that the joist can safely support a total load of 266 pounds per linear foot, and that a live load of 153 pounds per linear foot will produce a deflection of 1/360 of the span. Since the actual total load is 240 pounds per linear foot, which is less than 266, and the actual live load is 120 pounds per linear foot, which is less than 153, the 36LH07 joist is satisfactory (correct answer B). While the 36LH08 and 09 can also support the load, they are both heavier than the 36LH07. The 32LH06 may not be used, since it can only support 234 pounds per foot (less than the actual load of 240). Also, a live load of 119 pounds per foot will produce a deflection of 1/360 of the span (less than the actual live load of 120).

127. **D.** Trusses may be solved by a number of different methods. In the method of sections, which works very well in this case, the truss is cut by an imaginary section. A free body diagram is drawn of the portion of the truss isolated by cutting the section. Moments are taken about the intersection of two of the cut members to determine the force in the third member.

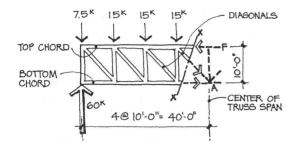

For a parallel chord truss, as in this problem, the internal force in the chord members is maximum at the center of the truss span. We therefore cut an imaginary section x-x as shown in the illustration and take moments about point A, where the bottom chord and diagonal intersect.

$\Sigma M = 0$
$60(40) - 7.5(40) - 15(30) - 15(20)$
$-15(10) - F(10) = 0$

$F = (2,400 - 300 - 450 - 300 - 150)/10$
$\quad = 1,200/10 = 120$ kips (correct answer D)

128. B. Concrete domes are stressed principally in compression. As they are generally very thin, they are not able to resist much bending moment. A and C are therefore incorrect. The forming of a concrete dome is expensive, and therefore D is also incorrect. B is the only correct answer.

129. C. A joist girder is a steel truss used to support equally spaced steel joists, which deliver concentrated loads to the top chord panel points. The load at each panel point is equal to the unit load (40 psf) multiplied by the joist spacing (6 feet) multiplied by the joist span (60 feet). Panel point load = 40 × 6 × 60 = 14,400# = 14.4 kips (C).

130. B. The closely spaced columns of layouts A and B considerably reduce the bending moment in both directions. The cantilevers on all four sides in layout B also reduce the moments at the center of

the spans, making it the most economical arrangement.

131. D. The slenderness ratio of a steel column is the effective length of the column KL divided by its least radius of gyration r. The effective length KL is the actual unbraced length L multiplied by the factor K, which depends on the support conditions at the ends of the column.

132. D. Although wind codes vary, the design wind pressure generally depends on the wind speed (I) and the exposure of the building, which is partially based on the terrain (II). Certain essential, hazardous, or assembly buildings are designed for increased wind pressures (III). And the wind pressures also depend on the part of the building under consideration (IV). Thus, all four factors listed affect the wind design (correct answer D).

133. C. Wind pressures increase with height (A and B are incorrect). This increase is incremental, as shown in correct answer C, not linear as in incorrect answer D.

134. B. The allowable shear in a fillet weld is based on the throat dimension, as shown.

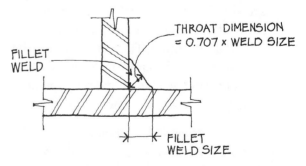

Thus, for a 1/4 inch fillet weld, the allowable shear per inch of weld = 0.25″ × 0.707 × 21.0 ksi = 3.71 kips per inch. The total length of weld required is 80 kips ÷

3.71 kips per inch = 21.6 inches. Half of this is required on each side of the beam web, or 21.6 ÷ 2 = 10.8 inches, which we round up to 11 inches.

135. **B.**   Statement A is incorrect because reinforced concrete columns must be designed for a minimum amount of eccentricity, which is equivalent to bending moment, even if the load theoretically is axial. C is also incorrect; the strength reduction factor ϕ is equal to 0.70 for spiral columns and 0.65 for tied columns, because of the greater toughness of spiral columns. Spiral columns are usually more expensive than tied columns because the spiral reinforcement costs more to fabricate (incorrect answer D). Only B is correct; a spiral column has about 14 percent more axial load capacity than a tied column with the same cross-sectional area and vertical reinforcement.

136. **D.**   All three statements are correct. Wind is an actual surface-applied force that depends only on the size, shape, and location of the building. The dead load and the type of lateral load resisting system do not affect the wind force. On the other hand, seismic forces are not real externally-applied forces, but are simulated forces that produce the same effect on a structure as the actual earthquake motion. The magnitude of the seismic forces depends on several factors, including the dead load and the type of lateral load resisting system.

137. **A.**   The strength design load combinations that must be considered with seismic loads in building design include dead load, floor live load (B and C), and snow load (D). Roof live load (A), however, is never combined with seismic loads when strength design load combinations are used. Answer A is therefore the correct answer.

138. **A.**   The Eiffel Tower, possibly the most recognizable structure in the world, was not the first great structure to be built of steel, but rather the last great structure to be built of iron (I is incorrect). III is also incorrect: several towers are taller, including the CN Tower in Toronto, the world's tallest. IV is a correct statement; the purpose of this magnificent iron structure was to attract visitors to the International Exposition of 1889, which celebrated the centennial of the French Revolution, after which it was to be dismantled. Happily, that never occurred. II is also correct: the narrowness of the tower near its top, combined with the openness of its structure, minimizes the wind forces and wind overturning moments that the tower must resist. Furthermore, the widening at the base reduces the forces on the legs caused by wind overturning. Because II and IV are correct statements, A is the answer.

139. **D.**   A diaphragm is a horizontal floor or roof system that transfers lateral wind or earthquake forces to the vertical resisting elements, which may be shear walls, braced frames, or moment-resisting frames (III is correct). A diaphragm is analogous to a horizontal girder, which resists shear in its own plane (analogous to the girder web) and tension and compression in chords at the diaphragm edges (analogous to the girder flanges). Thus, I and II are correct. Because I, II, and III are all correct, D is the answer to this question.

140. **A and B.**   The traditional method for structural steel design is Allowable Stress Design (ASD). In this method, the actual dead, live, and other loads are unfactored,

that is, not increased. The factor of safety varies depending on the type of stress to which the structural member is subjected. For example, for flexural stresses, the factor of safety Ω is equal to 1.67. Statements C and D therefore apply to Allowable Stress Design. Load and Resistance Factor Design, sometimes called limit states design, is a different and newer method of designing steel structures. In this method, which is similar to the strength design method for reinforced concrete design, the various loads (dead, live, etc.) are multiplied by their respective load factors (statement A). For example, the load factor for dead load only is 1.4, while the load factors for a member supporting dead, live, and roof live load are, respectively, 1.2, 1.6, and 0.5. The nominal strength, which is most often the yield strength, is multiplied by a resistance factor ϕ, which is generally less than 1 (statement B). For example, ϕ for flexure and compression is equal to 0.90. The primary objective of LRFD is to provide more uniform reliability for all steel structures under various loading conditions. As of this writing, the exam is likely to have only a few questions involving LRFD. However, as this method gains more widespread acceptance, we can expect the exam to include a greater number of questions on the subject.

141. **B.**   Wide flange sections are commonly used for beams, girders, and columns. They are efficient bending members because most of their material is in the flanges, at the greatest possible distance from the neutral axis. Looking at the other answers, wide flange beams have relatively thin webs (A is incorrect), their strength is much greater about the horizontal axis than the vertical axis (D is incorrect), and although they are symmetrical about both axes, that is unrelated to their efficiency as bending members (C is incorrect).

142. **C.**   The footing shown is called a cantilever footing or strap footing. It consists of an exterior column footing joined by a concrete beam to an interior column footing and is used where the exterior column is too close to the property line to have a symmetrical, concentric footing. A combined footing (B) is similar, except that it is one footing supporting both columns, not two separate, connected footings. A mat foundation (A) is essentially one large footing under the entire building area, and a pile cap (D) is a reinforced concrete element used to transmit a column load to a group of piles.

143. **A.**   Both wind and earthquake forces depend on the geographic location of the site. (I is correct.) Statements II and IV are also correct. Statement III, however, is incorrect; no increase in allowable stresses of any magnitude are permitted for either wind or earthquake forces. Answer A is therefore correct.

144. **A.**   As a rule, if the structural system resisting the vertical building loads is also designed to resist the lateral wind or earthquake forces, the additional cost to provide lateral resistance will be minimized. (A is correct, B is incorrect.) Visual expression of the lateral force resisting system is usually based on aesthetics, rather than economy. (C is generally incorrect.) The use of a base isolation system (D) does not necessarily result in the least additional cost, because in some cases the cost of such a system exceeds that of a conventional lateral force resisting system.

145. A.   The diaphragm is analogous to a horizontal girder, whose reaction at the east and west walls is $F/2 = wL/2 = 360\#/$ft. $\times$ 180 ft./2 = 32,400#. The diaphragm shear is the shear in the beam web = 32,400#/60 ft. = 540#/ft. (answer A).

146. C.   A cable only resists tension, and tends to pull away from its supports. The radial cables pulling away from the inner ring tend to open it up or stretch it, resulting in tension in the ring. Similarly, the cables tend to close or compress the outer ring. C is therefore the correct answer.

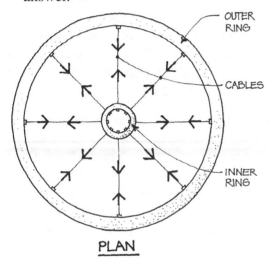

OUTER RING

CABLES

INNER RING

PLAN

147. C.   The truss without diagonals in this question is known as a Vierendeel truss, although it is actually a type of rigid frame. If its joints are rigid and capable of resisting moment, it is a stable structure (B and D are incorrect). As there are no diagonals, the chord members must resist shear, which produces bending moments in the chords. These moments are greatest where the maximum vertical shear occurs, near the supports (correct statement C). Vierendeel trusses tend to be uneconomical in the use of material, and also have high deflection (A is incorrect).

148. A.   The diagonal braces can only resist tension. Therefore, when the wind load acts to the left, brace 1 will be in tension and brace 2 will have zero stress, because it cannot resist compression. A free body diagram of the upper left joint looks like this:

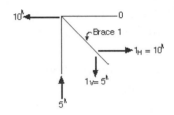

$\Sigma H = 0$

$-10 + 1 = 0$

$1_x = 10$ kips

The horizontal projection of brace 1 is 20 feet and the vertical projection is 10 feet, therefore

$1_x / 1_v = 20 / 10 = 2$

$1_v = 1_x / 2 = 10 / 2 = 5$ kips

$\Sigma V = 0$

$-1_v + $ Force in col. $= 0$

Force in col. $= 1_v = 5$ kips (compression)

149. A.   Buildings may be critical for overturning caused by wind or seismic forces if the overturning moment is high or the resisting moment is low, or both. The large height-to-width ratio in choice I results in both high overturning moment and low resisting moment. In choice B, the orientation of the building has no effect on overturning. The heavy equipment on the upper floors in choice C would result in high seismic forces and overturning moments, but has no effect on overturning from wind.

150. **B.** Wind forces cause a building's lateral force resisting system to deflect laterally or drift (I). The amount of drift must be limited to avoid damage to the nonstructural parts of the building or discomfort to the occupants of the building. Wind forces also cause overturning moment about the base of a building (IV), which must be resisted by the weight of the building. Liquefaction (II) and tsunamis (III) are both earthquake phenomena unrelated to wind.

151. **D.** When a flat roof deflects under load, a concave surface results. Rainwater can collect in such areas, increasing the deflection, which further increases the amount of ponded water, and so on. During intense rainstorms, therefore, ponding of flat roofs can result in problems, including even collapse. Because of their long span and relative flexibility, long-span joists are particularly vulnerable to this kind of trouble (A is incorrect). Therefore, the joists should be cambered or pitched sufficiently so that rainwater cannot build up (D is correct). Pitching the top chords of joists is one way to achieve slope, but is usually more expensive than using parallel chord joists that are sloped, or building in camber (B is incorrect). C is also incorrect: designing joists for a uniform amount of water is not required if the roof has sufficient slope, and may not be adequate if the roof is flat.

152. **C.** Choice I, conventional cast-in-place reinforced concrete, is not practical for a 62-foot span. Choice II, glued laminated beams, is not usually used for parking structures because of the required fire rating. Likewise, choice V would be unlikely because exposed steel girders have no fire rating. That leaves III and IV as possible choices, both of which are likely to be practical and economical. C is therefore the correct answer.

153. **C.** While there are exceptions, when one dimension of a typical bay is much greater than the other, the system generally requiring the least amount of material in the floor framing has short beams and long girders (scheme 2). However, the disadvantage of this system is the greater overall depth of construction required. Conversely, long beams and short girders (scheme 1) usually require more material, but result in less depth of construction. Answer C is correct.

154. **Peer review.** Because long-span structures are more vulnerable to failure than conventional structures, their designs are sometimes checked by independent third party architects or engineers—so-called peer review. This additional design check does not eliminate the need for checking by the design team or the building department, nor does it relieve the design team of responsibility. It does, however, provide an additional safeguard against design deficiencies.

155. **D.** In the detail shown, the vertical load is transferred from the joists to the ledger by the joist hangers, and from the ledger to the wall by the anchor bolts. If all the sizes are adequate, the detail is acceptable for transferring vertical load. The wall is required to be anchored to the diaphragm sufficiently well to transfer a force equal to $0.4S_{DS}I$ times the weight of the wall, 10 percent of the weight of the wall, 400 $S_{DS}I$ pounds per linear foot of wall, or 280 pounds per linear foot of wall, whichever is greater. The anchorage must be positive and direct, such as by means of metal straps. In the detail shown, there is no

direct, positive anchorage; instead, the lateral forces perpendicular to the wall would cause cross-grain bending and possible failure of the ledger. The detail is therefore unacceptable for anchoring the wall, making D the correct answer.

156. **C.**   Knowing that parapets are particularly vulnerable to earthquake damage, you might guess that a seismic force of 20 or 30 percent of the weight of the parapet is too low. It's not obvious whether 120 or 200 percent is the correct answer, so you would apply the formula

$$F = \frac{0.4a_pS_{DS}W_p}{\left(\dfrac{R_p}{I_p}\right)}\left(1+2\frac{z}{h}\right)$$

where F_p is the lateral seismic force on the parapet (component), $a_p = 2.5$, and $R_p = 2.5$ for a cantilevered parapet wall that is braced to the structural frame below its center of mass (from ASCE 7 Table 13.5-1), and I_p is the importance factor and is equal to 1.0 since this is not a high-occupancy, essential, or hazardous facility. Since the parapet is at the roof of the building, $z/h = 1.0$. Thus, with $S_{DS} = 1.0g$, $F_p =$

$$\frac{0.4\times2.5\times1.0\times W_p}{\left(\dfrac{2.5}{1.0}\right)}\left(1+2\right)=1.2W_p$$

or 120 percent of the weight of the parapet (correct answer C).

157. **B.**   A membrane can only resist tension. The vertical component of the tension in the membrane is an uplift force (III), while the horizontal component compresses the perimeter ring (I), making B the correct answer.

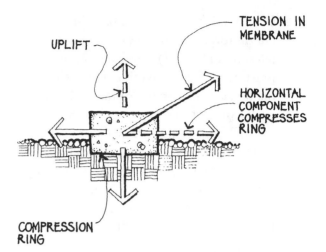

158. **B.**   The pressure exerted by a liquid is equal to the unit weight of the liquid multiplied by the depth of the liquid. At the top of the tank, the pressure is 62.4#/cu. ft. × 0 ft. = 0. At one foot down, the pressure is 62.4 × 1 = 62.4#/sq. ft., at two feet down, the pressure is 62.4 × 2 = 124.8#/sq. ft., and so on. At the bottom of the tank, the pressure is 62.4 × 10 = 624#/sq. ft. Thus, the pressure varies linearly, from zero at the top to 624#/sq. ft. at the bottom, as shown correctly in answer B.

159. **D.**   In this problem, we must determine the directions of the reactions but not their magnitudes. We draw a free body diagram and assume the reactions act in the directions shown.

$\Sigma M_2 = 0$

$+ (P \times L) - (1_H \times b) = 0$

$1_H = +PL/b$

Because 1_H comes out positive, our assumption that it acts to the left is correct. From $\Sigma H = 0$, $2_H = 1_H$ and acts to the right. We next draw a free body diagram of horizontal member 2-3-4.

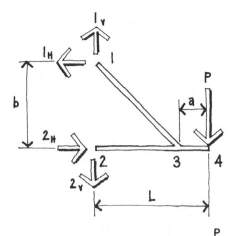

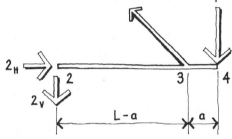

$\Sigma M_3 = 0$

$+(P \times a) - 2_v \times (L - a) = 0$

$2_v = +Pa/(L - a)$

Because 2_v comes out positive, our assumption that it acts downward is correct.

$\Sigma V = 0$

$+1_v - 2_v - P = 0$

$1_v = 2_v + P$

Because 1_v comes out positive, our assumption that it acts upward is correct. The directions of the reactions are shown correctly in answer D.

160. B. The formula for seismic base shear is $V = C_s W$, where $C_s = S_{DS}I/R$. S_{DS} is given as 1.50g. The importance factor I is equal to 1.0, since this is not a high-occupancy, essential, or hazardous facility. For buildings with special moment-resisting frames, R = 8,

which is given. Thus, $C_s = 1.5 \times 1.0/8 = 0.188$. Also, C_s need not exceed $S_{D1}I/TR$ where S_{D1} is given as 0.59g. T is the fundamental period of the building, and is equal to 1.0 second, as given. Thus, $C_s = (0.59 \times 1.0)/(1.0 \times 8) = 0.074$. Minimum $C_s = 0.01$. Therefore, V = 0.074W, or 7.4 percent of W.

161. C. The purpose of the earthquake regulations in the International Building Code is to make buildings resistant to ground shaking only (III), not to earth slides, subsidence, settlement, faulting in the vicinity of the structure, or soil liquefaction.

162. A. The basic IBC seismic formula includes an importance factor (I), which depends on the occupancy category of the building. In this case, both the original storage occupancy and the restaurant occupancy have an importance factor (I) of 1.0. Therefore, no additional design seismic force is required (A is correct). Certain high-occupancy, essential, or hazardous facilities have an importance factor greater than 1.0, thus requiring such facilities to be designed for increased seismic forces.

163. D. A space frame consists of a series of parallel and perpendicular trusses that are connected at their points of intersection to form a two-way system (IV). Since all the members of the space frame resist the applied loads (III), the space frame is stiffer than the one-way trusses (I) and consequently can be made shallower than the one-way trusses (II).

164. D. Deflection is the movement that a beam undergoes when subject to load. The immediate deflection is determined by four factors: the load (I), the span (III), the stiffness of the beam material (measured by its modulus of elasticity), and the moment of inertia of the beam (V). The modulus of elasticity of concrete is a function of its weight and its strength (VI). Concrete members deflect when the load is initially applied and then continue to deflect with time (II). The yield point of the reinforcing steel (IV) has no effect on the moment of inertia, and therefore the deflection, of the beam section.

165. **A.** Concrete has a certain amount of shear strength. However, if that shear strength is insufficient to resist the shear stress, web reinforcement in the form of stirrups must be added. Of the other choices, B describes compressive steel, C generally refers to top bars over supports, and D describes ties used to laterally brace compressive steel.

166. **B.** Short of looking it up in the beam diagram section of the AISC Manual, how does one answer this question? Intuitively, one should know that because the loading increases toward the right end of the beam, the right reaction must be greater than the left reaction. Consequently, the shear at the right end is greater than at the left end. C incorrectly shows the shear at the left end to be greater than at the right, while D incorrectly shows zero shear at the left end. That leaves A and B as possible choices. If the load were uniform, the shear would change at a uniform rate and so the shear diagram would be a straight line. But because the load increases toward the right end, the shear changes at an increasing rate, as shown correctly in B. A shows the shear changing at a decreasing rate, which is incorrect.

167. **D.** A rigid frame can be made of structural steel with welded joints (B), but it can also have bolted joints, or be made of reinforced concrete. It can have fixed bases (C), but it can also have hinged bases. The best, most inclusive definition is that in choice D. A is not a rigid frame at all, but rather a braced frame.

168. **D.** Because the horizontal load acts to the right, the horizontal reactions must act to the left (C is incorrect). If we take moments about the left base, the horizontal load causes a clockwise moment. The vertical reaction at the right base must therefore cause a counterclockwise moment, and so the vertical reaction must act upward at the right base and downward at the left base (B is incorrect). That leaves A and D as possible answers. We isolate the left column from the point of zero moment (contraflexure) to the base and show the horizontal and vertical forces acting in the known directions, as shown below. *H* causes a clockwise moment about the base, and therefore *M* must be equal and counterclockwise, as shown in correct answer D. See the illustration below.

169. **B.** A soft story is one whose stiffness is much less than that of the story above (correct answer B). It is considered a vertical structural irregularity, for which special provisions in the International Building Code are prescribed.

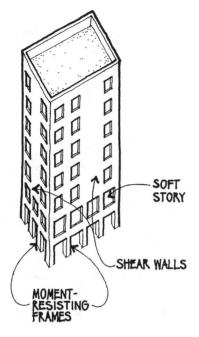

SOFT STORY

SHEAR WALLS

MOMENT-
RESISTING
FRAMES

170. D.   Infilling a moment-resisting frame with a nonstructural wall tends to stiffen the frame (correct answer D), thereby attracting more lateral load. There are two alternative solutions to this problem: either structurally separate the wall from the frame so it does not stiffen the frame, or adequately connect and reinforce the wall and frame so that they are able to resist the greater lateral load.

171. Drift.   Lateral wind or earthquake forces cause the levels of a building to move relative to each other. This story-to-story horizontal movement, or displacement, is called drift or story drift. The IBC limits the amount of drift in order to insure structural integrity, minimize discomfort to the building's occupants, and restrict damage to the brittle elements of the building.

172. C.   In this question, we have to determine which of the four buildings is a pyramid. The Marina City Towers in Chicago (A) is a round cylinder, the ABC Building in Los Angeles (B) is a triangular prism, and the Seagram

Building in New York (D) is a rectangular prism. The correct answer is C: the Transamerica Building in San Francisco, a prominent feature of that city's skyline, is in the shape of a pyramid, with the four corner columns joined at the top.

173. B.   Although there have been few numerical problems on the exam concerning arches or other long-span structures, candidates are expected to understand the concepts of such structures. An arch can resist both vertical and horizontal loads (D is incorrect). When an arch supports vertical loads, there is a horizontal reaction at each base, and the reactions are of equal magnitude and act in opposite directions (A is incorrect, B is correct). A pin or hinge in a structure cannot resist any moment, making C incorrect.

174. B.   In a moment-resisting steel frame, the moments in the beams produce tension in one beam flange and compression in the other flange. To transfer these forces from the beam flanges to the columns, moment-resisting connections are used, which must have adequate strength and not allow any slippage. For these reasons, the beam flanges are usually attached directly to the columns with full penetration groove welds (C), or with cover plates welded to the columns and welded (D) or bolted with high-strength bolts in slip-critical connections (A) to the beam flanges. ASTM A307 machine bolts are generally not used for moment-resisting connections because they rely on bearing to develop their strength, and in so doing allow some movement. B is therefore the correct answer.

175. B. Materials expand when heated and contract when cooled. The amount of expansion or contraction is equal to the product of three factors: the coefficient of thermal expansion of the material, the length of the member, and the temperature change. Thus Δ(expansion) = $(0.0000065) \times (24 \text{ ft.} \times 12 \text{ in./ft.}) \times (90 - 60) = 0.056''$ (answer B).

176. D. Once the total earthquake force has been determined, it must be distributed to the various levels of the structure. If the weights of all the stories of a short, stiff building are equal, the forces will be distributed in the form of a triangle, zero at the base and maximum at the top, with a horizontal force applied to each floor or roof level, as shown in correct choice D. This type of distribution is applicable to structures with a fundamental period of 0.5 seconds or less.

177. B. Re-entrant corners occur in L-, T-, U-, and cross-shaped plans, and tend to cause high stress concentrations under seismic loading.

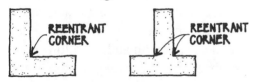

Therefore, they should be avoided if possible, such as by providing a seismic separation.

A re-entrant corner is considered to be a plan structural irregularity (correct answer B) and if it cannot be avoided, it must comply with special regulations in the International Building Code.

178. C. Each radial cable supports vertical load and resists tension, as shown.

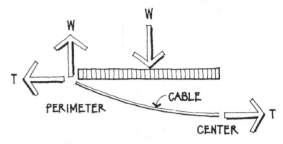

For equilibrium, the center ring must be *lower* than the perimeter ring (A is incorrect). Each cable *pulls* on the center ring, which tends to expand it, thus stressing it in tension. Each cable also *pulls* on the perimeter ring, which compresses it (C is correct, B and D are incorrect).

179. D. Candidates should be able to determine the reactions of any statically determinate beam subject to any load. To determine the reaction at R_1, we take moments about R_2.

$$\Sigma M_{R_2} = 0$$

$$+(5,000\# \times 8 \text{ ft.}) - (5,000\# \times 16 \text{ ft.})$$

$$-\left(1,000\#/\text{ft.} \times 24 \text{ ft.} \times \frac{24 \text{ ft.}}{2}\right) + (R_1 \times 24 \text{ ft.})$$

$$= 0$$

$$R_1 = (-40,000 + 80,000 + 288,000) \div 24$$

$$= 328,000 \div 24$$

$$= 13,667\# \text{ (answer D)}$$

180. C. The modulus of elasticity E of a material is defined as the ratio of unit stress to unit strain when the unit stress is below the elastic limit. Because unit stress = P/A and unit strain = Δ/L,

$$E = (P/A) \div (\Delta/L) = PL/A\Delta$$

$$= (50,000\# \times 10 \text{ ft.} \times 12 \text{ in./ft.})$$

$$\div \left[\frac{\pi(2 \text{ in.})^2}{4} \times 0.159 \text{ in.} \right]$$

= 6,000,000 ÷ 0.4995 = 12,012,000 psi
(answer C)

181. **D.**   When lateral forces act on a building that is not symmetrical with respect to rigidity, it causes torsion. In the four plans in this question, the lateral forces from wind or earthquake act through the center of gravity of the building, which is located close to the center of the building's plan. The center of the resistance to these lateral forces is called the center of rigidity. If the building is symmetrical with respect to resistance, that is, if opposite sides of the building are equally rigid, then the center of rigidity will be close to the center of gravity (plans I and II), and the torsional forces will be small. If the building is not symmetrical with respect to resistance, that is, if the shear resisting elements on opposite sides have very different rigidities (III), then the center of resistance will be located near the stiffer walls, resulting in larger torsional forces. In addition, buildings whose shear resisting elements are in a core far from the building's perimeter, particularly where the core is not at the center of the building, are subject to high torsional forces (plan IV). Answer D is correct.

182. **Shear wall.**   A shear wall resists lateral wind or earthquake loads parallel to itself by cantilevering from its base. Thus, a shear wall is essentially a very deep vertical cantilever beam.

183. **C.**   In general, buildings must be designed to resist the forces caused by either wind or earthquake, whichever is greater, but not both acting at the same time.

184. **A.**   The answer is *I, III, and IV.* The three-hinged gabled frame (I), moment-resisting frame (III), and braced frame (IV) are all stable under the action of horizontal forces. The post-and-beam (II) can support vertical loads, but would collapse if subject to horizontal forces.

185. **D.**   Wind and seismic forces are fundamentally different, in that wind forces are real exterior surface-applied forces, while seismic forces are simulated forces resulting from a building's inertia (B and C are correct statements). Seismic design forces are based on the assumption that inelastic behavior may occur in the structure as a result of major earthquake ground motion (A is a correct statement). Answer D is the incorrect statement: wind forces may or may not exceed seismic forces. They must each be evaluated, and the structure must be designed for whichever is larger.

186. **D.**   The basic structural component in all suspension structures is a steel cable, which has great tensile strength but practically no compressive or bending strength.

187. **A.**   The capacity of a wood column is determined by several factors: the modulus of elasticity (E) of the wood, which in turn depends on its species and grade; the reference compression design value (F_c), which also depends on the species and grade of the wood; the ratio *1/d*, where *1* is the unbraced height of the column and *d* is the least lateral dimension of the column, and the cross-sectional area of the column. Therefore B, C, and D are all correct. The radius of gyration is used in determining the capacity of steel columns, not wood, and thus A is the factor not used in the determination of the capacity of wood columns.

188. **A.**   In composite design, a concrete slab is connected to a steel beam with shear connectors that can develop the ultimate capacity of the concrete or the steel, whichever is less (D). Because the concrete and steel act together, a smaller size steel beam may be used than in conventional steel framing, which generally results in a more economical system (B). However, when a smaller steel beam is used, deflections tend to become greater, and thus more critical, in composite design than in conventional steel framing (C). Conventional steel framing can always be designed to carry the required loads, and thus A is the incorrect statement we are looking for.

189. **C.**   Candidates are not generally expected to memorize complex formulas. If a deflection problem of this kind appears on the exam, beam diagrams from the AISC Manual will probably be reproduced in the Exam Information Manual. For a simple beam supporting a uniform load, the deflection formula is

$$\Delta = \frac{5Wl^4}{384EI}$$

Since wl = W, the total load on the beam, the formula becomes

$$\Delta = \frac{5Wl^4}{384EI} = 5(2000)(28)(28 \times 12)^3$$

$$= 0.52''$$

Note that the length of 28 feet must be converted to (28 × 12) inches before being cubed.

.52″ is
answer
D on
p.42

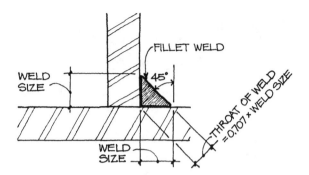

190. **A.**   We cut a section through the left column and apply the basic equation of static equilibrium ΣV = 0. Because the only vertical force acting at the joint is V, it follows that V (the force in the left column) = 0. From ΣV = 0, the force in the right column acts toward the upper right joint (compression) and is equal to $a_v = (16/12) \times 10 = 13.3$ kips. The correct answer is therefore A.

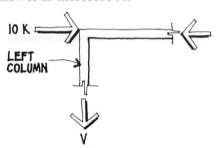

191. **C.**   Wind and seismic forces are fundamentally different, in that wind forces are real exterior surface applied forces, while seismic forces are simulated forces resulting from a building's inertia (A and B are incorrect). Seismic design forces are based on inelastic behavior of the structure (C is correct), which is not true of wind design forces (D is incorrect).

192. **A.**   The diagram shows a system in which glulam 2 is suspended between the cantilevered ends of glulams 1 and 3. Connections A and B therefore transfer the vertical reactions at the ends

of glulam 2 to glulams 1 and 3. This system has smaller maximum moments than a comparable simple span system, thereby permitting longer spans and/or larger loads for a given size member. The suspended member (glulam 2) can also be made shallower because of its reduced span.

193. **A.** This is a problem involving number crunching and conversion factors. In the deflection formula, because $wL = W$ (# per ft. × ft. = total #), the formula becomes $\Delta = 5WL^3/384EI$, where $\Delta = L/360 = 24$ ft. × 12 in./ft./360 = 0.8″

$W = 1,000\#/\text{ft.} \times 24 \text{ ft.} = 24,000\#$

$L^3 = (24 \text{ feet} \times 12 \text{ inches/foot})^3$

$E = 29,000,000 \text{ psi}$

$0.8 = 5(24,000)(24 \times 12)^3/384 \times 29,000,000 \times I$

$I = 5(24,000)(24 \times 12)^3/384 \times 29,000,000 \times 0.8$

$= 321.8 \text{ in.}^4$ (answer A)

194. **Joist girder.** A joist girder is an open web steel truss used as a primary framing member. It is designed as a simple span member supporting equally spaced concentrated loads from a floor or roof system, generally consisting of open web steel joists. These concentrated loads are considered to act at the panel points of the joist girder. Joist girders are standardized for various depths and spans.

195. **B.** Torsion is the rotation caused in a diaphragm when the center of mass does not coincide with the center of rigidity. The torsional moment is equal to the lateral earthquake force multiplied by the distance between the center of mass and the center of rigidity = 100(25 − 10) = 1,500 ft.-kips.

196. **B.** Base isolation is a relatively new approach to seismic design that has been used for a number of buildings. In this method, the structure is isolated from the ground by specially designed bearings and dampers that absorb earthquake forces and thus reduce the building's acceleration from earthquake ground motion.

197. **A.** The formula for seismic base shear is $V = C_S W$ where $C_S = S_{DS}I/R$. S_{DS} is given as 0.41g. The importance factor I is equal to 1.0, since this is not a high-occupancy, essential, or hazardous facility. For buildings with special steel moment-resisting frames, R = 8. Thus, $C_S = 0.41 \times 1.0/8 = 0.051$. Also, C_S need not exceed $S_{D1}I/TR$ where S_{D1} is given as 0.15g. T is the fundamental period of the building, and is equal to 1.2 seconds, as given. Thus, $C_S = (0.15 \times 1.0)/(1.2 \times 8) = 0.016$. Minimum $C_S = 0.01$. Therefore, V = 0.016W, or 1.6 percent of W.

198. **A.** Questions testing your understanding of structural behavior often appear on the exam. Structural steel columns fail by buckling. The ratio Kl/r is a measure of the buckling tendency of a steel column; the larger the value of Kl/r, the greater the tendency of the column to buckle, resulting in a lower column capacity. In this ratio, K is a constant determined by the end conditions of the column (I), that is, whether the column ends are pinned or fixed and whether the column is free to translate (move laterally). The actual unbraced length of the column is l and K$_l$ is the effective length (II is incorrect). The radius of gyration r is a property of the column cross section and is independent of the yield strength of the steel (III is incorrect). Because only I is a correct statement, A is the correct answer.

199. B.   Handrail problems, such as this one, sometimes appear on the exam. Such problems are easily solvable using the basic principles of statics. In this problem, we solve for the force in bolt A by taking moments about bolt B.

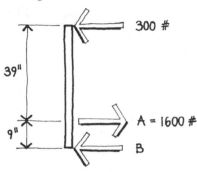

$$\Sigma M_B = 0$$

$$-300\#(39'' + 9'') + A(9'') = 0$$

$$A = (300 \times 48) \div 9 = 1,600\#$$

Bolt A is in *tension*, because the force acts *away* from the vertical post (correct answer B).

200. B.   In a reinforced concrete beam, if crushing of the concrete and yielding of the steel occur simultaneously, it is called a balanced design. In order to ensure that the steel yields before the concrete crushes (III is correct), a limit is placed on the strain in the reinforcing bars closest to the tension face (I is incorrect, II is correct).

201. B.   Steel columns bear on and are usually welded to steel base plates, which spread the column load over the supporting foundation. The bearing pressure is equal to the column load divided by the area of the base plate = 200,000#/16″ × 16″ = 781 psi.

202. D.   All three methods of splicing reinforcing bars are allowed. Lapped splices are usually the least costly and therefore the most common. Welded splices are also used extensively. There are several types of mechanical connection devices available for splicing reinforcing bars. In general, these devices are proprietary and not as widely used as the other two methods.

203. C.   A shell, or thin shell, is a structure with a curved surface that resists load by compression, shear, or tension in its own plane (I is incorrect), but that is too thin to resist any appreciable bending stresses (III is correct). Shells are strong in resisting uniform loads but cannot resist any substantial concentrated loads, which tend to induce bending (II is incorrect).

204. A.   If the reference screens furnished to candidates at the exam included the beam formulas for this condition, we would immediately see that the reaction at A is 7wL/16 = 7(1.0) (24)/16 = 10.5 kips. But can we solve this problem if the formulas are not given? Yes, pretty easily. We isolate span AB, as shown below.

The moment at B is equal to the reaction at C times the length of span BC = 1.5 kips × 24 feet = 36.0 ft.-kips, as shown. Take moments about B.

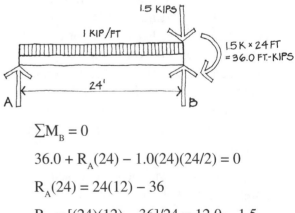

$$\Sigma M_B = 0$$

$$36.0 + R_A(24) - 1.0(24)(24/2) = 0$$

$$R_A(24) = 24(12) - 36$$

$$R_A = [(24)(12) - 36]/24 = 12.0 - 1.5$$

$$= 10.5 \text{ kips}$$

205. C. Composite beams, steel plate girders, and wood I-joists are examples of built-up members in which the flange-to-web connections must resist horizontal shear stress.

206. C. The earthquake regulations of the IBC are intended to provide resistance to ground shaking (IV), as noted in correct answer C. The code does not provide for resistance to ground ruptures (I); ground failure (II), such as landslides, subsidence, or settlement; or tsunamis (III), which are seismic seawaves.

207. D. Earthquake codes, especially the IBC, are periodically revised to keep pace with advancing seismic knowledge. The current earthquake regulations in the IBC consider all of the factors listed, except the Richter magnitude (D). Building configuration (A) is considered by classifying buildings as either regular or irregular, with special provisions prescribed for irregular structures. A building's occupancy category (B) determines its importance factor, which requires essential or hazardous facilities to be designed to resist greater seismic loads than other structures. The soil characteristics at a site (C) affect the seismic design force, so that structures on soft soil are required to resist greater seismic forces than those on firm soil.

208. A. The primary purpose of earthquake regulations in building codes is to safeguard against major failures and loss of life (A), not to limit damage, maintain functions, or provide for easy repair (B, C, and D).

209. D. Statements I, II, and IV are correct. Statement III is incorrect. The largest part of the structural framing cost in a suspension roof is in the fittings,

connections, and anchorage members. Statement V is also incorrect. The draped cable will assume the shape of a parabola. D is therefore the correct answer.

210. C. To calculate the horizontal thrust, we isolate the left half of the arch.

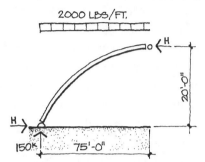

By symmetry, each vertical reaction is equal to one half of the total load on the arch

$$= 2{,}000 \times 150/2 = 150{,}000\# = 150 \text{ kips}$$

Take moments about the center hinge, where the moment is equal to zero

$$\sum M = 0$$

$$150(75) - 2.0(75)(75/2) - H(20) = 0$$

$$H = [150(75) - 2.0(75)(75/2)]/20$$

$$= (11{,}250 - 5{,}625)/20$$

$$= 5{,}625/20 = 281.25 \text{ kips (correct answer C)}$$

211. D. All of the statements are correct except I. A composite beam consists of a steel beam and a concrete slab that are connected so that they act together as a single structural unit to resist bending stresses. A composite beam is much stiffer than a noncomposite beam having the same depth, size, load, and span (III). However, because composite design usually allows us to use shallower beams (II), deflections should be checked (IV). The horizontal shear stress between the steel beam and the concrete slab, not moment, is resisted by shear connectors, such as studs, welded to the top flange of the beam and embedded in the concrete (I is incorrect).

212. **A.** The terms *ties* and *spirals* refer to the type of reinforcing used to wrap around the vertical reinforcing bars in reinforced concrete columns. Spirals are more effective than ties, and therefore spiral columns have greater axial load capacity than tied columns (I is correct). In plan, ties may be square, rectangular, or round, while spirals are always round. However, in both cases, the column may have any shape (III is incorrect). The use of ties or spirals has no effect on a column's fire resistance or forming (II and IV are incorrect).

213. **A.** I and II are rigid frames, which are able to resist horizontal loads in their own plane. Because III has a pin at the beam-column joints, it is not a rigid frame, and therefore it is unable to resist a horizontal load in its own plane.

214. **Drag strut.** Where a shear resisting element, such as a shear wall, braced frame, or moment-resisting frame, is discontinuous, a collector member called a strut or drag strut is used to collect seismic or wind load from the diaphragm to which it is attached and transfer it to the shear resisting element. An example follows.

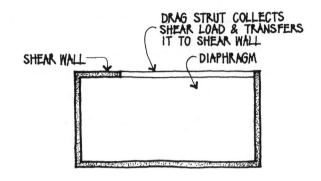

PLAN

215. **A.** The best definition of live load is that given in correct answer A. B is incorrect because a continuously applied load is usually considered to be dead load. C is incorrect because live load does not include wind or earthquake load. D is not as inclusive as A, and is therefore incorrect, because live load may include loads other than occupants and movable furniture.

216. **A.** In this question, we are not asking which building type has the greatest structural cost, but for which building type is the structural cost the lowest percentage of the total cost of construction. As a rule of thumb, the structural cost for commercial or office buildings averages about 25 percent of the total cost of construction (D is incorrect). For buildings with minimal architectural and mechanical requirements, such as warehouses and parking garages, the structural cost may be 50 percent or more of the total cost of construction (B and C are incorrect). For buildings that have complex or expensive architectural and mechanical requirements, such as hospitals, the structural cost may be only 10 or 15 percent of the total cost of construction. The correct answer is therefore A.

217. B. A structural system is an arrangement of structural components that resists a building's vertical and/or horizontal loads. There are many factors that influence the choice of structural system, including the building's spans and loads. This question tests your understanding of the appropriateness of various structural systems for the given conditions. The one-way concrete joist and beam system (I) is generally economical for spans of 35 to 40 feet, and would therefore not be economical in this case. Similarly, the flat slab system (III) is appropriate for spans of about 25 to 30 feet, and would not be economical. Prestressed concrete systems, such as those in choices II and IV, are usually able to span longer distances. The correct answer is therefore B. — *QUESTION HAS $\underline{C}$ AS OPTION FOR II & IV*

218. C. The exam often includes a few problems in statics, similar to this one, which can be solved by using the basic equations of static equilibrium: $\Sigma H = 0$, $\Sigma V = 0$, $\Sigma M = 0$. In this case, there is a pin at B, which means that there are vertical and horizontal reactions there, but no moment. At A, the horizontal bar pinned at both ends can resist an axial horizontal reaction only, but no vertical reaction or moment. We take moments about B to solve for A_H. See the illustration below.

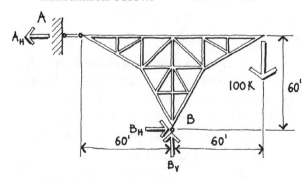

$$\Sigma M_B = 0$$

$+ 100 \text{ kips}(60 \text{ ft.}) - A_H(60 \text{ ft.}) = 0$

$A_H = 100 \text{ kips}$

$-A_H + B_H = 0$

$B_H = A_H = 100 \text{ kips}$

$\Sigma V = 0$

$-100 \text{ kips} + B_V = 0$

$B_V = 100 \text{ kips}$

The reactions are shown correctly in choice C.

219. B. A rigid diaphragm, such as concrete, distributes the horizontal forces from wind or earthquake to the vertical resisting elements in proportion to their relative rigidities. Rigidity is defined as resistance to deformation. Thus, a wall with a relative rigidity of 4 will resist twice as much lateral load as one whose relative rigidity is 2.

220. A. The three-hinged gabled frame (I), rigid frame (III), and braced frame (IV) are all stable under the action of horizontal forces. The post and lintel (II) can support vertical forces, but would collapse if subject to horizontal forces.

221. D. This question tests your understanding of various types of lateral load resisting systems. In a bearing wall system, the vertical load is supported by bearing walls or bracing systems and the required lateral forces are resisted by shear walls or braced frames. In other words, the shear walls or braced frames resist both vertical and lateral loads, as in choices A and B. If these elements should fail during an earthquake, their ability to support vertical loads may be eliminated and the structure may collapse. Consequently, such systems are not considered to be the most desirable for earthquake resistance and must be designed for relatively high seismic loads. Eccentric braced frames are ductile and therefore able to absorb a significant amount of energy without buckling the braces. However, such frames are only made of steel (C is incorrect). D is the correct choice: special moment-resisting frames, which can be made of steel or concrete, can absorb a large amount of energy in the inelastic range without collapsing or deforming unacceptably, and are therefore considered most desirable for earthquake-resistant design.

222. **A.**   The axial load-carrying capacity of a steel column is determined by the strength of the steel used in the column and the tendency of the column to buckle. The buckling tendency is a function of the length of the column (*1*), its radius of gyration (*r*), and the relative fixity of its ends (K). In this case, the base plate with two bolts has very little resistance to rotation and can therefore be considered pinned. Because the column is part of a moment-resisting steel frame, its top is more or less fixed against rotation, but it can translate (move horizontally). The correct answer is therefore A.

223. **D.**   Certain types of clay expand when wet and shrink when dried, and buildings supported on such expansive soils may suffer damage. To minimize or prevent damage, the foundations should be placed below the depth of seasonal moisture change, so that the moisture content of the subsoil remains relatively constant.

224. **C.**   In fillet welds, the stress is always considered to be shear stress on the minimum throat area, regardless of the direction of the applied load, and the throat area is assumed to be equal to 0.707 times the weld size. The correct answer is C.

225. **C.**   Reinforcing steel opposite the tension side of a reinforced concrete beam is called compressive reinforcement, as it is located in the compression side of the beam and resists compression (I is correct, III is incorrect). The deflection of concrete members increases with time, beyond the initial deflection. This additional deflection, caused by shrinkage and creep, can be reduced by using compressive reinforcement (IV). As with tensile longitudinal reinforcing, the compressive reinforcement does not resist shear stress (II is incorrect). As only I and IV are true, the correct answer is C.

226. **B.**   The formulas used to design columns are based on idealized pin-ended conditions, where the ends of the column are free to rotate, but not to move laterally (translate). Actual building columns, however, do not always meet these conditions: their ends may be free to rotate, or they may permit no rotation. Also, their ends may be free to translate, or they may be fixed against translation. To allow the column formulas to be used for all end conditions, the factor K was devised. This factor is multiplied by the actual unbraced length 1 to arrive at the effective length Kl, which is then used to design the column. B is therefore the correct answer.

227. **A.**   Every building has a natural or fundamental period of vibration, which varies inversely with its stiffness. Thus, a long-period building is relatively flexible (C is incorrect). The acceleration of a building during an earthquake and the resulting seismic force depend on the building's stiffness: the stiffer the building, the greater the acceleration and seismic force. Therefore, a long-period, flexible building has relatively low

acceleration and low seismic force (A is correct, D is incorrect). The overturning moment is not directly related to a building's period (B is incorrect).

228. C. This question requires the calculation of diaphragm shear. The approach is simple: the diaphragm acts as a horizontal beam spanning between the end shear walls. The reaction to each shear wall is therefore 200 lbs./ft. × 120 ft./2 = 12,000#. The maximum diaphragm shear is equal to this reaction divided by the diaphragm width = 12,000# ÷ 60 ft. = 200 lbs./ft. (correct answer C).

229. C. Earthquakes are measured by two different scales: the Richter scale and the Modified Mercalli scale. The Richter scale is a measure of energy released in an earthquake (D), while the Modified Mercalli scale measures an earthquake's intensity; that is, its effects on people and buildings (correct answer C).

230. D. Even if you are not familiar with specific code requirements, it should be obvious that a factor of safety against sliding should be provided. The only answer that has a factor of safety is D.

231. A. Although an arch is often subject to some bending moment, its internal stresses are primarily compression.

232. A. The design values for wood members and fasteners tabulated in building codes apply to normal duration of loading. For shorter durations of load, the design values may be increased; the shorter the duration, the greater the design values (correct answer A). For example, for two months' duration, as for snow, the design values may be increased 15 percent.

233. A. Most building codes require the dead load resisting moment to be at least 1.5 times the overturning moment caused by earth pressure, making A the correct answer. If the dead load resisting moment were less than 1.5 times the overturning moment, the simplest solution would be to make the footing wider. Making the footing deeper would increase the dead load resisting moment slightly, and increasing the amount of reinforcing steel would have no effect on the dead load resisting moment.

234. A. In general, buildings must be designed to resist wind or seismic load, but not both acting at the same time. In addition, floor live load must be considered to act on the structure, as well as permanent dead load.

235. A. In buildings with rigid diaphragms, which are usually concrete or steel, the lateral wind or earthquake loads are distributed to the vertical resisting elements in proportion to their relative rigidities (A). In other words, rigid elements resist more load than flexible elements. Shear walls are the most rigid elements, followed by braced frames and then moment-resisting frames, which are much more flexible than the other two.

236. A. The International Building Code specifies the maximum height-to-width ratios for plywood shear walls, which are called "vertical diaphragms" in the code. For a shear wall of a given height, the minimum width is determined by these ratios (correct answer A). The width may not be less than that determined by these ratios, even if the calculations should show that a lesser width would be adequate to resist the total shear force (C is incorrect).

237. A.   To answer this question, we take moments about point 2. Overturning moment = 10,000 × 16 = 160,000 ft.-lbs. Dead load resisting moment = 10,000 × 32 = 320,000 ft.-lbs. Because the dead load resisting moment exceeds the overturning moment, there is no net uplift.

238. A.   The columns of the rigid frame have a point of contraflexure (zero moment) approximately at mid-height. The free body diagram of the upper part of the frame is

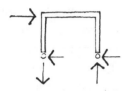

and the corresponding moment diagram is

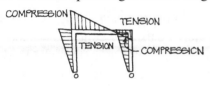

The free body diagram of the lower part of the frame is

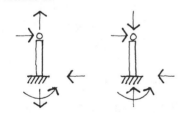

and the corresponding moment diagram is

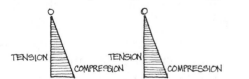

The stresses are correctly identified in A.

239. C.   Although most of the questions on the structural tests are conceptual, there are always some that require calculations, as in this case. Here we have a column that supports a roof and one floor. We first determine the column load per square foot, which is the total of the dead and live loads = (20 + 20 + 75 + 100) = 215 pounds per square foot. The total column load is equal to the load per square foot multiplied by the area tributary to the column = 215 × 500 = 107,500#. The required footing area is equal to the total column load divided by the soil bearing value = 107,500 ÷ 3,000 = 35.83 square feet. We therefore use a 6′-0″ × 6′-0″ pad (choice C), which has an area of 36.0 square feet.

240. C.   Long-span structures generally have little redundancy, or alternative ways of resisting load (A is incorrect). In a long-span structure, each connection supports a large area, so that the connections are more critical than in conventional structures (B is incorrect). C is correct: for a number of reasons, long-span structures are more vulnerable to overall collapse, in case of accidental overload or a defect or weakness in a member or joint, than conventional structures. D is incorrect; although certain types of long-span structures have a measure of instability, there is no requirement for a dynamic load analysis.

241. B.   A beam with compression reinforcement, in addition to tension reinforcement, is known as a doubly-reinforced beam. Compression steel may be used in cases where the concrete alone is inadequate to resist the compressive stress, or where it is desirable to reduce long-term deflection due to creep and shrinkage.

242. A.   The lateral load will be distributed to the four piers in proportion to their rigidities, where the rigidity is defined as resistance to deflection. The rigidity of a pier depends on its height-to-depth ratio. Since all four piers have the same height (four feet), their rigidities depend only on their depths: the deeper the pier, the greater the rigidity. Piers 1 and 4 are six feet deep and are therefore more rigid than piers 2 and 3, which are five feet deep. Consequently, piers 1 and 4 resist more lateral load than piers 2 and 3 (A is correct).

243. **B.** Torsion is the rotation caused in a rigid diaphragm when the center of mass does not coincide with the center of rigidity, as in this problem. Walls 2 and 4 resist seismic loads in the east-west direction, as shown. For wall 2, the shear caused by torsional moment is in the opposite direction from that caused by the applied seismic load. However, for wall 4, the shear caused by torsional moment is in the same direction as that caused by the applied seismic load, resulting in increased shear in wall 4 (correct answer B).

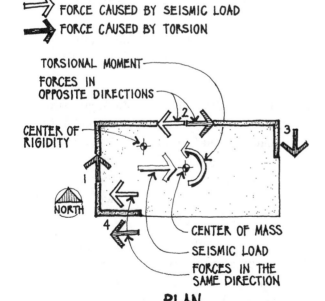

244. **B.** A moment-resisting frame, as the name suggests, resists forces by developing moments at the joints between beams and columns. The moments in the beams produce tension in one beam flange and compression in the opposite flange. To transfer these forces from the beam flanges to the columns, the flanges must be rigidly attached to the columns by plates welded to the columns and bolted to the beams, as shown in I, or the beam flanges must be directly welded to the columns, as shown in III. The shear forces in the steel beam webs are transferred to the columns by plates welded or bolted to the beam webs and welded to the columns, as shown in I and III. Steel beams that are not part of moment-resisting frames are simply supported, and need only have the shear in their webs transferred to the column, either by a beam seat, as shown in II, or a plate, as shown in IV. The top angle in II serves only to hold the top of the beam in place, but is too flexible to rigidly attach the beam to the column.

245. **D.** The midspan deflection is equal to the sum of the deflection caused by the uniform load and the deflection caused by the concentrated load. The deflection formulas may be found in a number of reference sources, including the AISC Manual.

The uniform load deflection =

$$\frac{5}{384}\frac{wl^4}{EI} = \frac{5}{384} \times \frac{200(30)(30\times12)^3}{29(106)(2,100)}$$

$$= 0.599''$$

The concentrated load deflection =

$$\frac{Pl^3}{48EI} = \frac{9,000(30\times12)^3}{48(29)(106)(2,100)} = 0.144''$$

The total deflection = 0.599'' + 0.144'' = 0.743'' (answer D)

Notice that the length of 30 feet must be converted to (30 × 12) inches before being cubed.

246. **A.** Because the frame has fixed bases, the angle between the columns and the base must be 90°. The moments in the beam and columns change from positive to negative, as shown below.

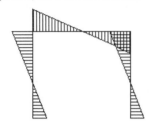

247. **D.** An eccentric braced frame has at least one end of each brace eccentric to the beam-column joint or the opposing brace, as shown below. The intent is to make the braced frame more ductile than a concentric braced frame (correct answer D) and therefore able to absorb a great amount of energy without causing the braces to buckle. Eccentric braced frames must be made of steel (B is incorrect), are permitted in buildings assigned to any Seismic Design Category (A is incorrect), and may be used in a dual system with moment-resisting frames (C is incorrect).

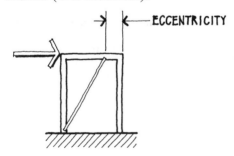

ECCENTRICITY

248. **A.** Candidates are expected to be able to solve simple problems in statics, as in this question.

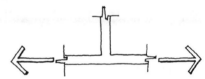

We isolate the bar. As member DB is a horizontal cable, it can only be stressed in tension. Therefore, it pulls away from the bar (to the left) in a horizontal direction. As $\sum H = 0$, H_A must be equal and opposite to H_B and act to the right. From the basic equation $\sum V = 0$, $-1,000 + V_A = 0$. $V_A = +1,000$, which means that V_A acts upward.

249. **A.** This problem can be solved very quickly if it is approached correctly. We simply isolate the joint between the vertical and bottom chord and apply the equation $\sum V = 0$.

As there are no vertical loads applied at the joint, the internal force in the vertical member is zero.

250. **B.** To answer this question, you simply need to know two things: (1) that a force that pulls on a member causes tension, and (2) that the grain of a wood member runs parallel to its length. Therefore, each 2 × 8 wood member is loaded in tension parallel to the grain.

251. **C.** Although there is some controversy surrounding the Imperial Hotel, this much is known: it survived the 1923 earthquake, although it sustained some damage; it was founded on very poor, spongy soil (I is incorrect); it was built of concrete and masonry, not steel (II is incorrect); and the building was divided

by seismic separation joints spaced about 60 feet apart (III is correct). This feature probably accounted for the good performance of the Imperial Hotel during the earthquake.

252. **C.** In general, the more flexible the building, the longer its fundamental period of vibration, which in turn results in lower seismic acceleration and consequently, smaller seismic load (C is correct).

253. **A.** In order to prevent two buildings from pounding against each other during an earthquake, they must be separated by an amount at least equal to the sum of the deflections (displacements) of the two buildings (correct answer A).

254. **D.** In a rigid frame, the joint between its beam and column members is rigid; that is, the angle between the members cannot change, and bending moment can be transferred. This enables the rigid frame to resist both horizontal and vertical loads.

255. **A.** B is the deflected shape of a simple beam supported by columns, without rigid joints. C is the deflected shape of a rigid frame with fixed supports, while D is the shape the hinged frame would take if horizontal reactions could not be resisted at the bases. A is the correct answer.

256. **C.** A truss, one of the oldest methods employed for long-span construction, is a structure designed to support vertical or horizontal loads and composed of straight members that form a number of triangles. Trusses may have a variety of configurations, but must always consist of triangles.

257. **C.** First of all, what is a circular dish roof? As implied by its name, it is a circular roof structure curving upward in all directions from its lowest point at the center (V is correct, VI is incorrect). A number of radial cables, which are in tension, are stretched between the outer ring and the inner ring. The cables pull outward on the inner ring, putting it in tension (IV). At the same time, they pull inward on the outer ring, compressing it (I). See sketch below.

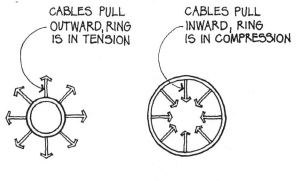

258. **A, B, and C.** Lateral bracing of trusses must be provided to prevent the compression members from buckling (A). Truss members are stressed principally in tension or compression only (D is incorrect). However, small secondary bending and shear stresses are produced by the restraint against rotation at the joints. These secondary stresses are often ignored for conventional trusses, but should be considered for long-span trusses (B). Trusses are always made up of triangles because the triangle is inherently a very stable shape; it is the only geometric figure that cannot be changed in shape without changing the length of one or more of its sides (C).

259. **B.** To solve this simple beam problem, you must know (1) the maximum moment in a beam supporting a concentrated load at midspan is PL/4, and (2) the required

plastic section modulus Z is equal to $M\Omega/F_y$ where the factor of safety $\Omega = 1.67$ for flexure. Thus, $M = PL/4 = 10(30)/4 = 75.0'k$. $Z = 75 \times 12 \times 1.67/50 = 30.1$ in.^{3} Note that we multiply the moment in ft.-kips by 12 to convert it to inch-kips, so that the plastic section modulus comes out in inches^3.

260. **A.** It is unnecessary to check the strength of wood beams in shear perpendicular to the grain, because the member will always fail first in shear parallel to the grain. A is therefore the incorrect statement we are looking for. B is correct: in all beams, the horizontal shear stress is always equal to the vertical shear stress. C is also correct: the design tension or compression parallel to the grain is many times greater than the design horizontal shear value (parallel to the grain). D is a correct statement; for example, if a 12″ deep beam is notched 2″ on its bottom face at the end, the actual shear stress is increased about 50 percent. In detailing wood construction, therefore, notches should be avoided.

261. **A.** The modulus of elasticity of concrete is approximately $w33\sqrt{f'_c}$, where w is the unit weight of the concrete in pounds per cubic foot and f'_c is the compressive strength of the concrete in psi. Thus, as the unit weight (I) or the strength (II) increases, the modulus of elasticity increases. The amount of reinforcing steel (III) is irrelevant, and the depth of the member (IV) affects the moment of inertia of the member, not the modulus of elasticity of the material.

262. **D.** Reinforcing steel must be protected against corrosion and fire by an adequate amount of concrete cover. The more severe the exposure (for example, concrete cast against earth), the greater the required concrete cover.

263. **B.** The margin of safety for reinforced concrete is provided by the load factor and φ, the strength reduction factor. The load factor, which is 1.4 for dead load and 1.7 for live load (A is correct), is based on the possibility that sometime during the life of the structure, the service loads may be exceeded (C is correct). The strength reduction factor φ allows for variations in material strengths and actual construction dimensions, as well as inaccuracies or approximations in design calculations (D is correct). Depending on the type of stress, φ varies from 0.65 to 0.90 (B is the incorrect statement).

264. **C.** The base plate tends to bend as shown and must be thick enough so that the allowable bending stress is not exceeded.

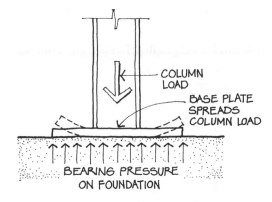

265. **Open web steel joists.** Open web steel joists are standardized lightweight steel trusses that are shop-fabricated. These members have no fire resistance capability unless they are combined with other materials.

266. **C.** All of the statements in this question are recommended seismic design practices, except C. To minimize overturning effects, buildings should have a low height-to-width ratio. A short, squat building (low height-to-width ratio) is less likely to overturn than a tall, slender building (high height-to-width ratio).

267. C. Earthquake ground motion causes buildings to vibrate back and forth. If a building consists of two dissimilar sections, as in this question, each section will tend to move differently. If the two sections are connected, stress concentrations will occur, which may result in excessive damage to the building. This is considered a structural irregularity, as defined by the IBC, which should be avoided by providing a complete structural separation between the two dissimilar portions, so that each can vibrate independently.

268. C. If the center of mass of a building coincides with its center of rigidity, there is theoretically no torsion. However, various factors may introduce accidental torsion if the diaphragm is rigid (correct answer C). To provide for this accidental torsion, the mass at each level is assumed to be displaced a distance equal to 5 percent of the building dimension at that level perpendicular to the direction of the force.

269. B. Exam questions often test candidates' understanding of structural concepts, as in this question. For a given load and span, a simple beam (A and D) will generally have the greatest deflection and positive moment. In arrangement B, beam 1-2 extends past support 2 and supports the end of the simple beam in span 2-3. This has the effect of reducing both the positive moment and the deflection in span 1-2. In arrangement C, beam 2-3 extends to about the midpoint of span 1-2 and will be subject to high negative moment at support 2, as well as high deflection. The correct answer is therefore B.

270. B. When purlins or other framing members are located at truss panel points, the chord and web members of the truss are stressed in axial tension or compression only and have no bending stress. However, if load is applied to a truss chord between panel points, the chord acts as a beam spanning between the panel points and is thus subject to bending stress in addition to the axial tension or compression caused by the truss action.

271. B. For elastic materials, such as steel, unit stress is proportional to unit strain at stresses below the elastic limit. If the stress is doubled, the strain is doubled, and so on. The stress-strain diagram in this region is therefore a straight line. The ratio of unit stress to unit strain is called the modulus of elasticity and is designated E. Materials with a high value of E are said to be stiff, which means highly resistant to deformation.

272. C. This truss resists both a vertical load and a horizontal load. Notice that support B is on a roller, which means that there can be no horizontal reaction at that support. Therefore, there must be a horizontal reaction of 10,000# acting to the right at support A, from $\Sigma H = 0$. To determine the vertical reaction at A, we take moments about B.

$$\Sigma M_B = 0$$

$$10,000(10 \text{ ft.}) - 10,000(10 \text{ ft.}) + V_A(40 \text{ ft.}) = 0$$

$$V_A = 0$$

From $\Sigma V = 0$, the vertical reaction at B equals 10,000# upward. The reactions are shown correctly in choice C.

273. C.   A braced frame is essentially a vertical truss which resists horizontal loads. We cut a section through the braces, as shown below.

$$\Sigma H = 0$$

$$10 - F_{1H} - F_{2H} = 0$$

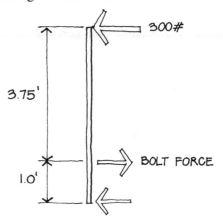

The internal force in brace 1 acts toward the upper left joint, which would mean that the brace is in compression. But the braces can only resist tension, not compression. Therefore, brace 1 is ineffective in resisting wind load applied to the right and has zero internal force.

$$10 - F_{1H} - F_{2H} = 0$$

$$10 - 0 - F_{2H} = 0$$

$$F_{2H} = 10$$

Stated in words, the horizontal component of the force in brace 2 is 10 kips. The internal force in brace 2 has the same relationship to its horizontal component as the length of brace 2 has to its horizontal projection.

The length of brace 2 = $\sqrt{(20)^2 + (15)^2}$ = 25 feet, and its horizontal projection is 20 feet. Therefore, the internal force in brace 2 = (25/20) × 10 kips = 12.5 kips. Answer C is correct.

274. B.   In this problem, we first calculate the overturning moment caused by the wind loads, which is equal to the sum of the products of each wind load and its distance from the bottom of the wall. Thus, the overturning moment = 10,000 lbs. × (15 + 15) ft. + 20,000 lbs. × 15 ft. = 300,000 + 300,000 = 600,000 ft.-lbs. The dead load resisting moment is equal to the dead load multiplied by the distance from the point of application of the dead load to the end of the wall, or 60,000 lbs. × 15 ft. = 900,000 ft.-lbs. The factor of safety against overturning is equal to the dead load resisting moment divided by the overturning moment = 900,000 ÷ 600,000 = 1.5. This design is unsatisfactory, since the dead load resisting moment is required to be at least 1.67 times the wind overturning moment. The design would be satisfactory if the structure was adequately anchored to its support.

275. C.   The load applied to each vertical support is 50#/lin. ft. × 6′-0″ = 300#. We solve for the force in the upper bolt by taking moments about the lower bolt.

$$\Sigma M = 0$$

$$-300(3.75 + 1) + \text{Bolt force}(1) = 0$$

Bolt force = (300)(4.75)/1 = 1,425#

As the force in the bolt acts *away* from the vertical support, the bolt is in tension.

276. B.   One of the basic concepts in structures is that of equilibrium. For a body to be in equilibrium, it must have no unbalanced force or unbalanced moment acting on it (A and D are correct). C is also correct, because if the lines of action did not meet at a point, it would result in an unbalanced moment. B is the incorrect statement: if the forces acting on a body are balanced, this does not necessarily mean that the body is in equilibrium. The moments must also be balanced, or the body would rotate.

277. **D.**   Rather than trying to memorize a formula, it is probably easier to remember that the modulus of elasticity of a material is simply the unit stress divided by the unit strain. Unit stress = P/A = 75 kips/1.0 in.^{2} = 75 ksi. Unit strain = Δ/L = 0.03"/12" = 0.0025. The modulus of elasticity = 75/0.0025 = 30,000 ksi.

278. **C.**   An opening in a beam has the least effect on the beam's load-carrying capacity if it is located where both the shear and bending stresses are low. The shear stress is usually greatest at the supports (A and B) and least near midspan (C and D). Thus, considering shear stress, an opening at C or D would least affect the beam's load-carrying capacity. But at which of these two locations is the bending stress less critical? The compressive bending stress is greatest near the top edge, while the tensile bending stress is resisted by the reinforcing steel, which is close to the bottom edge (D). Therefore, the only location where both the shear and bending stresses are low is C.

279. **A.**   A post-and-beam system can only resist vertical loads (A). It cannot resist lateral loads either in its own plane (B) or perpendicular to its own plane (C). Some type of bracing must be provided to resist the lateral loads.

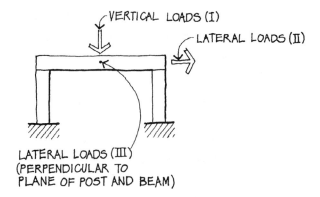

280. **D.**   The horizontal shear is transferred from the column to the footing by shear in the anchor bolts (correct answer D). The vertical load, not the horizontal shear, is transferred from the column to the footing by bearing of the base plate on the footing (A is incorrect). If there is movement in the column, it might be resisted by tension in the anchor bolts and bearing of the base plate on the footing (C is incorrect). Friction between the base plate and the footing is generally not considered to resist load (B is incorrect).

281. **B.**   Shear failure of a beam is most likely to occur where the vertical shear is maximum, which is adjacent to the supports (II is correct, I is incorrect). Horizontal shear stress in a beam varies from zero at the outermost fibers to a maximum value at the mid-depth of the beam (III is correct, IV is incorrect). Because only II and III are correct, the answer is B.

282. **D.**   After the total seismic force acting on a building has been calculated, it must be distributed to the various levels of the structure. A portion of the force is considered concentrated at the top of the structure. In general, the shape of the distributed load is parabolic, as shown in answer choice D. If the weights of all the stories of a short, stiff building are the same, the seismic forces will be

distributed in the form of a triangle—zero at the base and maximum at the top—with a horizontal force applied to each level.

283. **D.**   The IBC earthquake regulations are intended to limit damage caused by ground shaking, but not by earth movement or soil liquefaction (A is incorrect). Answer B is also incorrect, since seismic design forces are expected to be exceeded in a major earthquake. While nonstructural elements must be adequately connected to minimize damage, they are not necessarily connected rigidly (C is incorrect). Sometimes, flexible connections that allow movement are used. Answer D is the correct statement; structures designed in accordance with the IBC are expected to survive a major earthquake, but with structural and nonstructural damage.

284. **B.**   The lateral load in this question acts to the right, and the horizontal reaction at each column base must therefore act to the left. Since the column bases are fixed, there is a moment at each base, which in this case is counterclockwise. The overturning moment causes a downward reaction at the left column and an upward reaction at the right column. These are summarized in the sketch below. If we draw the moment diagram on the compression side of each member, we will arrive at correct answer B. Answer A is incorrect because it shows no moment at the column bases, which is not possible since the bases are fixed. Answer C is arbitrary and incorrect, and D is incorrect because it shows (1) no moment in the middle column, and (2) parabolic moment diagrams for the beams, which would be correct for uniform vertical loads, but not for lateral loads.

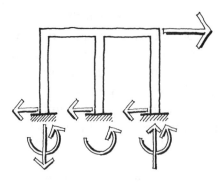

285. **C.**   In the seismic formula $V = C_S W$, V is the total lateral force or shear at the base; W is the total dead load; and C_S is the seismic response coefficient, which is equal to $S_{DS}/(R/I)$. Also, C_S need not exceed $S_{D1}/T(R/I)$. S_{DS} and S_{D1} are the short-period and one-second design accelerations that account for the seismic risk for the area and the soil characteristics at the site. I is the importance factor and is related to the occupancy of the building. T is the building's fundamental period of vibration. R is the response modification factor, determined by the type of lateral load resisting system used (correct answer C).

286. **B.**   The exam includes both numerical and conceptual questions, although there are usually more of the latter. This question tests your understanding of the concept of deflection. All beam deflection formulas are essentially in the form $\Sigma = KL^3/EI$, where K is a constant that depends on the load and the loading condition. Thus, to reduce the deflection, one must increase the moment of inertia I (correct answer B). A and D are incorrect because all steel, regardless of yield strength, has the same modulus of elasticity E. C is also incorrect: while a beam with a greater section modulus has a greater ability to resist flexural stress, it does not necessarily have a greater value of moment of inertia I.

287. A and B. Statements A and B are correct. Statement C is incorrect; the horizontal thrust at each end of a cable is inversely proportional to the sag of the cable. Thus, the greater the sag, the smaller the thrust.

288. C. Hooke's Law states that up to a certain unit stress, called the elastic limit, unit stress is directly proportional to unit strain. This constant ratio of unit stress to unit strain for a given material is called the modulus of elasticity (C) and is represented by the letter *E*.

289. A. Candidates should understand basic structural terminology. The stiffness of a member refers to its resistance to deformation (correct answer A). For a member with axial load, the stiffness is a function of the modulus of elasticity E of the material and the cross-sectional area A of the member. For a flexural member, the stiffness refers to its resistance to deflection and depends on E and on the moment of inertia I of the member.

290. B. Simple beams differ from continuous beams in a number of ways: the maximum positive moment in the simple beam is greater (A), the maximum deflection of the simple beam is greater (C), and the continuous beam has negative moment over its interior supports, while the simple beam never has any negative moment (D). Thus, A, C, and D are all correct statements. B is the incorrect statement we are looking for: the maximum shear in the simple beam is wL/2, which is less than that in the continuous beam, which is 5wL/8.

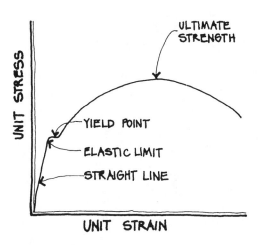

291. Elastic limit. Candidates should have some familiarity with typical stress-strain diagrams, such as that shown in the right column, for steel in tension. The elastic limit is defined as the maximum unit stress that can be developed in a material without causing permanent deformation when the stress is released.

292. Counterfort wall. A retaining wall consisting of a vertical stem supported at intervals on the back side by triangular buttresses connected to the base is called a counterfort wall. Other types of retaining walls include gravity walls, crib walls, and cantilever walls. Candidates should be able to identify all of these structures.

293. D. Exam questions often test candidates' understanding of how structures respond to load. In this case, the pressure of the retained earth against the wall varies from zero at the top to a maximum at the bottom, which causes the wall to cantilever off its footing. The soil pressure under the footing varies from a maximum under the toe to a minimum under the heel. The resulting distortions and stresses are shown on the next page.

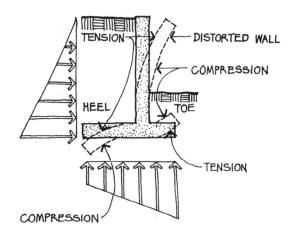

TENSION — DISTORTED WALL

COMPRESSION

HEEL   TOE

TENSION

COMPRESSION

294. D. This question tests conceptual knowledge regarding space frames and trusses. Space frames are stiffer than one-way trusses (C), and their two-way action permits them to be shallower than trusses (A). Trusses act independently of each other (B), while a space frame acts more or less as one integral system. Trusses are statically determinate, while space frames are highly indeterminate. Answer D is the incorrect statement and therefore the answer to this question.

295. C. Re-entrant corners, such as those in plans II, III, and IV, should be avoided if possible, since these are points of high stress concentration under seismic loading. There are two ways to strengthen re-entrant corners: adding drag struts or providing seismic separations. Plan I is square, which is ideal for seismic resistance.

296. B. In answering this question, we first review a few basic definitions and formulas. Unit stress is equal to axial load P divided by cross-sectional area A, or P/A. Unit strain is equal to total strain Δ divided by length L, or Δ/L. Modulus of elasticity E is equal to unit stress divided by unit strain, or $E = (P/A) \div (\Delta/L) = PL/A\Delta$. Transposing, $\Delta = PL/AE$. Thus, the change of length Δ is directly

proportional to the load P (I) and the length L (II) and inversely proportional to the cross-sectional area A (IV) and the modulus of elasticity E (V). The moment of inertia (III) does not affect the change of length. B is therefore the correct answer.

297. B. The flexural stress in a rectangular beam varies from a maximum value at the outer fibers to zero at the neutral axis, as shown in answer A. The shear stress varies parabolically, from zero at the outer fibers to a maximum value at the neutral axis, as shown in correct answer B. Answers C and D are arbitrary diagrams.

298. D. A three-hinged gabled frame has a hinge at the center and at each support and is statically determinate (A is correct). The hinges at the supports permit rotation (B is correct), and the hinge at the center also permits rotation, which prevents any moment from being developed at the center (C is correct). D is the incorrect statement and is therefore the answer to this question: the maximum moment does occur at the intersection of the column and the sloping beam, but this moment is generally less than in a rectangular rigid frame.

299. C. In general, the distribution of lateral seismic forces to building levels is parabolic in shape, with the force being zero at the base and maximum at the top of the building. C is the correct answer. For relatively short, stiff buildings with natural periods less than 0.5 seconds and with equal weights at each floor level, the distribution is essentially in the form of a triangle, with the force being zero at the base and maximum at the top level. Answer A shows the distribution of wind—not seismic—pressure. B shows a uniform distribution, such as the wind pressure on a leeward wall. Answer D shows pressure increasing uniformly from top to bottom, such as soil pressure acting on a retaining wall.

300. **B.** Structures must be designed to resist seismic forces coming from any horizontal direction (B is correct, C is incorrect). The vertical earthquake motions are not usually considered in design because they are generally smaller than the horizontal. Also, buildings usually have excess strength in the vertical direction since they are basically designed for vertical gravity loads. Structures must be designed to resist seismic forces, regardless of their Seismic Design Category (A is incorrect). Not all structures must always be designed for seismic forces acting concurrently in the direction of each principle axis of the structure (D is incorrect). Seismic forces acting at the same time must be considered only for certain structures assigned to SDC C and higher.

301. **A.** A parallel chord truss is analogous to a steel beam: the truss chords are like the beam's flanges, while the truss web members are similar to the beam's web. Just as the beam flange forces increase toward the center of the span, the forces in the truss chords increase toward the center of the span. And just as the shear in the beam web decreases toward the center of the span, similarly the forces in the truss web members decrease toward the center of the span. A is therefore the correct answer.

302. **D.** Exam questions sometimes test candidates' understanding of the economics of various structural systems and components. This is that kind of question. The connections used in structural steel systems comprise a significant part of the cost of these systems, and can even influence the type of structural steel system selected (A is correct). It is true that fillet welds are usually more economical than full penetration welds (B is correct). Shop connections are usually preferred over field connections because they are less costly (C is correct). In addition, good quality control is easier to achieve in the shop than in the field. Depending on the circumstances, welded connections are not necessarily more economical than bolted connections. D is therefore the incorrect statement.

303. **B.** This can be a troublesome question because the choices are similar, but have subtle differences. When a rigid frame supports a uniform vertical load, the horizontal member deflects downward, as in choices A, B, and C. D is the shape of the deflected frame when it resists a lateral load, such as wind or earthquake, and is therefore incorrect. C is the deflected shape of a simple beam supported by columns, not a rigid frame, and is therefore incorrect. A is the deflected shape of a rigid frame with hinged bases, not fixed (note that the column bases are rotated, not vertical). B is similar to A, but note that the bottoms of the columns are vertical where they meet the ground, which indicates a fixed condition. B is therefore the correct choice.

304. **B.** The retaining walls illustrated are all cantilever walls, which resist the lateral soil pressure by bending. The reinforcing steel must be placed in the tension side of the wall, which is the face closest to the retained earth. Thus, the wall reinforcing is correctly located in all of the illustrations, except B. C has reinforcing in both faces, which may be required

in some situations. The bottom of the footing is in tension at the toe, while the top is in tension at the heel. Thus, all four cases show the footing reinforcing steel correctly.

305. C. Generally, rock is the best bearing material, followed by sands and gravels (I and II). Fine-grained soils, such as silts and clays, are usually adequate to support building foundations (III), but may require investigation. However, organic soils, such as peat (IV), are usually unacceptable for the support of buildings.

306. A. The pressure of the retained earth against a retaining wall varies linearly, from zero at the top to a maximum value at the bottom, as shown in A, B, and C. The bearing pressure under the base is maximum under the toe and minimum under the heel, as shown in A and D. Only A shows the correct pressure diagrams for both the stem and base.

307. A and D. Design wind pressures for each element of a structure are determined from various code tables and charts. However, even without referring to any code, it should be obvious that the wind causes a direct, inward pressure as it is stopped by the windward side of the building (A). Somewhat less obvious is the fact that the wind acts outward on the leeward side (D), creating negative pressure or suction.

308. D. In the equation of the velocity pressure q, the coefficient K_z is the velocity pressure exposure coefficient, which is a function of exposure and height (answer choice A). G is the gust factor in the basic formula for design wind pressure, which is $p = qGC_p - q_i(GC_{pi})$ (answer choice B). Figure 1609 in the IBC shows very high basic wind

speeds in areas subject to hurricanes, such as the Gulf Coast (answer choice C). Only tornadoes (answer choice D) are not considered in the IBC wind design provisions.

309. B. In this question, you should know the wind pressure formula $p = qGC_p$, ignoring internal pressure. Since the values of all the factors are given, it's simple to multiply them to obtain the wind pressure. Thus, $p = 17.3 \times 0.85 \times 0.8 = 11.8$ pounds per square foot.

310. D. The wind pressures used in the design of buildings in accordance with the IBC take into account the high wind speeds of hurricanes (A is correct). The wind pressure is greater for buildings on flat, open terrain than on terrain with buildings or surface irregularities close to the site (B is correct). Answer C is also correct; as the height increases, the wind pressure increases. Answer D is the incorrect statement we are looking for, because wind pressure acts inward on windward walls, but outward on leeward walls.

311. B. Candidates should be aware that this kind of question has appeared on the exams before, and therefore might appear again. According to the Building Code Requirements for Reinforced Concrete (ACI 318), which has been incorporated into many building codes, the minimum concrete coverages are 3″ for footings cast against earth (correct answer B).

312. C. The answer is I, II, and IV. Live load is the load superimposed by the use and occupancy of the building, such as furniture (III), and does not include wind load, snow load, earthquake load, or dead load. (I, II, and IV are not live load.)

313. B. The answer is 150 kips. To solve this problem, we use Table 10-1 from the AISC Manual of Steel Construction (see page 103). Using the upper portion of the table, the bolt and angle available strength is equal to 165 kips for 5-7/8 inch ASTM A325-X bolts (threads excluded from shear plane) and a ½ inch angle thickness. From the lower portion of the table, the beam web available strength is equal to 341 kips per inch of thickness for an uncoped beam. For the 0.44 inch web thickness of the W24 × 76 beam, the web available strength is equal to $341 \times 0.44 = 150$ kips. This is the governing value, as it is less than the allowable load in shear of 165 kips. The allowable load on the connection is therefore 150 kips.

314. A. When the use or occupancy of a building changes, the building must comply with all building code regulations for the new use, including live load requirements (A). The new use is not required to be less hazardous than the existing use (B is incorrect); in fact, it can even be more hazardous, provided that the building complies with the code regulations for the greater hazard. C is obviously incorrect, as an architect has no proprietary interest in a building after its completion. D is also incorrect; the structural design of the building would be checked only if the new use has more severe requirements than the existing use.

315. B. The staggered truss system (correct answer B) consists of story-high trusses spanning transversely between exterior columns and arranged in a staggered pattern. It is often an efficient and economical structural system for high-rise apartment buildings.

316. C. The ideal steel column to resist buckling is one whose radius of gyration r is the same in both directions, such as a pipe column or tubular section, rather than a wide flange section (C is correct). All the other statements are incorrect. The buckling tendency of a steel column depends on its end conditions, its length, and its radius of gyration, not on its yield point (A). The maximum allowable slenderness ratio Kl/r is 200, not 50 (B). And if the value of r is different in each direction, as with a wide flange section, the lower value is used to compute Kl/r (D).

317. B. Using the upper portion of Table 10-1 on page 103, the bolt and angle available strength is equal to 144 kips for 5-7/8 inch ASTM A325-N bolts and a 1/2-inch angle thickness. We can determine the beam web available strength from the lower portion of the table. Since we are not given any information on the size of the cope at the top of the beam, let's assume a 3″ by 1-3/4″ cope. The beam web available strength for this cope size is equal to 237 kips per inch of thickness. For the 0.44 inch web thickness of the W24 × 76 beam, the web available strength is equal to $237 \times 0.44 = 104.3$ kips. This is the governing value, as it is less than the allowable load in shear of 144 kips. The allowable load on the connection is therefore 104.3 kips.

318. D. Exam questions involving trusses may be conceptual, or they may require calculations, as in this question. We first determine the value of each reaction. By symmetry, each reaction is equal to one-half of the total load on the truss = $(10 + 10 + 10 + 10 + 10) \div 2 = 25$ kips. We next cut a section through the truss panel that contains member a, as shown, assuming member *a* to be stressed in tension (pulling away from the joint).

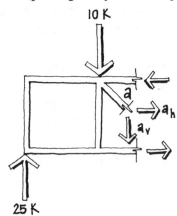

$\Sigma V = 0$

$+ 25 \text{ kips} - 10 \text{ kips} - a_v = 0$

$a_v = +15 \text{ kips}$

Since member *a* is inclined at 45°,

$a_h = a_v = +15 \text{ kips.}$

Therefore, the internal axial force in member $a = \sqrt{15^2 + 15^2} = 21.2 \text{ kips.}$ Since we assumed member *a* to be in tension, and the sign of its internal force comes out positive, our assumption is correct and member *a* is in tension (D is correct).

319. **C.**   All of the factors shown affect the wind design. Although wind codes vary, the design wind pressure generally depends on the wind speed (I) and the exposure of the building, which is partially a function of the terrain (III). Certain essential, hazardous, or assembly buildings are designed for increased wind pressures (II), and the building's size and shape (IV) determine the total wind force.

320. **C.**   The north and south walls are 100 feet long, while the east and west walls are 50 feet long. Therefore, the wall surface area subject to north-south wind is twice as great ($100 \div 50$) as that subject to

east-west wind. Hence, the total wind load in the north-south direction is twice as great as in the east-west direction (correct answer C). Incidentally, the gust factor in choice D depends only on the building's height and exposure, not on the wind direction.

321. **C.**   In the tubular concept, the entire structure acts like an immense, hollow, tubular column that cantilevers from its foundation under the action of wind loads. The Sears Tower in Chicago consists of nine tubes (a "bundle"), each 75 feet square, placed next to each other to form a pattern of three squares in each direction. The tubes end at varying heights.

322. **B.**   We solve for R_2 by taking moments about R_1.

10 kips(4 ft.) + 10 kips(20 + 10) ft.
$\times R_2(20 \text{ ft.}) = 0$
$40 + 300 = 20R_2$
$R_2 = 340/20 = 17.0 \text{ kips}$
$\Sigma V = 0$
$R_1 + R_2 - 10 - 10 = 0$
$R_1 = 10 + 10 - R_2 = 10 + 10 - 17 = 3.0$
kips.

323. **C.**   The section modulus of a beam (S), which is expressed in inches[3], is equal to the moment of inertia (I) divided by the distance from the neutral axis to the outermost fiber (*c*). Thus, S = I/*c*.

324. **D.**   In a beam, the material close to the outermost fibers is highly stressed in flexure, while the material close to the neutral axis is understressed. By concentrating most of the beam's material toward the outer fibers and away from the neutral axis, as in a wide flange section, we obtain a very efficient bending member.

325. B. The first step is to calculate the value of the left reaction by taking moments about the right end.

R_L(20 ft.) − (1 kip/ft.)(20 ft.)(20 ft./2)
−10 kips (6 ft.) − 15 kips(16 ft.) = 0

$20R_L$ = 200 + 60 + 240

R_L = 500/20 = 25 kips

The shear at section $x - x$ = +25.0 − 15.0 −1(9) = 1 kip, or 1,000#. It may be helpful to study the shear diagram for this beam, which is shown below.

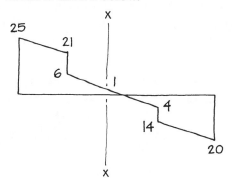

326. C. One way to solve this problem is to determine the loading on the beam. Let's look at the shear diagram again.

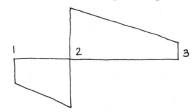

At point 1, the shear is negative, which corresponds to a downward vertical load. From 1 to 2, the shear diagram is a sloping line, which signifies a uniform load. At point 2, the shear changes from negative to positive, corresponding to an upward reaction. From 2 to 3, the shear diagram slopes the same as 1 to 2, and so we know that the uniform load is the same as from 1 to 2. At point 3, the shear is positive, which corresponds to a downward reaction. We can now draw the loading diagram.

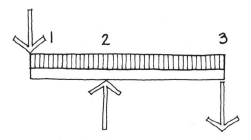

At 1, there is zero moment. From 1 to 2, there is negative moment, whose value increases to a maximum at support 2. From 2 to 3, the negative moment decreases and becomes zero at 3. C is therefore the correct moment diagram. Although D has the correct shape, it is incorrect because it shows positive moment in span 2–3.

327. C. The John Hancock Center's huge diagonal bracing was designed to resist wind loads and is visible on the exterior of the building. This makes the building one of the most recognizable landmarks in Chicago.

328. D. Because a steel rod can only resist tension, rod a is effective, and rod b has no internal force. Isolating the upper right joint, and applying the equation $\Sigma H = 0$.

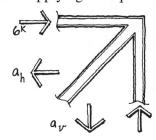

$6 - a_h = 0$

a_h = 6 kips

The ratio of a_v to a_h is the same as the ratio of the vertical projection of the length of rod a to its horizontal projection, or
$\dfrac{a_v}{a_h} = \dfrac{16}{12}$

$$a_v = \frac{16}{12} a_h = \frac{16}{12}(6) = 8k$$

The force in rod a = $\sqrt{\left(a_h\right)^2 + \left(a_v\right)^2}$ = $\sqrt{(6)^2 + (8)^2}$ = 10 kips tension (answer D).

329. C. The total wind force on the sign is equal to the design wind pressure multiplied by the area of the sign = 12.74 × 5 × 15 = 955.5 lbs. This force effectively acts at the center of the sign, which is located at (20 + 5/2) = 22.5 feet above the ground. The overturning moment is equal to 955.5 × 22.5 = 21,499 ft.-lbs.

330. D. A braced frame is essentially a vertical truss that resists horizontal loads. We cut a section through the brace, as shown.

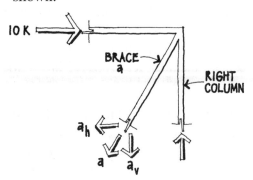

Assume that the brace is stressed in tension (acting away from the upper right joint).

$\Sigma H = 0$

$+ 10 - a_h = 0$

$a_h = +10$ kips

Because the answer comes out positive, our assumption that the brace is in tension is correct. The brace has a horizontal projection of 12 feet and a vertical projection of 16 feet. Therefore, its length $= \sqrt{12^2 + 16^2} = 20$. The force in the brace = (20/12) × 10 kips = 16.7 kips tension (correct answer D).

331. D. Since the area of the sign = 10 ft. × 30 ft. = 300 sq.ft., the total wind force = 16.8 psf × 300 sq.ft. = 5,040# (answer D).

332. D. The terrain surrounding a building has a great effect on the wind speed, and therefore, the wind pressure. If the surrounding area is built up with buildings or other features, the resulting turbulence reduces the wind velocity and pressure (I is correct). On the other hand, buildings on open sites, such as those facing large bodies of water, must bear the full brunt of the wind and thus have greater pressures (II is correct). The size and shape of a building can also affect wind pressures as narrow buildings allow the wind to flow around them while wide buildings block more of the wind, resulting in high pressures (III is correct). Finally, friction between the wind and the found causes wind velocity, and thus the pressure, to decrease close to the ground and, conversely, to increase as the height increases (IV is correct).

333. D. In this problem, we must determine the magnitude of the horizontal thrust. Taking moments about the crown,

VL/2 − (wL/2)(L/4) − Hh = 0
Hh = (wL/2)(L/2) − wL²/8 = wL²/8
H = wL²/8h
Therefore, if w and h remain the same, but L becomes 2L, the new value of H = w (2L)²/8h = 4wL²/8h, which is 4 times the original value of H.

334. A. Shear stress in a rectangular homogeneous beam varies parabolically, from zero at the top and bottom fibers to a maximum value at the neutral axis.

335. A. One of the factors in seismic design is the importance factor I, which is equal to 1.0 for the standard occupancy structures. For essential facilities, such as fire or police stations, I increases to 1.5 for seismic design (A is correct). Thus, fire or police stations are designed for 50 percent more seismic load than standard occupancy structures.

336. C. The answer is *II and III.* An open-front building tends to have high torsional stresses during and earthquake because the rear wall, which usually has minimal openings, is very stiff, while the open front is very flexible. One solution is to make the front wall approximately as stiff as the rear wall, as in choices II and III. Choice I is irrelevant, since it does not address the problem caused by the great difference of stiffness between the front and rear walls.

337. A. Retrofitting older buildings to improve their seismic performance has become a major concern to architects in earthquake-prone areas. As with new buildings, the primary objective is to provide for life safety by minimizing the likelihood of collapse. In this regard, the elements of older buildings that are most vulnerable are unreinforced masonry walls.

338. C. Truss I is a Vierendeel truss, which is actually a type of rigid frame, while truss II is a typical triangulated truss. For the same load, span, and depth, the axial stresses in the chords of both trusses are equal (A is incorrect). The absence of diagonals in truss I does not cause instability (B is incorrect), but it does require the chords to resist shear, which results in bending moments in the chords. The verticals are also subject to bending moments (C is correct). Vierendeel trusses also tend to have high deflection (D is incorrect).

339. A. A Vierendeel truss has no diagonals. Therefore, the web is unencumbered (I) and the joints have a simple appearance (II). However, Vierendeel trusses tend to have high deflection (III is incorrect). Also, as the members must be adequate to resist both bending moment and direct stress, a Vierendeel truss requires much more material than a triangulated truss (IV is incorrect).

340. D. In the stub girder system, steel floor beams sit on top of a stub girder, instead of framing into a girder. Because the beams are clear of the girder, they may be designed for simulated continuity (IV). The space between floor beams can be used for the mechanical and electrical distribution systems. Short lengths of filler beams the same depth as the floor beams are welded to the top of the stub girder to provide a connection between the girder and the slab for composite action. The main advantages of the stub girder system are reduced weight of steel (I), reduced story height (II), and simplified steel erection (III).

341. A. A flat slab is a two-way concrete slab supported directly by columns, without the use of beams or girders. In this system, a portion of the slab at the columns is thickened, which is termed a drop panel. The tops of the columns are flared, and these are known as column capitals. Both drop panels and column capitals are used to reduce shear stress in the slab near the columns and to provide greater effective depth for negative bending moment.

342. C. In the staggered truss system, story-high trusses spanning the full width of the building are arranged in a staggered pattern: trusses in the odd-numbered column lines are erected in a given story, while those in the even-numbered column lines are in the stories above and below. Thus, the floor system is supported alternately by the top chord of one truss and the bottom chord of the next. This provides an efficient framing system for the tall, narrow buildings typically used for hotel and residential occupancies (III is correct). The staggered truss system is not generally economical for buildings of less than 8 or 10 stories (II is incorrect). Similarly, the system is usually not efficient for spans less than about 45 feet (I is correct).

343. **D.** Because the allowable compressive stress depends on the slenderness ratio KL/r, the section with the greatest value of r will have the greatest allowable compressive stress. Closed sections, such as pipes and steel tubes, usually have greater r values than wide flange sections (B) or sections built up from angles (A and C). Note that in the slenderness ratio KL/r, we always use the least value of r if the value is different in each direction.

344. **B.** This question tests your ability to use bolt tables in the AISC Manual. The bolts have one value in shear and a different value in bearing, and the lower of these two values governs. Because there are two angles, the bolts are in double shear. From Table 7-1 on page 100, each bolt has an allowable load in shear of 18.6 kips. From Tables 7-5 and 7-6 on pages 101–102, each bolt has an allowable load in bearing on the 3/8″ plate of at least $(3/8) \times 52.2 = 19.6$ kips. The shear value governs, as it is lower. The number of bolts required is 50 kips/19.6 kips per bolt = 2.55; therefore we require 3 bolts.

345. **D.** The height limits for a building assigned to SDC D are tabulated in ASCE 7-05 and vary from 35 feet to no limit, depending on the lateral load resisting system used for the building. The maximum allowable height is therefore unlimited (correct answer D).

346. **A.** This question tests your understanding of the quantities that make up the basic seismic formula $V = C_S W$. The quantity C_S is equal to $S_{DS}I/R$, not to exceed $S_{D1}I/TR$. W is the total dead load. The quantity S_{DS} is the short-period design acceleration, S_{D1} is the one-second period design acceleration (B is incorrect), I is the importance factor (C is incorrect). T is the fundamental period of the building, and R is the response modification factor, which is determined by the type of lateral load resisting system (D is incorrect). A is the correct answer.

347. **C.** All buildings, including those assigned to SDC D and higher, must be designed for either wind or earthquake, whichever governs, but not both acting at the same time (C is correct, A and B are incorrect). Answer D is incorrect because many different types of lateral load resisting systems may be used in buildings assigned to SDC D and higher, not limited to special moment-resisting frames.

348. **B.** In this problem, you must solve for the base shear V, which is equal to $C_S W$. First we compute $C_S = S_{DS}/(R/I)$ where I = 1.0 because this is not a high-occupancy, essential, or hazardous facility. Thus, $C_S = 0.45 \times 1.0/6 = 0.075$. Also, C_S need not exceed $S_{D1}/T(R/I) = (0.27 \times 1.0)/(2.0 \times 6) = 0.023$. Minimum $C_S = 0.01$. Therefore, $V = 0.023 \times 5000 = 115$ kips (correct answer B).

349. C. The deflected shape of a beam is always a curve. B and D are composed of straight lines and are therefore incorrect. A shows the deflected shape for a simple beam. The beam in this question has fixed ends, which means that the ends are restrained against rotation, as shown in correct answer C.

350. B. A three-hinged arch is statically determinate; that is, its reactions can be computed using only the basic equations of equilibrium. The supports of a three-hinged arch permit rotation, while those of a fixed arch do not. Fixed arches are therefore stiffer than hinged arches (A is incorrect). Three-hinged arches are able to resist horizontal loads (C is incorrect), and can have a variety of profiles, not limited to semicircular shapes (D is incorrect).

351. C. The structural divisions of the exam invariably include a number of questions on architectural history, such as this one. One of the features of Byzantine architecture was the dome, which, during the later Renaissance period, was sometimes raised on a drum and surmounted by a lantern. The transition from the round dome or drum to the square base was effected by spherical pendentives, triangular in form, which rested on pillars at the four corners of the space below. See the illustration in the top right-hand corner of this page.

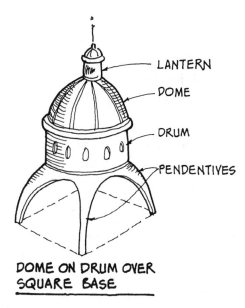

DOME ON DRUM OVER SQUARE BASE

352. D. The campanile of the Cathedral of Pisa, better known as the Leaning Tower of Pisa, is probably the world's most famous example of differential settlement (II). The tilting began during the tower's construction (I) and continues to this day; its top is now out of plumb by 16 feet, not 16 inches (III is incorrect). The tilt of the tower cannot be blamed on its structure; it is an elegant piece of architecture, consisting of a cylindrical core surrounded by marble columns that form a balanced, symmetrical design.

353. B. Pier Luigi Nervi was one of the giants of 20th-century architecture and engineering. Although trained as an engineer, his aesthetic sense and design vision led him to design structures of exceptional beauty. He was the first designer to successfully use ferrocement (A), a combination of steel mesh and cement mortar. His concrete lamella roofs (C), such as the airplane hangar roofs he built during the 1940s, were among the largest and most elegant roofs of this kind ever built. For the Borgo paper plant, Nervi designed a roof that hung from the cables of a suspension bridge (D).

However, Nervi is not associated with the tubular frame (B), a concept used by Fazlur Khan and others in the design of very tall buildings.

354. C.   In buildings with rigid diaphragms, which are usually concrete or steel, the lateral wind or earthquake loads are distributed to the vertical resisting elements in proportion to their relative rigidities (A). In other words, rigid elements resist more load than flexible elements. Shear walls are the most rigid elements, followed by braced frames and then moment-resisting frames. In this question, since the shear walls are all the same thickness, the longest wall, on line 3, is the most rigid, and will therefore resist the greatest amount of lateral load. The shear wall on line A, although very rigid, will only resist lateral load in the east-west direction.

355. A.   Anchor bolts (I) and bracing (II) may be used to resist seismic forces. However, because of possible vertical seismic accelerations and other reasons, friction resulting from gravity loads may not be used to resist seismic forces.

356. A, C, and D.   All of the provided answers are correct except B. Moment-resisting frames have great ductility (A), that is, they are able to absorb a large amount of energy by deforming in the inelastic range when the material is stressed above its yield point, without failure. Because of this ability, they usually are designed for smaller seismic loads than other systems (D). Since they absorb energy by inelastic deformation, they tend to deflect more, not less, than other systems (B is incorrect).

357. C.   The horizontal seismic force on a parapet is equal to

$$\frac{0.4 a_p S_{DS} W_p}{\left(\dfrac{R_p}{I_p}\right)}\left(1+2\frac{z}{h}\right)$$

where (from ASCE 7 Table 13.5-1) a_p = 2.5 and R_p = 2.5 for a cantilevered parapet wall that is braced to the structural frame below its center of mass. Also, I_p, the importance factor, is equal to 1.0 since this office building is not high occupancy, essential, or hazardous. Since the parapet is at the roof of the building, z/h = 1.0. The weight of the parapet (W_p) is given as 100 pounds per square foot. Thus, with S_{DS} = 0.29g,

$$\frac{0.4 \times 2.5 \times 0.29 \times 100}{\left(\dfrac{2.5}{1.0}\right)}(1+2)=35$$

pounds per square foot. Maximum F_p = $1.6 S_{DS} I_p W_p$ = 1.6 × 0.29 × 1.0 × 100 = 46 pounds per square foot, and minimum F_p = $0.3 S_{DS} I_p W_p$ = 0.3 × 0.29 × 1.0 × 100 = 9 pounds per square foot. The horizontal force is therefore 35 × 4 = 140 pounds (answer C).

358. D.   Candidates should have some knowledge concerning the efficiency, economy, and appropriateness of various structural systems and components. In general, we try to keep everything as simple, regular, and conventional as possible. For example, as moment or rigid connections are more expensive than simple or shear connections, the number of moment connections should be kept to a minimum (I is incorrect). Rolled sections should be used wherever possible; while the use of built-up sections may save weight, the additional labor cost often results in a higher in-place cost (II is incorrect). III is also incorrect; high-strength steel is stronger than ASTM A36 steel, but it is also more costly and therefore not always the more economical choice for connection members. IV is the only correct statement (D is correct). Most steel floor decking today is composite because it is more economical than non-composite decking.

359. D. In the post-and-beam, the maximum moment in the beam is equal to $wL^2/8$ and there is no moment in the columns. In the rigid frame, the beam ends are restrained by the columns, which reduces the maximum moment in the beam (II) and results in moment in the columns (I). The axial force in the columns is the same for both the rigid frame and the post-and-beam (III). The column bases of the rigid frame have a horizontal reaction, which the column bases of the post-and-beam do not (IV). Because all four statements are correct, the answer is D.

360. A. All structures tend to expand when the temperature increases and contract when the temperature decreases. As the bottom of a dome is prevented by its foundation from expanding and moving outward when the temperature rises, the only way the dome can expand is to move upward (correct answer A).

361. C. Studies have shown that the optimum bay shape for steel framing is rectangular with a length-to-width ratio of about 1.3 (A and D are incorrect). The beams should preferably span in the long direction and the girders in the short direction (C is correct, B is incorrect).

362. Rigid frame. A rigid frame is a frame with rigid joints capable of resisting moment. In contrast, a frame with diagonal braces (A) is a braced frame.

363. D. The lateral load will be distributed to the four piers in proportion to their rigidities (rigidity is resistance to deflection). The rigidity of a pier depends on its height-to-depth ration, where the height is that of the smaller adjacent opening and the depth is the pier dimension parallel to the length of the wall. Because all four piers have the same height (six feet), their rigidities depend only on their depths: the deeper the pier, the greater the rigidity. Piers 1 and 4 are five feet deep and therefore less rigid than piers 2 and 3, which are eight feet deep. Consequently, piers 2 and 3 resist more lateral load than piers 1 and 4 (D is correct).

364. A. The answer is *The ability of a structure to redistribute seismic loads to other elements, if a particular element fails or is damaged.* If a particular element of a building's lateral load resisting system should fail or be damaged during an earthquake, it is very desirable that the seismic load be redistributed to other elements and thereby avoid collapse. This is called redundancy and can be provided in various ways, including the use of multiple lines of resistance rather than a single line, and multiple bents in each line of bracing rather than a single bent. The use of two systems (incorrect choice B) results in a specific type of lateral load resisting system, called a dual system.

365. D. The intensity of an earthquake is measured by the Modified Mercalli scale (A is incorrect), while the Richter scale measures the amount of energy released in an earthquake (correct answer D). Neither scale measures duration or frequency (B and C).

366. B.   Because the columns have the same length and cross section, their rigidities are equal. Therefore, each column resists one-half of the lateral load = 24 kips / 2 = 12 kips. The maximum column moment occurs at the beam-column joint and is equal to 12 kips × 15 feet = 180 ft.-kips. We take moments about either base to determine the vertical reaction, which is resisted by the internal force in the column.

$\Sigma M = 0$

$(24 \text{ kips} \times 15 \text{ ft.}) - R(25 \text{ ft.}) = 0$

$R = 360/25 = 14.4 \text{ kips}$

The frame reactions and moment diagram are shown below.

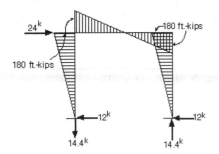

367. D.   Drift is the lateral deflection of a structure caused by seismic or wind loads. Although it is not possible to design a building to have zero drift (A is incorrect), the amount of drift is limited in order to insure structural integrity, minimize discomfort to the building's occupants, and restrict damage to brittle nonstructural elements (D is correct and C is incorrect). The actual displacement of a structure is expected to be much greater than that calculated based on the design seismic forces because it is anticipated that the structure will behave inelastically when subject to major earthquake ground motions (B is incorrect).

368. D.   It is practically impossible to make butt joints sufficiently strong or permanent to adequately join laminations end to end. Instead, scarf joints (I and II), finger joints (III), or other similar joints must be used (D is correct).

369. B.   The flat slab floor system is a two-way reinforced concrete system that is supported directly on the columns, generally without any beams or girders. A and D are therefore correct statements. The flat slab system is usually economical for heavy loads, as in warehouses (C is correct). B is incorrect and is therefore the answer to this question; flat slabs are relatively thin and are therefore not economical in reinforcing steel.

370. C.   Candidates should be able to determine the shears and moments in a simple beam subject to any type of loading, as in this question. We first calculate the left reaction by taking moments about the right end.

$\Sigma M = 0$

$-1.0(20)(20/2) - 20(6) - 10(8 + 6) + R_L(20) = 0$

$R_L = (200 + 120 + 140)/20 = 460/20$

$= 23.0 \text{ kips}$

We next determine the point of zero shear.

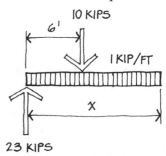

$+23.0 - 10.0 - 1.0(x) = 0$

$x = (23.0 - 10.0)/1.0 = 13.0 \text{ ft.}$

Finally, because we know that the moment is maximum where the shear is zero, we calculate the moment at that point.

M = +23.0(13.0) − 1.0(13.0)(13.0/2) −10.0(13.0 − 6.0) = 299.0 − 84.5 − 70

= 144.5 ft.-kips

371. D.   This is a very simple problem, particularly as we're given the formula I = bd^3/12. In the formula, b = width = 4″ and d = depth = 12″. Thus, I = 4(12)³/12 = 576 in.⁴

372. C.   Dead load is the vertical load due to the weight of all permanent structural and nonstructural components of a building. Live load is the vertical load caused by the use and occupancy of a building, not including wind, earthquake, or dead loads. Building structures must be designed to resist various combinations of loads, the most basic of which is dead load plus live load.

373. A.   This problem involves a two-step solution. First, the beam is considered to expand freely due to the temperature change, and the amount of this expansion is calculated. Second, because the beam cannot expand, we calculate how much compressive stress is required to push the beam back to its original length. Expansion due to temperature change = coefficient of expansion × length × temperature change = (6.5×10^{-6}) × (24 × 12) × (100 − 40) = 0.11232″. (Note that we multiply the length of 24 feet by 12 to convert it to inches.) How much compressive stress is needed to push the beam back to its original length, that is, to shorten it 0.11232″? Unit stress divided by unit strain = modulus of elasticity E, or (P/A) ÷ (Δ/L) = E, or P/A = EΔ/L = (29×10^6) × (0.11232)/24 × 12 = 11,310 psi compression.

374. B.   The connection shown is a seated beam connection, in which the load is transferred from the beam to seat angle B by bearing, and then through bolts F to the column. Bolts E connect the beam to the seat angle, but do not resist any calculated load. Top angle A and bolts C and D serve to stabilize the beam, not support it.

375. A.   Here we have a typical moment connection, as might be used in a rigid frame. The beam moment is basically resisted by the flanges, while the shear is resisted by the web. Therefore, the moment is transferred to the column by the flange plates, which are welded to the column and bolted to the beam flanges. The shear is transferred to the column by the web plate, which is welded to the column and bolted to the beam web.

376. B and C.   Questions about structural costs sometimes appear on the exam. A is incorrect: moment connections are more expensive than nonmoment or simple connections, and should therefore be used only when necessary. B is correct; rolled sections should be used whenever possible, as they are generally less expensive than built-up sections. For economy, a good rule is to use as few members as possible (C is correct). High-strength steel has a higher unit cost than conventional A992 steel, and therefore its use is not generally economical except for highly stressed members (D is incorrect).

377. B.   Every building has a natural or fundamental period of vibration, which is the time in seconds that it takes for the building to go through one complete back-and-forth motion when a horizontal load acts on it. A building with a long period, such as a tall building with moment-resisting frames, is flexible (I) and has relatively low seismic forces (IV). Conversely, a short-period building is stiff and has relatively high seismic forces.

378. D.   There are four basic types of structural systems used in seismic design. The bearing wall system (B) does not have a complete vertical load carrying frame; gravity loads are supported by bearing walls or bracing systems and lateral loads are resisted by shear walls or braced frames. The moment-resisting frame system (C) has an essentially complete frame supporting gravity loads and moment-resisting frames that resist lateral loads. The dual system (A) has an essentially complete frame that supports gravity loads and a combination of shear walls or braced frames plus moment-resisting frames which resist lateral loads. The problem statement correctly defines the building frame system (D).

379. D.   The Richter scale measures the magnitude of an earthquake, that is, the amount of energy it releases. The scale is logarithmic, with each number representing 10 times the ground motion, or about 33 times the energy of the lower number. Thus, the magnitude 8.0 earthquake release 33 times more energy than one of magnitude 7.0, about 1,000 times (33×33) more energy than one of magnitude 6.0, about 33,000 times more energy than one of magnitude 5.0, and about 1,000,000 times ($33,000 \times 33$) more energy than one of magnitude 4.0.

380. A.   Drift is the lateral deflection of a structure caused by seismic or wind load. The drift of a given story relative to the stories above and below is called story drift. The amount of drift is limited in order to insure structural integrity, minimize discomfort to the building's occupants, and restrict damage to brittle nonstructural elements.

381. B.   A hinge or pin is free to rotate and therefore has no resistance to moment. Actual hinges or pins are rarely used in modern construction. However, a joint that has little moment resistance or restraint against rotation is generally considered to be a hinge or pin.

382. A.   In problems of this kind, we cut an imaginary section through the truss that cuts through the member whose internal force is to be determined. We then draw a free body diagram and apply the equations of equilibrium.

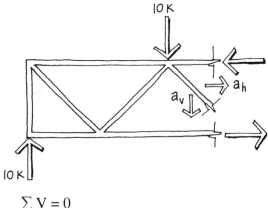

$$\sum V = 0$$

$$+10 - 10 - a_v = 0$$

$$a_v = 0$$

As the vertical component of the force in member a is zero, the force in member a must be zero.

383. B.   A cable is essentially the reverse of an arch: an arch is stressed principally in compression, while a cable is stressed in tension. But where arches almost always have some bending moment combined with compression, cables are too flexible to have any significant resistance to bending.

384. A.   In a simple beam, where is the bending moment, and hence the bending stress, maximum? It varies with the loading, but it is usually close to midspan (B and D are incorrect). Within the depth of the beam, the bending stress is maximum at the outer fibers (A is correct) and minimum at the neutral axis (C is incorrect). These concepts apply to beams of any material, and the fact that the beam in this question is a glulam is immaterial.

385. C.   To solve this problem, we resolve the 1,500# force acting at 45° with the horizontal into its horizontal and vertical components. Its horizontal component = 1,500 cos 45° = 1,500(.707) = 1,060.5# to the right, and its vertical component = 1,500 sin 45° = 1,500(.707) = 1,060.5# upward. The sum of the horizontal forces is 1,500# + 1,060.5# = 2,560.5# to the right. The only vertical force is 1,060.5# upward. The resultant is

$$\sqrt{2,560.5^2 + 1,060.5^2}$$

= 2,771#. Tan θ = 1,060.5/2,560.5 = 0.414, from which θ = 22.5°, as shown below. C is therefore the correct answer.

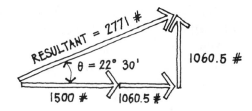

386. P-delta effect.   When lateral seismic forces act on a building, the stories deflect horizontally relative to each other. This story-to-story horizontal movement is called the story drift. If the story drift is Δ (delta) and the vertical load in a column is P, then the bending moments in the story are increased by P times Δ, or P-delta.

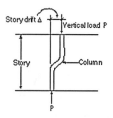

The effect must be taken into account unless it is very low relative to the story bending moments.

387. C.   Seismic forces are generally evaluated in the two horizontal directions parallel to the axes of a building. Structures assigned to SDC A and B and structures assigned to SDC C with no irregularities must be capable of resisting the stresses caused by the seismic forces in each direction, but not in both directions at the same time. For structures assigned to SDC C with nonparallel systems horizontal irregularity and all structures assigned to SDC D through F, certain members need to be designed for seismic forces acting in both directions at the same time (C is correct, and A and B are incorrect). D is incorrect because seismic forces are not considered to act at the same time as wind forces.

388. A.   With the meager amount of information given in this question, we can only make a rough approximation. Most of the additional cost to provide seismic resistance would be structural; the architectural, mechanical, and electrical costs would not increase significantly. The additional structural cost might be 5 to 25 percent of the original structural cost, averaging perhaps 15 percent. Because the structural cost is about 25 percent of the total cost of construction, the additional cost to provide seismic resistance would be roughly 15 percent of the 25 percent, which amounts to 3.75 percent of the total cost of construction.

389. Liquefaction. The shear strength of some soils, particularly loose, saturated sands, can be substantially reduced by liquefaction, the soil's tendency to flow like a liquid, caused by earthquake ground motion. The result may be severe settlement of tilting buildings because of the reduced soil bearing capacity, such as occurred in Niigata, Japan, in 1964.

390. C and D. In seismic isolation, the structure is isolated from the ground by specially-designed bearings and dampers that absorb earthquake forces, thus reducing the building's acceleration and story drift caused by earthquake ground motion (C and D). The total displacement is similar to that of a building with conventional seismic design (B is incorrect). Providing a gap between adjacent buildings to prevent pounding is called seismic separation, not isolation (A is incorrect).

391. C. When the fundamental period of vibration of a building coincides with that of the shaking ground, the building is said to be in resonance with the shaking ground. This tends to greatly amplify the seismic forces and deformations and can lead to severe damage and even collapse. Therefore, it is desirable that the period of the building and that of the shaking ground be out of resonance, that is, that the periods be very different.

392. C. All elements and components of a building and their attachments must be designed to resist the seismic forces prescribed by the building code. In general, the seismic forces that must be resisted by a given element, such as the parapet walls in this question, are greater than those used

for the design of the building as a whole (C is correct). There are a number of reasons for this, including the fact that individual elements usually lack the redundancy and ductility that the structure as a whole has.

393. D. There are a number of ways to reduce the deflection of a reinforced concrete beam. The moment of inertia I of the beam may be increased by making the beam wider or deeper, the modulus of elasticity E of the concrete may be increased by using higher strength concrete, or additional reinforcing steel may be used. Of these, the most efficient way to reduce the deflection is to deepen the beam (choice D), because the I value of the beam is proportional to the third power of the depth. For example, doubling the depth increases the value of I eightfold ($2 \times 2 \times 2$), which would reduce the deflection to 1/8 of its original value.

394. C. In this question, referring to the AISC Manual is helpful, but not necessary, to solve this problem. In the Manual, the maximum moment for a beam with a uniformly increasing load is given as 0.1283 Wl. In this case, W = $1,200 \times 24/2 = 14,400$#, and M = 0.1283 (14,400) (24) = 44,340'# (correct answer C). Without the Manual, one would determine the left reaction by taking moments about the right end.

$-1,200(24/2) (24/3) + R_L (24) = 0$

$R_L = 4,800$#

The maximum moment occurs where the shear is equal to zero. Since the load increases at the rate of 1,200/24 = 50#/', we determine the distance x from the left end to the point of zero shear, as shown on the next page.

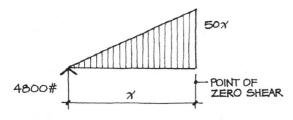

$50 (X) (x/2) = 4,800$

$x^2 = 4,800/25 = 192$

$x = \sqrt{192} = 13.856'$

The maximum moment $= 4,800(13.856)$ $-4,800(13,856/3) = 44,340'\#$, the same as we determined previously.

395. B. Reinforcing bars are furnished with rolled-in markings. The top mark identifies the rolling mill (Y in this case). The mark immediately below the top one gives the bar size according to a system of metric sizes. The "13" corresponds to a #13 bar, which has a diameter of 12.7 mm. This bar size is equivalent to a #4 bar, which has a diameter of 0.5 in. The next mark designates the type of steel: "S" is for billet steel (A615). The mark of "4" corresponds to Grade 420 bars, which have a yield stress of 420 MPa or, equivalently, 60 ksi (Grade 60).

396. Elastic limit. See the study guide for a complete explanation, including descriptions of the elastic limit, modulus of elasticity, yield point, and ultimate strength. Candidates should become familiar with all of these terms and their meanings.

397. A. The truss in this question is called a *King Post truss*, in which the internal force in the vertical member is zero (correct answer A). To prove this, we isolate joint D and apply the basic equation of static equilibrium $\Sigma V = 0$.

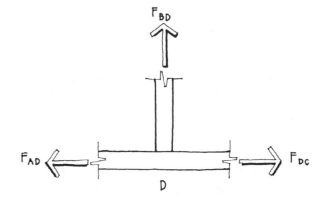

Since the only vertical force acting at the joint is $F_{B\text{-}D}$, it follows that $F_{B\text{-}D} = 0$.

398. C. In composite design, a steel beam and the concrete slab above it are connected so that they act together as a single structural unit to resist bending stresses. The concrete slab becomes part of the top flange and resists compressive bending stresses (C is correct). Connectors welded to the top flange of the steel beam resist shear, not flexural stresses (A is incorrect). Adding these connectors changes the beam from noncomposite to composite and makes the beam stiffer. However, as composite design usually allows the designer to use shallower beams, it is necessary to check deflections (D is incorrect). Composite construction is most efficient with heavy loads and long spans (B is incorrect).

399. B. Stirrups are small U-shaped bars, such as #3 or #4, which are placed vertically in a reinforced concrete beam to reinforce the web where the shear stresses are excessive (correct answer B). A is incorrect, as compressive reinforcement consists of longitudinal bars placed in the compressive area of a beam to resist part of the compressive stress. Reinforcement is anchored by mechanical devices and/or embedment (C is incorrect), and lateral buckling of compressive reinforcement is prevented by the use of ties, not stirrups (D is incorrect).

400. D.   One of the factors in wind design is the importance factor I, which is equal to 1 for the standard occupancy structures. For hazardous or essential facilities, such as fire or police stations, I increases to 1.15 for wind design. Thus, fire or police stations are designed for 15 percent more wind load than standard occupancy structures.

401. D.   The basic formula for design wind pressure is $p = qGC_p - q_i(GC_{pi})$ where q is the velocity pressure, which is equal to $0.00256K_zK_{zt}K_dV^2I$; G is the gust effect factor; C_p is the external pressure coefficient; and $q_i(GC_{pi})$ is the internal pressure. In the formula for q, K_z is the velocity pressure exposure coefficient, which is a function of exposure and height (II and III are correct); K_{zt} is the topographic factor; K_d is the directionality factor; V is the wind velocity (IV is correct); and I is the importance factor, which depends on the building's occupancy category (I is correct).

402. D.   Wind pressures used in design according to the IBC take into account the higher wind speeds in hurricanes, but do not account for the much greater speeds often associated with tornadoes (A is incorrect). The greater the height and amount of surface irregularities, the more interference with the wind and consequently, the lower the wind pressure used in design. Thus the design wind pressures decrease when there are greater surface irregularities (B is incorrect). The wind pressures at corners, discontinuities and irregularities in the building shape are higher than those on the wall and roof

surfaces, and thus C is also incorrect. The correct answer is D: wind creates both positive inward pressures and negative outward pressures on vertical surfaces.

403. D.   This is a typical steel beam problem that you should be able to solve very easily. The maximum moment in a simple beam supporting a uniform load is equal to $wL^2/8$ (a formula you should probably memorize). Thus, maximum moment M = 1,800#/ft. $\times$ (30 ft.)$^2 \div 8$ = 202,500 ft.-lbs. We convert this to in.-lbs. by multiplying by 12 = 202,500 $\times$ 12 = 2,430,000 in.-lbs. The required plastic section modulus Z = $M\Omega/F_y$ = 2,430,000 $\times$ 1.67/50,000 = 81.2 in.^{3} Using Table 3-2 on page 105, we locate the first group of beams that have a value of Z greater than or equal to 81.2 in^3. The beam in boldface type at the top of the group is the lightest beam that is adequate, in this case a W21 $\times$ 44 (correct answer D). While this is a fairly straightforward procedure, an even simpler procedure is to locate the group of beams that have a value of M_p/Ω greater than or equal to 202.5 ft.-kips and select the beam in boldface type at the top of the group (again, W21 $\times$ 44).

404. A.   The stub girder system is a steel beam-and-girder system in which the floor beams sit on top of the main girders, rather than framing into them. Short lengths of stub girders the same depth as the floor beams are welded to the tops of the main girders to provide a connection to the slab for composite action (A is correct). The advantages of the stub girder system are reduced weight of steel and reduced story height.

405. A.   Unlike structural steel, which has a constant value of modulus of elasticity, the modulus of elasticity of concrete varies with its strength and unit weight (I is correct). A reinforced concrete beam continues to deflect after it reaches its initial deflection (II is correct). III is incorrect because adding compressive reinforcement reduces the creep and hence the long-term deflection of a reinforced concrete beam. Since I and II are correct statements, A is the correct answer.

406. A. In buildings with an irregular shape, such as L, T, or cruciform configurations (C and D), the less rigid wings tend to rotate about the more rigid elements during an earthquake. This torsional movement can result in severe damage, particularly where two wings join. That leaves us with choices A and B. The best basic plan shape is one which is symmetrical and equally capable of resisting earthquake forces imposed from any direction. The square plan (correct answer A) is therefore preferable to the rectangular plan (B).

407. D. Because the building has a special steel moment-resisting frame, its height is not limited by the code, making D the correct answer.

408. C. We construct a force triangle, consisting of the 1,000# load, the tension in cable A, and the tension in cable B.

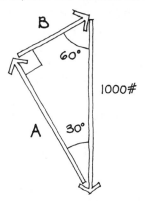

From basic trigonometry, sin 60° = A/1,000.

A = 1,000 sin 60° = 1,000(0.866) = 866#. sin 30° = B/1,000. B = 1,000 sin 30° = 1,000(0.500) = 500#.

409. A. Hydrostatic pressure, which is the pressure exerted by a liquid, is equal to the unit weight of the liquid (I) multiplied by the depth of the liquid (II). The width of the tank that contains the liquid (III) is irrelevant.

410. D. An arch is primarily a compression member. In fact, under a given loading, it may be stressed purely in compression. Any other loading will result in some bending, in addition to compression. Therefore, in general, an arch supports load by a combination of compression and bending.

411. C. Each force produces a moment about point O equal to the magnitude of the force multiplied by its distance from point O. The total moment is equal to the algebraic sum of the moments caused by all the forces. The 1,000# horizontal force produces a clockwise moment equal to 1,000# × 4 feet = 4,000 ft.-lbs. The 1,000# vertical force produces no moment, because its line of action passes through point O. The moment caused by the 1,000# force at 30° is determined by resolving the force into its vertical and horizontal components. The vertical component is 1,000 sin 30° = 500#, and the horizontal component is 1,000 cos 30° = 866#. The vertical component causes no moment, because its line of action passes through point O. The horizontal component produces a clockwise moment of 866# × 4 feet = 3,464 ft.-lbs. The total moment is the algebraic sum of the moments = 4,000 + 3,464 = 7,464 ft.-lbs. (answer C).

412. C. Steel columns rest on and are generally welded to steel base plates, which transfer the column load by bearing on the concrete foundation. The bearing pressure under the base plate is equal to P/A, where P is the column load and A is the area of the base plate = 300,000# ÷ (20 in. × 20 in.) = 750 psi (correct answer C). This is as simple a calculation as you're likely to see on the exam.

413. A. If a parabolic arch supports a uniformly distributed vertical load, it will be stressed only in compression, with no bending (A is correct). Under any other loading, it will be subject to some bending moment (C). B (pure bending) describes the stress in a beam, not an arch, and D (pure tension) describes the stress in a cable, not an arch.

414. B. The dead load of a structure acts continuously, but the live load can vary from zero to the full design load. In the design of the structural framing of a building, the live load must be arranged so as to produce the maximum moments. For a simple beam, the full design live load acting on the entire span will produce the maximum positive moment. For a continuous beam, the live load arrangements that will produce the maximum moments are as follows: (1) live load on two adjacent spans will produce the maximum negative moment over the support, and (2) live load on alternate spans will produce the maximum positive moment between supports. In this case, therefore, arrangement C (live load on spans 1-2 and 2-3) will produce the maximum negative moment over support 2, while arrangement B (live load on spans 1-2 and 3-4) will produce the maximum positive moment in spans 1-2 and 3-4. Arrangements A and D will not produce either maximum positive or negative moment. B is therefore the correct answer.

415. B and C. The maximum stress that a steel column can resist without buckling is a function of its slenderness ratio Kl/r, where K is a factor that depends on the column end conditions, l is the unbraced length of the column, and r is the radius of gyration of the column section, which is equal to $\sqrt{I/A}$. I is the moment of inertia of the column section (choice B) and A is the cross-sectional area of the column section (choice C).

416. D. In order to prevent the two adjacent elements from pounding against each other during an earthquake, the separation should be at least equal to the sum of the drifts (deflections) of the two elements (correct answer D). Answer A is not correct, because it is not necessary to extend the separation through the foundation. Answer B is an arbitrary rule of thumb, which does not necessarily provide adequate separation. Answer C is also incorrect, because joints do not reduce drift; they simply allow the movements to take place in a safe manner.

417. Epicenter. The location in the earth's crust where slippage begins is called the focus or hypocenter, and its projection on the ground surface is the *epicenter*.

418. D. A braced frame is a vertical truss that resists lateral forces, in which the members are subject primarily to axial stresses. Its behavior is closest to that of a shear wall (D). Moment-resisting frames (A and B) have joints capable of resisting moment, are not braced, and are relatively flexible. An appendage (C) is a nonstructural element applied to a building.

419. C. See the explanation for answer 421.

420. D. See the explanation for answer 421.

421. B. Questions about the stress-strain diagram have appeared on past exams, and candidates are therefore urged to become familiar with it. If we test a steel bar in tension in a testing machine and plot unit stress vs. unit strain, we will arrive at a diagram like the one shown in question 419. Hooke's Law states that up to the elastic limit (point A), unit stress is directly proportional to unit strain—in other words, the stress-strain diagram is a straight line. The constant ratio of unit stress to unit strain in this region, which can also be expressed as the tangent of angle θ, is called the modulus of elasticity. As we continue to test the bar, we reach a point where the bar continues to stretch with no increase in load, and the unit stress at which this occurs is called the yield point (point B). If we continue to increase the load on the steel bar, we will eventually reach the maximum unit stress that can be developed before it fractures. This stress is called the ultimate strength (point C).

422. B. We can use Table 104.5-1 on page 104 to determine the required number of rows of top chord bridging for the 32LH06. The maximum spacing of lines of bridging for the 32LH06 is 12'-0". The number of bridging spaces is equal to the joist span divided by the maximum spacing = 62/12 = 5.2. Because this must be a whole number, we use 6 spaces, or 5 lines of bridging, as shown in the sketch.

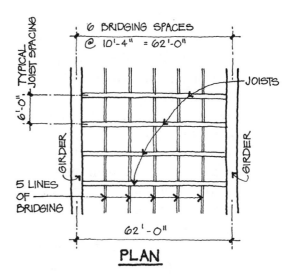

PLAN

423. A, B, and C. A and C are true statements. B is also correct; truss chord members are normally subject to axial stress only, unless they support loads between the panel points, which causes bending. D is incorrect, because the optimum depth to span ratio is about 1/10. E is also incorrect; increasing the depth of a truss decreases the stress in the chord members, but the stress in the web members depends on their slope, not on the truss depth.

424. B. For spans longer than 150 feet, steel arches are often trussed to increase their bending resistance (A is false, B is true). C is also incorrect: the horizontal thrust is unaffected by the trussing, and depends only on the load, span, and rise. D is irrelevant; all types of arches may be fixed, two-hinged, or three-hinged.

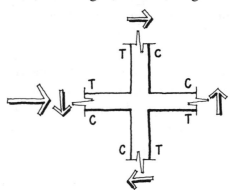

425. C.   We isolate the joint in question, as shown above. Because the seismic loads act to the right, the internal force in the lower column must act to the left for equilibrium. That results in clockwise moments in the columns, which for equilibrium must be balanced by counterclockwise moments in the beams. The shear in the left beam therefore acts down, while that in the right beam acts up. The face of the beam or column that tends to open up because of the moments is in tension (T), while the face tending to close or crush is in compression (C) as shown. Answer C is therefore the correct answer.

426. B, C, and D.   Drift is the displacement of one level of a building relative to the adjacent levels, caused by lateral loads. It is limited for the reasons in B, C, and D, namely, to insure structural integrity, minimize discomfort to the building's occupants, and restrict damage to brittle elements. Answer A is the incorrect statement: a building *is* expected to undergo inelastic deformation during a major earthquake, even if the drift is limited.

427. D.   Irregular structures are those with significant discontinuities. If these discontinuities occur in plan or in the diaphragm, they are termed plan structural irregularities and must be dealt with in accordance with special regulations in the IBC. Included are re-entrant corners (I), torsional irregularity resulting from an unsymmetrical arrangement of shear resisting elements (II), unsymmetrical mass distribution (III), and diaphragm discontinuity (IV). Since all four plans are considered plan irregularities, the correct answer is D.

428. A.   Providing seismic resistance may add 5 to 20 percent to the structural cost of a building, or 1.25 to 5 percent to the total construction cost (correct answer A), because the structure usually represents about 25 percent of the total cost of construction.

429. D.   Because parapets are particularly vulnerable to earthquake damage, they must be designed to resist substantial seismic forces. The seismic force (F_p) acts perpendicular to the face of the parapet and is equal to $F_p =$

$$\frac{0.4 a_p S_{DS} W_p}{\left(\dfrac{R_p}{I_p}\right)}\left(1+2\frac{z}{h}\right)$$

where (from ASCE 7 Table 13.5-1) $a_p =$ 2.5 and $R_p = 2.5$ for a cantilevered parapet wall that is braced to the structural frame below its center of mass. We can assume that the importance factor I_p is equal to 1.0, because we have no information to the contrary. Since the parapet is at the roof of the building, $z/h = 1$. We are given that $S_{DS} = 1.0g$, so that $F_p =$

$$\frac{0.4 \times 2.5 \times 1.0}{\left(\dfrac{2.5}{1.0}\right)}(1+2)W = 1.2W.$$

Maximum $F_p = 1.6 S_{DS} I_p W_p = 1.6 \times 1.0 \times 1.0 \times W = 0.3W$. Thus, F_p is equal to 120 percent of the weight of the parapet for the case when $S_{DS} = 1.0g$. Other percentages can easily be found for other short-period design accelerations.

430. A.   One of the primary considerations in hospital design is providing maximum flexibility without interruption of service. In this regard, interstitial trusses about eight feet in depth (A) offer unusual layout flexibility by providing a walk-through ceiling space above each column-free hospital floor. This interstitial space is utilized for all mechanical and electrical services, which can be maintained or changed without disrupting normal hospital functions on the floor above or below.

431. A. The traditional method for structural steel design is Allowable Stress Design (ASD), in which the actual dead and live loads are unfactored, that is, not increased. The factor of safety varies depending on the type of stress to which the structural member is subjected. For example, for flexural stresses, shear stresses, and axial compression stresses, the factor of safety Ω is equal to 1.67, while for tension stresses on the net section and shear stresses in bolts, the factor of safety is equal to 2.00.

Therefore, I is correct. Load and Resistance Factor Design, sometimes called limit states design, is a newer method of designing steel structures, in which the various loads (dead, live, etc.) are multiplied by their respective load factors. The nominal strength, which is most often the yield strength, is multiplied by a resistance factor ϕ, which is generally less than 1. Thus, II is correct. The primary objective of LRFD is to provide more uniform reliability for all steel structures under various loading conditions (III is incorrect). A is therefore the correct answer.

432. B. In this question, the four choices are all well-known Chicago buildings of the late-19th century. Burnham and Root's 16-story Monadnock Building (A) was the last of the pure masonry towers, with six-foot-thick walls at its base. Louis Sullivan's Carson Pirie Scott Store (C), with its metal frame, broad windows, and unique decoration, was the most modern building of the Chicago School. For the

Marshall Field Warehouse (D), H. H. Richardson designed exterior masonry piers and arches with interior framing of wood and iron. But it was Jenney's Home Insurance Building (correct answer B) that is considered the first iron and steel-framed skyscraper. Although only ten stories high, it was the predecessor of all the tall metal-framed buildings that followed.

433. A. Three of the buildings in this question are essentially hollow steel tubes that cantilever from their foundations when subject to lateral wind or earthquake forces. The Sears Tower in Chicago (C) consists of nine tubes that end at varying heights. The John Hancock Building in Chicago (D) and the Bank of China Tower are both gigantic trussed tubes. Only the Water Tower Building in Chicago (correct answer A) is not a tubular steel building, but rather a very tall reinforced concrete skyscraper.

434. D. Pier Luigi Nervi designed buildings that expressed their structure in bold and imaginative ways. His work is associated with all four structural concepts listed (correct answer D). He made use of ferrocement (I), a material consisting of layers of wire mesh embedded in concrete mortar. The Palazzeto Dello Sport has a prefabricated ribbed concrete shell dome (II), and the airplane hangars he built for the Italian Air Force in the 1930s had prefabricated concrete lamella roofs (III). Nervi's Borgo Paper Plant utilized a suspension bridge to achieve a span of 830 feet.

435. Catenary. If the only load acting on a cable is its own weight, the shape the cable assumes is a catenary. If the loads were uniformly distributed horizontally across the span, the cable would assume the shape of a parabola.

436. C. A thin shell is a structure with a curved surface that supports load by compression, shear, and tension in its own plane (I, II, and III), but is too thin to resist any bending stresses (IV is incorrect). C is therefore the correct answer. Among the more popular thin shell shapes are the dome, the cylindrical or barrel shell, the vault, and the hyperbolic paraboloid.

437. D. The section modulus of a beam (S) is equal to the moment of inertia of the beam (I) divided by the distance from the outermost fiber of the beam to the neutral axis (c), or $S = I/c$. The maximum bending stress $f = M/S$, so the greater the section modulus, the lower the bending stress for a given moment. Therefore, the section modulus is a measure of the beam's bending strength (D is correct).

438. Composite deck. A composite deck is steel decking manufactured with deformations that mechanically bond the deck to the concrete slab above it, so that the deck and slab act together as a single structural element to span between floor beams. Composite beams are often confused with composite decks.

439. D. Identification marks are rolled into the surface of reinforcing bars to denote the producing mill, the bar size, the type of steel, and the minimum yield strength. In this case, the producing mill has the symbol H. The mark immediately below the mill stamp gives the bar size according to a system of metric sizes. The "32" corresponds to a #32 bar, which has a diameter of 32.3 mm. This bar size is equivalent to a #10 bar, which has a diameter of 1.27 in. The next mark

designates the type of steel: "S" is for billet steel (A615). The mark of "4" corresponds to Grade 420 bars, which have a yield stress of 420 MPa or, equivalently, 60 ksi (Grade 60). Thus, the correct answer is D.

440. D. I-shaped wood joists have a profile that looks like the illustration in the right column. As with any I-shaped member, such as a steel plate girder, the flanges substantially resist the flexural tension and compression, the web resists the shear, and the connections between the flanges and the web resist horizontal shear (D is correct).

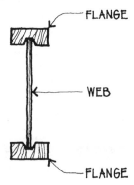

441. C. A soft first story, that is, one whose stiffness is considerably less than that of other stories, should generally be avoided if possible, because it can result in severe distortion and stress concentration in an earthquake (A is incorrect). Answer B is also incorrect; wood frame buildings usually perform well in an earthquake and do not pose a significant threat to life, although such buildings and their contents may be damaged. Adjacent buildings may move differently during an earthquake and pound against each other. To minimize this possibility, they should be adequately separated (C is correct). Answer D is incorrect, because wood stud walls should be bolted to the foundation to prevent the structure from sliding off in an earthquake.

442. A. Ground motions in an earthquake are both horizontal and vertical. Earthquake design accounts for the horizontal motions, but not usually the vertical effects (A). The acceleration of a building and that of the ground beneath are not usually the same, and thus B is false. A special moment-resisting space frame has the greatest ability to withstand earthquakes without damage, whereas a shear wall system usually does not perform as well in earthquakes (C is incorrect). The overturning moment is considered in earthquake design, and thus statement D is also false.

443. C. This question tests candidates' conceptual understanding of trusses. A truss is analogous to a steel beam; for a given load and span, the deeper the beam, the smaller the tensile and compressive forces in the flanges. Likewise for a truss: the deeper truss B has smaller chord forces than the shallower truss A (I is correct). From $\Sigma V = 0$, the vertical component of the force in the first diagonal of each truss is equal to R. For truss A, the horizontal component is also equal to R, as the truss depth and the panel length are both 10 feet. The total force in the diagonal is $\sqrt{R^2 + R^2}$ = 1.41R. For truss B, the horizontal component is 10R/15 = 0.67R, as the truss depth is 15 feet and the panel length is 10 feet. The total force in the diagonal is $\sqrt{R^2 + (0.67R)^2}$ = 1.20R. Therefore, the diagonals in truss B have lower axial tension forces than those in truss A (II is incorrect). Finally, we cut a section through the first vertical of each truss, as shown in the next column. From $\Sigma V = 0$, the force in the vertical of each truss is equal to R (III is correct).

444. C. The flat plate system (A) has inexpensive formwork, but it is not generally economical for heavy loads or spans longer than 25 feet. The flat slab system (B) is economical for heavy loads, but not when the spans are much longer than 25 feet. The pan joist system (D) might be economical in this case, but it is generally more appropriate for moderate loads and spans where the bays are rectangular. The waffle slab system (C) is appropriate for heavy loads, square bays, and spans up to about 40 feet.

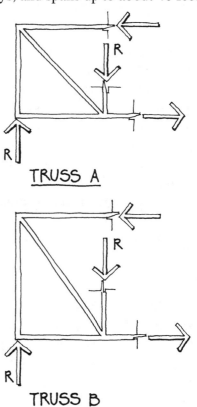

TRUSS A

TRUSS B

445. C. The combined effect of prestress and the applied loads usually results in compression over the entire cross section of a beam, which prevents tension cracks (A) and allows smaller sections to be used (D). Offsetting these advantages are greater labor and material costs (B). C is the incorrect statement we are looking for: pretensioned members are usually produced at a casting yard away from the building site, while posttensioned members are generally cast in place.

446. D. From the beam diagrams on page 109, we read that the maximum deflection Δ of a cantilever beam with a concentrated load at the free end is equal to $PL^3/3EI$. Substituting, we have $0.67 = 10,000(10 \times 12)^3/3 \times 29 \times 10^6 \times I$. $I = 10,000(10 \times 12)^3/3 \times 29 \times 10^6 \times 0.67 = 296.4$ in^4. Notice the units: 10 kips becomes 10,000 pounds, and 10 feet becomes (10×12) inches. In that way, I will be expressed in inches^4.

447. B. In scheme B, simulated continuity is provided by hanging the center beam from the outer beams, thereby reducing the positive moment in the end spans (I). In addition, the effective span of the center beam is reduced from L, the column spacing, to the distance between hinges, resulting in a smaller positive moment in the center span (II). Scheme B results in greater loads in the interior columns and smaller loads in the exterior columns (III is not correct). As I and II are advantages of scheme B, B is the correct answer.

448. D. If the upper soils are strong enough to support the building loads, then footings at a relatively shallow depth can be used. In this case, as the upper soils consist of loose fill, these loose soils must be removed and recompacted (III), if they are to support building loads. Alternatively, the footings could extend through these loose upper soils into the stronger soils below (II or IV), or the building loads could be spread over a large area (I), so that the average bearing pressure will be low and the system made rigid to bridge over localized areas of poor soil. Because all four systems might be appropriate, D is the correct answer.

449. A. The pressure applied to a retaining wall by the retained earth is usually assumed to vary uniformly from zero at the top to a maximum at the bottom, as shown in A and C. The soil pressure under the footing is maximum at the toe and minimum at the heel, as shown in both A and B. Only A has both correct diagrams, and is therefore the correct answer.

450. A and D. Ductility, as it relates to lateral loads, is correctly defined in choices A and D. The stiffness of a system refers to its resistance to deformation, not to its ability to absorb seismic loads (B is incorrect), and the ability of a system to redistribute seismic loads to other elements is termed redundancy, not ductility (C is incorrect).

451. B. Determining the location of the center of rigidity is similar to determining the location of the center of gravity, only using rigidities instead of weights. The north wall has a rigidity of 10 and the south wall has a rigidity of 1 and is 50 feet from the north wall. We take moments about the north wall. $[1 (50) + 10 (0)] \div (1 + 10) = 50/11 = 4.55$ feet from the north wall (B is correct).

452. D. A space frame is a series of trusses that intersect in a grid pattern and are connected at their points of intersection. Space frames are often economical for enclosing large, square, column-free spaces, as in this question. The key to their economy is the use of repetitive members and connections (I). Other advantages include greater stiffness (II) and reduced depth (III). However, space frames are statically indeterminate and their structural analysis is complex (IV is incorrect). D is therefore the correct answer.

453. C. A drilled caisson bears on the soil at its bottom and is constructed by pouring concrete into a drilled shaft. The bottom of the shaft is often enlarged, or belled, in order to increase the bearing area and hence the bearing capacity of the caisson (correct answer C).

454. C. The shear capacity of a reinforced concrete beam depends on its width, its depth, and the ultimate 28-day compressive strength of the concrete (C is correct). If the shear capacity is insufficient to resist the shear force, web reinforcement may be added. The cross-sectional area of the longitudinal tension reinforcing is irrelevant in this regard (A is incorrect), and the beam's load and span affect the shear force on the beam, not its shear capacity (B and D are incorrect).

455. C. In this question, you must determine the maximum bending moment that can be resisted by a 6 × 12 wood beam. Using the formula $F_b = M/S$, we rearrange the terms so that $M = F_bS = 1,600\#/in.^2 \times 121.229\ in.^3 = 193,966$ in.-lbs. We convert this to ft.-lbs. by dividing by 12. 193,966 ÷ 12 = 16,164 ft.-lbs. (answer C).

456. D. The problem of selecting a steel joist has come up on some exams, and solving such a problem is very easy if you know how to use the Steel Joist Institute tables, such as that on page 106. In this case, the total load supported by each joist is equal to (20 + 30) lbs./sq. ft. × 6 feet = 300 pounds per linear foot. The live load per joist is equal to 30 × 6 = 180 pounds per linear foot. You will note that each joist in the table has two numbers corresponding to each span: the upper number represents the total load in pounds per linear foot that the joist can safely support, and the lower number represents the live load in

pounds per linear foot which will produce a deflection of 1/360 of the span. In order to satisfy both load and deflection criteria in this problem, we must find a joist whose upper number is at least 300 and whose lower number is at least 180, and further, we must select the lightest such joist. For the 36LH10, we read 295 and 140, and the joist is inadequate for load (295 < 300) and deflection (140 < 180). The 36LH11 and 36LH12 are both adequate for load, but not for deflection. Only the 36LH13 is adequate for both load (451 > 300) and deflection (213 > 180). Other 36LH joists are adequate, but they weigh more than the 36LH13.

457. A, B, and D. This question tests your understanding of several reinforced concrete design concepts. Failure due to crushing of the concrete is sudden and without warning, while failure due to yielding of the tensile steel is more gradual and gives adequate warning of approaching collapse. In order to ensure that failure due to yielding of the steel takes place before failure of the concrete, the code sets an upper limit on the reinforcement ratio by limiting the strain in the reinforcement closest to the tension face. A is therefore a correct statement and C is an incorrect statement. B and D are also correct; the reinforcing steel is generally assumed to resist all the tensile stresses, and the ultimate load factors are greater for live load than for dead load because a specified live load is more apt to be exceeded than dead load, which is fixed.

458. A. Curtain walls are generally attached to a building's frame and are nonstructural. However, in Mies van der Rohe's Lake Shore Drive Apartments, steel plate cladding, bonded with studs to the concrete fireproofing, acts not only as a curtain wall, but also provides additional lateral stiffness for wind loads. Answer A is therefore correct.

459. B. The Empire State Building (A), Stonehenge (C), and the Chrysler Building (D), have forms that do not reflect the structural concepts of wind resistance. The Eiffel Tower (correct answer B) has a tapered profile, which reduces the wind load as the height increases (reducing the overturning moment) and provides greater stability because its legs are spread (increasing the dead load resisting moment). Thus, its form clearly reflects the concepts of wind resistance.

460. B. IBC Table 2306.3.1 is used to determine the allowable shear force for wood structural panel diaphragms for wind or seismic loading. The panel grade is given in the first column of the table, the nail or staple size is in the second column, the nominal panel thickness is in the fourth column, and the nominal width of the framing members at the panel edges and boundaries is in the fifth column. In this case, the allowable shear force is read under the column labeled Blocked Diaphragms with a fastener spacing of 6 inches. Thus, the allowable shear force is equal to 300 pounds per foot (B).

461. A. The answer is *The minimum width of the shear wall is determined by its height.* Table 2305.3.4 of the International Building Code specifies the maximum height-to-width ratios for plywood shear walls. For a shear wall of a given height, the minimum width is determined by these ratios. For example, if the maximum height-to-width ratio is 3½:1 and the height of the shear wall is 9 feet, then the minimum width is 9 / 3½, or 2.57 feet. The width may not be less than

that determined in this manner, even if the calculations should show that a lesser width would be adequate to resist the shear (D is incorrect).

462. C. In this question, four different diagrams are presented, and you are asked to select the one representing the flexural stresses in a reinforced concrete beam at failure. Diagram A represents the flexural stresses in a homogeneous rectangular beam, such as wood, and diagram B represents the flexural stresses in a reinforced concrete beam at working stresses. This is the basis of working stress design, which has been largely superseded by the strength design method. Diagram C correctly shows the flexural stresses in a reinforced concrete beam at failure, which is the basis of strength design. The bunched arrows represent the compressive stress in the concrete and the single arrow represents the tensile stress in the reinforcing steel. Diagram D represents the flexural stresses in a steel beam when the entire beam profile is stressed to the yield strength. This is the basis of limit states design in steel, which is analogous to the strength design method used for reinforced concrete.

463. A. This truss problem can be solved in various ways, but the simplest way is to isolate the joint where the 20 kip load is applied and draw a free body diagram.

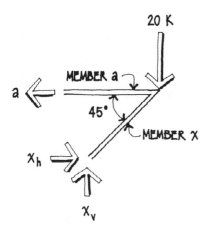

Assume member *a* is stressed in tension (pulling away from the joint) and diagonal member *x* is stressed in compression (pushing toward the joint).

$\Sigma V = 0$

$-20 + x_v = 0$

$x_v = +20$ kips

Since member *x* slopes at 45°, $x_h = x_v = 20$ kips

$\Sigma H = 0$

$+x_h - a = 0$

$a = +x_h = +20$ kips

Since all the signs come out positive, our assumptions about the directions of the stresses are correct, and member *a* is stressed in tension. A is therefore the correct answer.

464. B.   A three-hinged arch is the only type of arch that is statically determinate, no matter what the loading is (B is correct). In the answer to Question 466, we show how the horizontal thrust at each end of a three-hinged arch is calculated.

465. C.   When a flat roof deflects under load, a concave surface results. Rainwater can collect in such areas, increasing the deflection, which further increases the amount of ponded water, and so on. During intense rainstorms, therefore, the ponding of flat roofs can result in problems, including even collapse. Because of their long span and relative flexibility, long span open web joists are particularly vulnerable to this kind of trouble. Therefore, the joists should be cambered or pitched sufficiently so that rainwater cannot build up. Building pitch into the top chords of the joists is one way to achieve slope, but is usually more expensive than using parallel chord joists which are sloped, or building in camber (I is incorrect, II and IV are correct). Further, a slope of 1/8 inch per foot is sometimes used; although this slope is considered minimum, it is considered acceptable practice (III is correct). C is therefore the correct answer.

466. C.   A three-hinged arch is the only type of arch that is statically determinate. To calculate the horizontal thrust, we draw a free body diagram of the left half of the arch.

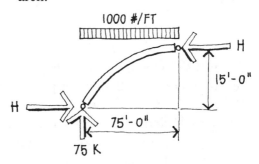

By symmetry, each vertical reaction is equal to one-half of the total vertical load on the arch = 1,000 lbs./ft. × 150 ft./2 = 75,000# = 75 kips. Take moments about the center hinge, where the moment is equal to zero.

$\Sigma M = 0$

$(75 \text{ kips} \times 75 \text{ ft.}) - (1.0 \text{ kips/ft.} \times 75 \text{ ft.}$
$\times \dfrac{75 \text{ft}}{2}) - (H \times 15 \text{ ft.}) = 0$

H   = [(75 × 75) − (1 × 75 × 37.5)] ÷ 15

= (5,625 − 2,812.5) ÷ 15 = 187.5 kips
(answer C)

467. D.   The bolts in this question are in double shear, as there are two planes through each bolt that resist shear. From Table 11-F of the NDS Specification, which is reproduced on page 107, the reference lateral design value for each 7/8″ bolt in double shear parallel to grain when the thickness of the main member is 3-1/2″ (nominal 4″) and the side member is 1-1/2″ (nominal 2″) is 3,180#. The total load that can be transferred by two bolts is therefore 3,180 × 2 = 6,360# (correct answer D).

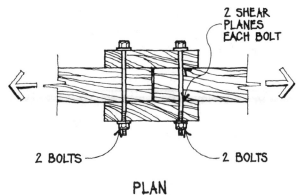

PLAN

468. Modulus of elasticity.   All steel, regardless of strength or other properties, has the same value of modulus of elasticity E, about 29,000,000 psi. Other properties such as yield point, ultimate strength, and weldability will vary depending on the type of steel.

469. A.   In this question, definitions of four different long-span roof systems are given, and you are asked to select the one which refers to a lamella roof. Answer A correctly defines a lamella roof. B is the definition of a space frame, and C and D describe systems that have been used but do not have specific names.

470. D.   All four statements are correct (answer D). Air-supported membranes that enclose a space are pressurized by fans (I). Since the internal air pressure is slightly greater than the outside pressure, airlocks or special doors are required to get in and out of the space (II). Loss of pressure can cause the roof to deflate (IV); however, in that event, the velocity of the fans could be increased so that the deflation would take place over a long period of time. Large air-supported fabric structures are usually reinforced with steel cables (III).

471. C.   The top chord of a simply supported truss is stressed in compression. As with all steel compression members, the capacity of the truss chord is based on its Kl/r value. K is usually assumed to be *1* and the value of *r* is the lower value, which may be with respect to either the *x-x* or the *y-y* axis (correct answer C).